BY SEA AND BY RIVER

By Sea and By River

The Naval History of the

CIVIL WAR

by Bern Anderson

A DA CAPO PAPERBACK

Library of Congress Cataloging in Publication Data

Anderson, Bern.
  By sea and by river.

(A Da Capo paperback)
  Reprint. Originally published: New York: Knopf, 1962.
  Includes index.
  1. United States—History—Civil War, 1861-1865—Naval opera-
tions. 2. United States—History—Civil, 1861-1865—Campaigns. I.
Title.
E591.A54 1989   973.7′5   89-11793
ISBN 0-306-80367-4

This Da Capo Press paperback edition of
By Sea and By River is an unabridged
republication of the edition published in
New York in 1962. It is reprinted by
arrangement with Alfred A. Knopf, Inc.

Published by Da Capo Press, Inc.
A Subsidiary of Plenum Publishing Corporation
233 Spring Street, New York, New York 10013

PREFACE

THE NAVAL HISTORY of the Civil War, probably because it is less spectacular on the whole, has not received attention commensurate with the history of the land campaigns. Only recently have historians recognized that the Union naval blockade of the South was an important factor in the outcome of the war. While some of the more familiar naval events of the war are known to every schoolboy, such as the battle between *Monitor* and *Merrimack* and Farragut at Mobile Bay, to learn that the Union Navy had an important part in McClellan's Peninsula campaign and Grant's final campaign in Virginia requires special study beyond the usual general histories of the war.

Naval histories of the Civil War are few in number. Charles B. Boynton's *The History of the Navy During the Rebellion*, in two volumes (1870), was prepared at the request of the Secretary of the Navy as a quasi-official history of the Union Navy in that war. It was criticized at the time it was published because of its inaccuracies and it reflects a strong prejudice against the South. David D. Porter's *The Naval History of the Civil War* (1886) is also an account of the Union Navy's part, but it suffers both from errors in fact and because it presents Admiral Porter's own part in too favorable a light. The admiral's *Incidents and Anecdotes of the Civil War* (1885) is a readable and amusing account, but it is subject to the same criticism as his *History* and should be regarded with caution. The best of the early histories of the Union Navy is the three-volume *The Navy in the Civil War* (1883–90) in the Scribner's series of volumes on the war. The three-volume *Diary* of Gideon Welles, first published in 1911 and revised and corrected by Howard K. Beale in 1960, is an invaluable personal record, revealing the inner workings of Lincoln's cabinet and the direction of the Union naval effort. As a personal diary it reflects Welles's own prejudices and this must be kept in mind in reading it. Richard S. West's *Mr. Lincoln's Navy* (1947) is the first modern history of the Union Navy. Most of the recent works in the naval field have dealt with only limited aspects of the story. J. T. Scharf's *History of the Confederate States Navy* (1887) is the only one devoted to the general history of that Navy.

All these works are historical narratives relating the bare naval events of the Civil War. What has not yet been written is a study of those events from the viewpoint of their strategic impact on the progress and outcome of the war. Alfred T. Mahan, who wrote *The Gulf and Inland Waters* in the Scribner's series, made only a few references to events of the Civil War in his later extensive writings on sea power, although he did recognize the part the Union Navy played in that war. His historical studies were mainly concerned with earlier wars, but the Civil War does provide an excellent, if somewhat limited, illustration of the application of his doctrine of the influence of sea power.

Were there strategic plans for the employment of the Union and Confederate navies? If so, how well were they carried out? What was the purpose of the various operations undertaken by both navies? What did they contribute to the outcome of the war?

The events and incidents described in this study have been selected with such questions in mind. In relating the course of the battles and actions, I have included only sufficient tactical details to round out the description of the event. I have tried to avoid becoming involved in unimportant details and thereby possibly obscuring the main point.

Inasmuch as this is an interpretation of the significance of the naval aspects of the Civil War rather than a documentary account, there is no formal bibliography. The facts stated and conclusions reached are not always derived from a single source but from whatever bears on the subject. In an effort to get behind the emotional atmosphere of the times in order to find out what really happened and why, it has been necessary to study works which emphasize social, economic, and political rather than purely military events.

Within that framework, my main reliance has been on the standard sources, the thirty-volume *Official Records of the Union and Confederate Navies in the War of the Rebellion* and, when applicable, the corresponding 128-volume *Official Records of the Union and Confederate Armies*. The first is incomplete and in some cases the contents have been edited, but it provides an adequate record for the purposes of this study. When cited in a footnote these sources are indicated by the abbreviations ORN and ORA, with the volume and page reference. All volumes cited are in Series I. The Century Company's four-volume *Battles and Leaders of the Civil War* (1877), compiled from articles published in the *Century Magazine*, is valuable for its wealth of personal accounts of leading events, but it too has to be used with reserve, as human memory is fallible. It is cited in the text as *Battles and Leaders*. Two other standard sources have been used only to a very limited extent. *The Rebellion Record*, edited by Frank Moore, is a twelve-volume collection of documents, narratives, anecdotes, poetry, etc., published as the war progressed. It is of value in revealing some of the heated atmosphere and distorted reporting of the period. With few exceptions, newspapers shaded their reports to fit the editorial policy of the paper, resulting in biased accounts which add little to the true record in the naval field. The many personal memoirs and biographies of participants are necessary sources to round out this historical study.

Whenever conflicting or varying accounts of an event exist in the sources, it has been necessary to select either the most authoritative or the most plausible, or to reconcile the differences in order to reconstruct the event as it probably occurred. In interpreting the significance of an event, my own studied opinion is given. I have been careful to phrase these opinions so that their nature should be apparent to the reader. I have also found that Civil War statistics must be used with caution, as their accuracy is apt to be questionable. For that reason, whenever a statistical figure is given, it is usually qualified with an "about" and given in round numbers. The figure used is the one that I believe to be as close to the correct one as possible. Battle casualties are an exception to this statistical generalization. There can be errors in them, but usually they are reliable. Whenever a difference in spelling exists between current usage and that of the Civil War period, I have used the earlier form.

In developing a method of using these sources, I have had the benefit of eight years of close association with Samuel E. Morison in the preparation of his *History of U.S. Naval Operations in World War II.* During that time I had access to hundreds of plans and strategic and tactical studies and thousands of action reports of commanders at all levels, and have learned to recognize shortcomings as well as virtues in individual reports. Civil War records are not as formal or complicated as those of World War II, but they show that naval officers have not changed much in preparing their reports.

Throughout, I have been guided by Alfred T. Mahan's standard, as given in his autobiographical *From Sail to Steam:* ". . . to be accurate in facts and correct in conclusions, both as to appreciation and expression, . . ." I have also made a conscious effort to be objective and fair—not easy when dealing with records which reflect the emotional and partisan influence that existed in those fateful years.

A personal visit to the scene of the important naval actions on the Southern coast is rewarding, but there are also disappointments. Those forts which are national or state monuments are generally well preserved, marked and tended, and accessible. Unfortunately many of them are no longer owned by the government, and these are usually neglected and all but inaccessible to the visitor. The channel of the Mississippi River has been so changed by nature and man that it is necessary to revert to maps of the Civil War period for geographical details. Dr. Erwin Raisz, of Cambridge, Massachusetts, produced the map for this volume.

Professor Keener Fraser, of the University of North Carolina, first brought the general subject of this study to my attention and urged me to undertake it. Most of my research has been done in the library of the U. S. Naval War College, Newport, Rhode Island, where the Director of Libraries, Mr. Charles Di Napoli, and his excellent staff have been most helpful in every way. In using other facilities, I have found the staffs, from the expert specialists in the National Archives and the Library of Congress to the part-time attendants at local historical societies, to have been without exception most accommodating, and I am grateful to all of them who have contributed to the preparation of this study.

BERN ANDERSON,
Rear Admiral, U. S. Navy (RETIRED)

Jamestown, Rhode Island
May 1962

CONTENTS

PLATES

BY SEA AND BY RIVER

NOTE: *A map illustrating the naval history of the Civil War appears on pages 122–3.*

Chapter I

The Men and the Tools

THE NORTH

No STUDY of the Union Navy's part in the Civil War can go very far before coming upon the towering figure of Gideon Welles, Lincoln's Secretary of the Navy. His full white beard and flowing brown wig made Welles conspicuous in any company, but behind his picturesque appearance was an agile mind; he was one of the ablest and most loyal of Lincoln's close advisers.

Gideon Welles was a Connecticut lawyer, journalist, and editor, but above all he was a shrewd and honest politician. The only time he ran for the national Congress, he lost, and he knew in advance that he would lose in 1856 as the Republican candidate for governor, but he wanted to get that new party established in Connecticut. His strength was in organization. He was chairman of his state's delegation to the Republican National Convention in Chicago in 1860. Though he was un-instructed, his chief interest was to prevent the nomination of the leading candidate for the Presidency, William H. Seward, who he felt lacked the necessary qualifications. His personal choice was Salmon P. Chase, but on the third ballot he shifted and helped to nominate Lincoln.

Lincoln chose Welles for a post in the cabinet soon after his election. He had Vice President-elect Hamlin sound Welles out in a roundabout way to insure that his political views were closely enough in accord with Lincoln's to make him acceptable. Welles was not informed of his appointment at that time. Not until March 1, 1861, did he receive a telegram from Hamlin summoning him to Washington, and he did not see Lincoln until the morning of Inauguration Day. It was only then he learned that he was to be named to the naval post. This rather casual handling of an important office was in keeping with tradition, for the Secretary of the Navy was considered among politicians as one of the least desirable cabinet offices and usually was one of the last to be filled. Down to World War II, at least, it generally was given to somewhat less than distinguished men. Gideon Welles was a conspicuous exception to that rule, and Abraham Lincoln was indeed fortunate in his choice.

Although he showed a keen interest in naval operations, Lincoln only rarely intervened in their conduct. This may have been due in part to a little-publicized but intimate relationship formed with a naval officer early in his administration. During the critical days of April and May 1861, after the attack on Fort Sumter, when Washington was believed to be in great danger, Lincoln inspected the defenses of the Washington Navy Yard. There he met Commander John A. Dahlgren, the ordnance expert and one of two officers at the yard who did not cast his lot with the Confederacy. Thereafter Lincoln became a frequent visitor, and he found relaxation and relief from the cares of office in Dahlgren's company. What advice he sought or what passed between them we do not know, for Dahlgren's private journal gives us few details. His influence with the President was considerable, but there is no evidence that he used it for personal advantage. His journal also reveals that he was on close, if not intimate, terms with several cabinet officers and Senators. Welles was cool in his relations with Dahlgren, a natural reaction in view of the latter's friendship with those in high office.

There was little in Welles's record to indicate his fitness for the post. For his help in electing President Polk he had been made chief of the Navy Department's Bureau of Provisions and Clothing in 1845. Under the pressure of the Mexican War he completely overhauled that small bureau, and by the time President Taylor ousted him in 1849, it was an efficient and economical bureau.

The Civil War leaders on both sides were burdened with an army of armchair strategists who regularly offered unsolicited advice on every aspect of the war. The pros and cons of projected campaigns were freely discussed in the press of North and South alike, although the mainly partisan and critical nature of such discussion was more nearly an exercise of license rather than the traditional freedom of the press. Welles avoided newspaper reporters, and when he instructed naval officers not to talk to the press about naval matters, he was vigorously attacked for imposing censorship. He was branded as the "Rip van Winkle of the Navy Department," one of the less opprobrious nicknames he was to collect, in common with his colleagues. He was a favorite of the free-wheeling cartoonists of the era.

Another excellent choice was the man Welles made his Assistant Secretary, Gustavus V. Fox. An officer in the regular Navy for many years, Fox had resigned to become a successful businessman. Early in the Lincoln administration he submitted to the President a scheme for the relief of Fort Sumter. That failed, but it brought Fox to his new post, where he proved to be an excellent administrator. With Fox handling the multitude of details, Welles was free to concentrate on the broader problems of the naval war. The pair formed a working team almost unique in American political life.

Because the United States Navy was completely unprepared to undertake the task which was suddenly handed to it in April 1861, historians have generally accepted its contemporary critics' claims that it was obsolete, decayed, and moribund at the outbreak of the Civil War. Generally that is an inaccurate and unfair charge. The Navy's record for the twenty years before 1861 shows that it was active, progressive, and possessed of much initiative.

Up to 1862 the highest rank in the United States Navy was that of captain. Officers commanding squadrons were formally designated flag officers and they were entitled to display a personal flag or pennant from their flagships. The title of commodore was in common use for such officers, and it sometimes crept into official correspondence, but it was not an official rank. There was no system of retirement. This was the greatest handicap for the Navy, for the only way a superannuated officer could be removed from the active list was by death. In 1861 the senior officer on the Navy List was a captain, aged about seventy-five, who had held that rank for thirty years. This condition made promotion very slow and caused many younger officers to resign and enter more promising fields. Many Navy Secretaries had tried to correct this undesirable condition, but it was not until 1855 that Congress enacted a law establishing a naval retirement board. This board thereupon found 201 officers incapacitated for sea duty and recommended that they be separated from the active list. When the list was published, the retirement board was subjected to such a barrage of criticism and abuse that Congress amended the law to such an extent as to practically nullify it. The problem still existed in 1861. Most Secretaries handled it by means of an unofficial retired list; overaged and unfit officers were not given active duty posts, but that was not a satisfactory solution.

On the credit side was the founding of the Naval Academy at Annapolis, Maryland. The idea had been developed by Secretary George Bancroft in 1845, in order to improve the existing method of instruction of midshipmen on ships at sea. A naval school was established at old Fort Severn in Annapolis. In the beginning only the first and fifth years of training there were ashore and the second through fourth years were spent at sea. In 1850 it became the Naval Academy with a full four-year resident course. By 1861 it was well established and flourishing, giving future officers a solid and uniform education to fit them for their careers.

The quarter century before the Civil War saw the Navy very active in science and exploration. Lieutenant Matthew F. Maury had a deserved world-wide reputation for his work in oceanography and marine meteorology. The Navy Observatory, the Nautical Almanac Office, and the Hydrographic Office were established during this period. Lieutenant Charles Wilkes returned from a noteworthy exploring expedition in the Pacific and Antarctic Oceans in 1842. Numerous other naval exploring and scientific expeditions to many parts of the world followed him. The best-known achievement of the period was Commodore Perry's successful diplomatic expedition to Japan in 1852–4.

Like other navies throughout the world, the U.S. Navy was at this time in the midst of the transition from sail to steam. Steam was generally an auxiliary to sail in seagoing ships during the Civil War, for steam installations were then inefficient and required a heavy consumption of coal.

In 1842 Congress had authorized the first steam screw-propeller warship, *Princeton*. The engine and propeller were designed by John Ericsson, better known for his later *Monitor*. Also mounted in *Princeton* was a huge twelve-inch gun of Ericsson's design. Her naval promoter and future commander, Captain R. F. Stockton, designed a second twelve-inch gun for the ship. *Princeton*'s trials, early in February 1844, were so successful that in less than a month she was sent up the Potomac to be shown off to high government officials in Washington. There the featured event was a demonstration of the big guns, with President Pierce, the Secretaries of State and Navy, and other officials on board as observers. Ericsson's gun, which he named Oregon (the Oregon Boundary Dispute was then nearing its climax), and Stockton's Peacemaker showed their power with great effect until a final round from the Peacemaker blew up the gun, killing Secretary of State Abel P. Upshur, Secretary of the Navy T. W. Gilmer, and other high-ranking officers. Fortunately, President Pierce had gone below just before the fatal accident. The incident put a damper on experimentation with big guns, but not for long. Ericsson spent many years trying to collect his just fee for his work on the *Princeton*, and even after he obtained a judgment from the Court of Claims, Congress was slow in producing the funds.

Also in 1842 Congress authorized the construction of an ironclad steam warship, to be built by Robert L. Stevens of Hoboken, New Jersey. Construction of this harbor defense craft dragged out until Stevens's death in 1856, and it was never completed. The delays were due partly to changes in his design and partly to Congress's refusal to appropriate additional funds. Although in the end nothing came of this project, a start had been made and the Navy was conscious of the growing trend toward armored ships. In the Crimean War the French had used armored floating batteries with some success. Thereafter Napoleon III encouraged his naval architects to build armored warships. In September 1860, *Gloire*, the first of four, completed her trials very successfully. At the time the most powerful warship in the world, she made wooden warships obsolete. England, sensing the threat to her sea supremacy, was not far behind, and her *Warrior* was completed a year later.

In the 1850s Congress awoke to the need for modernizing the United States Navy. Up to 1853 only eighteen steamers had been built or acquired, but in the five years beginning in 1854 no less than thirty were added. Six of these were first-class steam frigates with screw propellers. Probably the best known of this class was *Merrimack*,[1] later converted to an ironclad by the Confederates. Twelve of the new ships were steam sloops with propellers. Farragut's famed flagship *Hartford* was of this class. Southern Senators made sure that the draft of these new ships was too great for them to enter Southern harbors before they voted to approve them. By 1861 the Navy had ninety ships on its list, but twenty-one of them were classed as unserviceable and only forty-two were in commission.

One of the important changes in this period was in the design of heavy ordnance for the new ships. In 1847 Lieutenant John A. Dahlgren began his studies in this field. By measuring barrel pressures when the guns were fired, he was able to design successfully guns of large caliber. Dahlgren guns of nine-inch, ten-inch, and eleven-inch bore were adopted for the new steam frigates. Some even larger guns of thirteen-inch caliber were also built. The dahlgrens were smooth bore but they could fire shells as well as solid shot. Many guns under eight-inch caliber had rifled bores and were more accurate than the smooth bores. By 1861 there was a wide assortment of naval guns ranging from those of the period of the War of 1812 to thirteen-inch monsters throwing a projectile weighing 280 pounds. *Hartford*'s main battery of twenty nine-inch guns made her a very formidable "sloop of war."

In both navies the officers and men were professionals and the nature of their profession was such that amateurs seeking high rank were not attracted to it. There was nothing to compare with the "political generals" that burdened both armies in the Civil War. Many of the sailors in the Union Navy were foreigners, having enlisted in the Navy for reasons of their own. When that Navy was called upon to ex-

---

[1] This is the correct spelling. In 1863 Union forces captured a blockade runner which was converted to a gunboat and named *Merrimac*.

pand very rapidly, it had a pool of merchant marine officers to draw upon. They lacked naval training and discipline, but they were experienced sailors and quickly made up their deficiencies.

The normal peacetime organization of the Navy consisted of stations, or squadrons, of which there were six. Most of the ships were assigned to foreign stations and only the Home Squadron, as its name implies, was based in home ports. The others were the Mediterranean Squadron, the African Squadron for the suppression of the slave trade, the Brazilian Squadron, the Pacific Squadron, and the East Indies Squadron. The duties of each foreign squadron were to look after and protect American interests within the limits of its station.

It was essentially a deep-water navy, ill trained and unprepared for the inshore and coastal tasks it would be called upon to perform in the Civil War. There was a limited employment of the Home Squadron in this type of operation during the Mexican War, when it was called upon to transport troops, blockade Mexican ports, and bombard shore fortifications in support of troop landings.

With most of the ships far away on foreign station, their officers were not in close touch with the developments at home during the 1850s that led to the break between the North and South. It is unlikely that any active officer, as the crisis approached, could foresee any really important part for the Navy in a civil war. There was no naval preparation for such an eventuality, and one reason for that may be found in the policies of President Lincoln's predecessor.

When Lincoln took office in March 1861, seven states of the cotton belt had seceded from the Union and formed the Confederate States of America, with Jefferson Davis as President and Montgomery, Alabama, as its capital. From the time that South Carolina started the procession in December 1860, President Buchanan followed a policy of doing nothing to aggravate the situation. His position was that the states had no right to secede from the Union but that the Federal government was powerless to stop them from doing so. Lincoln came into office after three months of inactivity in which no important action had been taken to meet the crisis.

The heart of Lincoln's policy was that the Union must be preserved, peaceably if possible but by force if necessary. At first he had no desire to interfere with the institution of slavery other than to insure that it was contained within its existing limits. Eight slave states had not yet taken a stand on secession, and his first concern was to avoid any action which would provoke them into seceding. This seeming inactivity on Lincoln's part caused his Secretary of State, William H. Seward, to submit to him an amazing and arrogant memorandum on April 1, 1861. Seward pointed out the necessity for the government to have a policy, that there now was none, and that the President should set such a policy, but if he were unwilling or unable to do so, he, Seward, was available to take over. Lincoln slapped down this brazen bid to be Prime Minister firmly but gently. Seward's ambition to be considered Lincoln's first minister irritated Gideon Welles and was to cause the Secretary of the Navy some embarrassment, but Welles soon had Seward understanding who was running the Navy Department.

With the North divided on the issue, Lincoln realized that he could depend upon no solid support for the use of force. There was a vocal minority clamoring to send troops to put the impertinent Southerners in their place, but on the whole apathy reigned in the North. Many thought: "Let them go— good riddance"; others professed to be amused by what was happening. Lincoln felt that the only way in which he could get the necessary unity and support in preserving the Union was for the Confederacy to commit the first overt act of war. In his inaugural address on March 4, 1861, he made this clear:

> In your hands, my dissatisfied fellow-countrymen,
> and not in mine, is the momentous issue of civil war.

The government will not assail you. You can have no conflict without being yourselves the aggressors.[2]

Tragically, the Confederacy did commit that first overt act. Fort Sumter solidly united the North—not for long but long enough to permit Lincoln to act. It was only then that naval preparation for the conflict began.

THE SOUTH

IN THE BEGINNING, of course, the Confederacy had no navy, but it did have an able Secretary of the Navy in Stephen R. Mallory of Florida, who did a remarkable job with the limited resources available to him. He was one of two members of Davis's cabinet who held his office throughout the life of the Confederacy. In the 1850s he was a Senator from Florida; in 1853 he became Chairman of the Senate Naval Affairs Committee and was an active backer of the naval shipbuilding modernization program that began in 1854. In that position he became thoroughly familiar with naval affairs and naval developments in Europe. He was enabled, with such a background, to create a substantial Confederate Navy.

Less than half of the officers of the United States Navy were Southern born and only about 300 of those resigned to join fortunes with their native states. These were well distributed among the various ranks, so that at the start Mallory had an adequate pool of officers upon which to draw as needed. Many Southerners remained with their flag for reasons of their own. Commander Charles Steedman of South Carolina, for example, wrote to an old friend in Buenos Aires that he was a Union man and knew no duty but to country and flag. It is ironic and indicative of the high passions of the times that later, after the Union occupation of Port Royal,

---

[2] James L. Richardson (ed.): *Messages and Papers of the Presidents* (Washington; 1897), Vol. VI, p. 111.

South Carolina, he and other South Carolinians who remained with the Union had a price put on their heads as traitors by South Carolina. Among them was Commander Percival Drayton, whose brother commanded the defenses of Port Royal.

The South had no ships for its Navy other than a few small public vessels, such as revenue cutters, which were seized in Southern ports by the seceding states. Nor did the South have a pool of seamen to draw upon. The maritime-minded part of the nation was Yankee and the South had been content to let others haul away her products and to bring in the necessities which she did not produce. Other than small coastal shipping and river craft, there was no indigenous shipping.

To a lesser extent than the army the Confederate Navy was bothered by the inherent weakness of the South—the primacy of the individual states and state rights. As each state seceded, it organized a state navy of its own. These were supposed to be absorbed by the Confederate States Navy within the first year, but the problem of independent state navies was never completely solved.

The basic economy of the South was a plantation economy in which slaves did the field work. The propertied class lived an aristocratic life and took great pride in its observance of the code of gentlemen. Cotton, rice, tobacco, and naval stores were the chief products. These were exported to New England and Europe in exchange for manufactured goods, almost none of which was produced in the South. There were no important factories, no mines to speak of, and no private shipyards except at New Orleans. The Tredegar Iron Works in Richmond was the South's only major foundry. Irish and German immigrants provided most of the skilled craftsmen and the heavy labor for which slaves were unsuited. The economy of the South was obviously very unbalanced, and this was one of the major factors contributing to its downfall.

There were only about 300,000 slaveowners in the Confederacy and less than one third of these owned ten or more slaves. The political leaders of the South came from this group. Those elected to national office tended to hold their offices for long periods, and for that reason, then as now, the chairmanships of the major committees in the national Congress were apt to be held by Southerners, giving them influence and power out of proportion to their numbers.

One disastrous belief, held by almost all Southern leaders, was the doctrine that "Cotton is King." England was easily the South's best customer for its cotton, which provided 95 per cent of British needs. Five million people in England depended upon the textile industry for their livelihood. For twenty years before 1861, English economists had been alarmed by the fact that the source for such an important raw material was outside the British Empire, and they foresaw dire calamities if that source was ever cut off.

Southerners seized and expanded upon that theme. Stop the flow of cotton, they argued, and there would be revolution in England. The North would not dare to interfere with this movement of cotton, for such an action would force England to intervene. One Southern Senator predicted in 1858 that if cut off from its cotton supply for three years, ". . . England would topple headlong and carry the whole civilized world with her save the South. No, you dare not war on Cotton. No power on earth dares make war on cotton. Cotton is King." [3] The conviction that the Union could not interfere with the flow of Southern cotton to England without instant retaliation was universally held in the South, and the disillusionment, when it came, was a bitter one.

---

[3] Senator Hammond (S.C.), March 4, 1858, during the debate on the admission of Kansas to the Union. *Congressional Globe*, 1st Session, 35th Congress, p. 961.

RELATIVE STRATEGIC POSITIONS

IF WE MAY IMAGINE ourselves looking at the South from a spaceship high over the Caribbean Sea, the distinguishing feature is that the entire region consists of a flat coastal plain extending for 3,000 miles from the capes of Virginia to the Rio Grande. Reaching deeply into this plain are the Appalachian and related mountain chains, which form barriers in the inland parts of Virginia, the Carolinas, and Georgia, and to a limited extent in Alabama and eastern Tennessee. Numerous rivers flow outward from these mountains toward the sea. The Mississippi River extends the coastal plain to the northern limits of the Confederacy, but it also separates Arkansas, Texas, and most of Louisiana from the rest of the South. The mountainous regions were generally non-slave areas, and Northern sympathy was strong there throughout the Civil War. Thus the Confederacy, for strategic purposes, consisted primarily of the coastal plain and piedmont regions where the bulk of its one-sided economy was located.

The South's long seacoast contains hundreds of bays, inlets, river mouths, and deltas, but only a few of them were important. In most, the water was too shallow for use by any but small craft. Only ten seaports had rail connections with the interior: Norfolk, Virginia; New Bern and Wilmington, North Carolina; Charleston, South Carolina; Savannah, Georgia; Fernandina and Pensacola, Florida; Mobile, Alabama; and New Orleans. Of these, Wilmington, Charleston, Savannah, Pensacola, Mobile, and New Orleans were the only ones with interstate rail connections. Except for Norfolk, these harbors were relatively shallow, limiting their use to ships of less than twenty feet draft. Almost all of the exports and imports of the South, before the Civil War, went through those six ports, with New Orleans and Mobile the busiest. In volume of goods handled, New Orleans was exceeded only by New York as a seaport.

East of the Mississippi there was a fairly well-developed railroad system, although it was not as extensive as that in the North. Southern railroads were dependent upon the North for locomotives, rolling stock, and rails, a weakness that was to prove critical as the war progressed. Hard-surface or macadam roads were almost unknown, and in Richmond only the business district was paved with cobblestones.

For transportation the South depended less on its railroads than on its river and coastal steamers and schooners. In 1861 there were regular packet services between the principal Southern and Northern ports. In all of the South, however, there were only three shipyards—the Navy Yard at Norfolk, another naval repair yard at Pensacola, and private shipbuilding facilities at New Orleans.

With its long coast line and numerous inlets the South was especially vulnerable to attacks from the sea. The naval attacker has mobility and the choice of time and place to launch an attack, but by and large the North failed to take full advantage of the great strategic assets in this form of military operation.

The population of the South was about 9,000,000, of which about 3,500,000 were slaves. The North had a population of over 20,000,000. Offhand the North would seem to have had a vastly superior pool of manpower to draw on, but the nature of the Civil War was such that to achieve its objectives the North had to invade and occupy the South. This gave the defender a decided natural advantage. There were but three main avenues of invasion by land open to the North—the coastal region of Virginia with many rivers crossing it, the Shenandoah Valley, and the Mississippi Valley. Each route had serious military obstacles. At the outset, at least, the South was much more united than the North, where factional and regional differences were divisive elements. Also, the military spirit was more highly developed in the South, which was a region of horsemen where no white man would walk when he could ride. In light of these factors, the South was by no means hopelessly outclassed in a contest of arms.

The greatest single advantage possessed by the Union was that it contained the industry of the United States and was diversified enough to provide the means for conducting a major war. The rich farming regions of the West were already producing exportable surpluses of grains and other foodstuffs. Economically there was no real comparison in the relative strength of the North and the South, but before that disparity was exploited by the Union—and how that happened is a central theme of this study—many blunders would be made and much blood would be needlessly shed.

Chapter II

Opening Moves

THE RELIEF OF FORTS SUMTER
AND PICKENS

As each Southern state seceded from the Union it seized the Federal ships and buildings within its limits. By the time of Lincoln's inauguration there were but two outposts in those states still in Federal hands, Fort Sumter in the harbor of Charleston, South Carolina, and Fort Pickens at the entrance to Pensacola harbor in Florida.

At the time of South Carolina's secession, on December 20, 1860, Major Robert Anderson commanded the harbor defenses of Charleston with a token garrison of about seventy men. To South Carolinians, who firmly believed that the act of secession was the exercise of the constitutional right of a state to withdraw from the Union whenever it so desired, the Union flag flying over the harbor forts was an alien flag. There was a clamor to drive the "foreigners" out. As tension grew, Major Anderson prudently withdrew his small garrison to the most inaccessible fort, Fort Sumter, built on a shoal near the harbor entrance. South Carolina troops occupied the other forts in the harbor and busily built other fortifications aimed at isolating and surrounding Fort Sumter. In March 1861 Major Anderson reported to Washington that he could no longer obtain provisions in Charleston and that if he was not relieved by April 16, he would have to surrender. What to do about Fort Sumter thus became one of the most pressing problems that Lincoln had to face.

At this time the Union Army was headed by the aged General Winfield Scott, hero of the Mexican War and the battle of Lundy's Lane in 1814. Most of the Army, which had only about 15,000 troops, was deployed against the Indians along the Western frontier. General Scott felt that it was then too late to withdraw troops from the West to reinforce the Southern forts still in Union hands. Lincoln's cabinet was divided on the question. Secretary of State Seward was negotiating with Southern commissioners in Washington, through intermediaries, for the evacuation of the two forts. On March 15 Lincoln placed before the cabinet the proposal of Gustavus V. Fox to relieve Fort Sumter, using shallow draft vessels and force if necessary. Gideon Welles thought Fox's plan would result in civil war and, plagued as he was by resignations of Southern officers and with the Navy unprepared, he advised against it. Lincoln sent Fox to Charleston to bring back a first-hand report of conditions, and on his return late in the month, Fox convinced the President that his plan was feasible. On March 29 Lincoln reached the decision to relieve Fort Sumter. Welles then promptly ordered the naval vessels requested by Fox to be made ready by April 6.

The steam sloop *Powhatan* had returned to New York from Vera Cruz on March 14 and on March 28 Welles had ordered her placed out of commission. Now, after the decision to relieve Fort Sumter, he ordered the ship to be prepared for sea service. Welles felt that the powerful *Powhatan* would provide added insurance for the success of Fox's plan.

Fox sailed from New York on April 10 with transports carrying 200 troops, provisions, and supplies, and arrived off Charleston early on the 12th, where he expected to join the assigned naval vessels. Two of them were already there, but

Powhatan failed to appear, for reasons which will become apparent shortly.

Meanwhile the Confederate commissioners in Washington were sending frantic telegrams to their government about the expedition and its possible destination. The latter was clarified on April 8; a special emissary from Lincoln arrived in Charleston to inform General Beauregard, commanding the South Carolina forces, and the governor that Fort Sumter was shortly to be reprovisioned peaceably, but by force if necessary. On learning of this, Jefferson Davis, with his cabinet's approval, authorized General Beauregard to demand the surrender of the fort at his discretion. The demand for its surrender was made on April 10, but Major Anderson rejected it. A bombardment of the fort commenced on April 12, the day Fox arrived off the harbor, and Major Anderson was forced to surrender late the next day. Fox then had the humiliating experience of embarking the major and his troops under parole and carrying them north instead of reinforcing them.

At about the same time occurred one of the most bizarre series of incidents in American military history—the efforts to relieve Fort Pickens at Pensacola.

Buchanan's Secretary of the Navy, Isaac Toucey of Connecticut, is usually considered to have been a strong Southern sympathizer who deliberately did nothing in the closing months of the Buchanan administration to prepare for possible trouble. Yet when talk of secession was running high in Florida at the end of 1860 and in early 1861, he was alert to developments and ordered the commandant of the Pensacola Navy Yard to be ". . . vigilant to protect the public property." The commandant sent provisions to Fort Pickens and ordered the steamer *Wyandotte* to co-operate with the fort in case of attack. He also transported the small garrison at Fort Barrancas, near Pensacola, to Pickens, which was on an island at the harbor entrance.

On January 12 a force of about 350 militia from Florida and

Alabama appeared at the Navy Yard and demanded its surrender. The Union flag was hauled down without a shot being fired and with no effort to send movable property to Fort Pickens or to evacuate anyone. A later court of inquiry found that the commandant had taken no steps for the defense of the yard, although he had heard rumors of troops moving against it several days before they appeared. The lieutenant commanding Fort Pickens was made of sterner stuff, for he notified the Florida troops that he would defend the fort if attacked.

Within two weeks Toucey sent out the steam sloop *Brooklyn*, loaded with troops for Fort Pickens and artillery for Fort Jefferson on Dry Tortugas Island, near Key West, Florida. He also ordered the Home Squadron commander, who was then off Vera Cruz, Mexico, to send two warships to Pensacola. At the end of January the then Senator Mallory of Florida arranged a truce with Buchanan providing that the fort would not be attacked if the troops then en route were not landed. There followed an uneasy respite at Pensacola until after Lincoln took office and Gideon Welles learned that the troops were still on board *Brooklyn*. In the middle of March he ordered the senior officer at Pensacola to land them.

On April 1 Lincoln's personal secretary handed Welles an order signed by Lincoln himself, directing that he send his chief detail officer to take command at Pensacola and that the post of chief detail officer be given to Captain Samuel Barron. Barron was a Southerner whose loyalty was in doubt and Welles was much agitated by the order. Leaving an unfinished dinner, he hurried to the White House. When he entered the President's office, Lincoln noticed his discomposure and asked: "What have I done wrong?" It developed that that afternoon Seward had been in Lincoln's office with some officers and that Lincoln had signed some papers at the Secretary's request. Welles drew out that the officers present were Captain Montgomery Meigs of the Army and Lieutenant

David D. Porter of the Navy. Lincoln told him to disregard the order about Barron and promised that he would not handle such papers again.

Welles determined to make it clear to the Secretary of State that he could not interfere with the affairs of the Navy Department. What he did not know as yet, since Lincoln did not tell him about Seward's project, was that the latter, with the help of Meigs and Porter, had concocted a scheme for the reinforcement of Fort Pickens. Seward believed that involvement in a foreign war would divert attention from the crisis at home and might bring the South back into the Union. On March 30 he received word from his consul general in Havana that a Spanish expedition had left that port for the presumed purpose of invading Santo Domingo, which feared conquest by Haiti and as a result had requested annexation to Spain. But Seward did not know this, and he sent a stiff note to the Spanish minister in Washington protesting the apparent invasion. In view of the possibility of war with Spain, he felt that the Gulf forts, especially Forts Jefferson and Pickens, should be strengthened. He had already talked with Meigs about this and now he called him in to work out the details. Porter became a willing accomplice. Seward took the two to the White House, where it was stressed that secrecy was essential to success, and Lincoln's approval was obtained.

Meigs and Porter then drew up several orders which Lincoln signed. One sent Meigs in command of the troops to be used. Another assigned Porter to command *Powhatan* to support Meigs and his transports. This was the ship that Welles had already assigned to the Fort Sumter expedition. What was behind Porter's draft of the order about Barron is not known, as Porter's own memoirs are silent on it. He justified bypassing the Secretary of the Navy in this affair by the need for absolute secrecy and the rampant disloyalty in the Navy Department.

A few days after his meeting with Lincoln, Welles received

some vaguely worded telegrams from Captain Andrew H. Foote, acting commandant of the New York Navy Yard, relative to *Powhatan* and the Army and Navy officers who had special instructions from the government. Suspecting that this had something to do with Seward's meeting with the President, Welles wired Foote to hold *Powhatan* until further orders. Meanwhile an officer from Pensacola appeared in Welles's office to report that the senior officer there had still not landed the troops because of the earlier agreement. Welles then sent Lieutenant John L. Worden, later to command *Monitor*, posthaste overland to Pensacola with a firm order to land the troops at once.

That evening Seward appeared at Welles's quarters complaining that Meigs and Porter were having trouble carrying out their orders because of conflicting orders from the Secretary of the Navy. Welles then let the Secretary of State have full salvos of wrath for his effort to interfere with the affairs of the Navy Department. He did not record the tongue-lashing he gave Seward, but on the way to the White House —Welles insisted on straightening out the matter at once— Seward told him that he had learned a lesson from this experience; from now on he would confine himself to his own department and not interfere with others.

It developed that Lincoln had not read and did not know what was in the papers he had signed for Seward and he directed the Secretary of State to recall Porter. Seward's telegram to Porter telling him to restore *Powhatan* to her captain reached New York after she had sailed, but the New York commandant, Captain Foote, sent a tug in pursuit. The telegram was delivered just as the ship was about to clear the harbor. Porter sent back an arrogant reply to the effect that he was operating under direct orders from the President and would carry them out. He continued his run to Pensacola.

Meanwhile Worden delivered Welles's order at Pensacola and the troops were landed without incident, though the indignation of General Braxton Bragg, commanding the Confederate forces at Pensacola, was aroused. Four days later, on April 16, Meigs arrived from New York with his transports; the troops were landed and set to work to strengthen and improve the defenses of Fort Pickens. Porter arrived in *Powhatan* the next day. With some difficulty, Captain Meigs dissuaded him from forcing the harbor and engaging the inner Confederate forts. Horses and supplies for the troops were still being unloaded and the Army officers naturally did not want to precipitate a fight when they were not ready for it. *Powhatan* then joined the naval squadron off Pensacola under Captain H. A. Adams. Fort Pickens remained in Union possession and the use of Pensacola harbor was denied to the Confederates.

AFTERMATH OF FORT SUMTER

THE ATTACK on Fort Sumter triggered a chain of events which led to the Civil War itself. The people of the North were angered, aroused, and unified to a degree comparable to that of a later generation of Americans after Pearl Harbor. Lincoln was then in a position to take positive action to preserve the Union.

On April 15 he issued a proclamation stating that an insurrection had occurred in certain Southern states that was beyond the power of the normal law-enforcing agencies to handle. He called upon the remaining states, including the other slave states that had not yet seceded, for 75,000 volunteers to serve for three months. With them he would recover the forts, arsenals, Navy Yards, and public buildings that had been seized by the seceding states. He also called a special session of Congress for July 4.

The fine hand of Seward may be seen in this proclamation. Southerners believed that the states involved in secession were exercising a perfectly legal constitutional right. To label these secessions an "insurrection" meant that the constitutional question was brushed aside and the citizens of those states became "Rebels," a term that was bitterly resented in the South at the time. Lincoln did not have to have the sanction of Congress in calling for volunteers to put down an internal disturbance, and the delay in calling Congress into session was deliberate. Under the old law of 1795, on which Lincoln relied, the militia could be kept in service for thirty days after Congress convened. The lesson was not lost on another President ninety years later when President Truman sent United States armed forces into Korea in what was described as a "police action."

Jefferson Davis, who had already called for 21,000 volunteers following Lincoln's notice that Fort Sumter was to be relieved, met the challenge promptly. In a proclamation of April 17 he announced that Lincoln's proclamation indicated that the South would be invaded and that it was the duty of the Confederate government to repel the invasion. Thus both sides were committed to war by Presidential proclamation. Neither side realized the tremendous effort that would be required to carry on such a war.

Davis went one step farther and precipitated the action which would become the principal basis of Union naval strategy. In his proclamation he called for volunteers to take out Confederate letters of marque, a commission or license for privately owned and armed vessels to capture Northern merchant ships at sea. This was a revival of the privateers of earlier wars. Since the Confederacy then had no navy, it was hoped that the privateers would so disrupt Northern commerce that European countries would intervene on the side of the South. Anticipating that a blockade of Southern ports might be attempted, it was also hoped that the privateers would so occupy Union naval forces that no blockade could be established. This was the first great and tragic miscalculation in the Confederate naval effort. Southern leaders, except Secretary Mallory, were not maritime minded and did not anticipate the consequences of this call. Unwittingly in the proclamation, with its call for privateers, Jefferson Davis signed the death warrant of the Confederacy.

Lincoln countered the Confederate move on April 19 by proclaiming a naval blockade against the ports of the seceded states. That it was in retaliation for Davis's proclamation is clear, for Lincoln added that any vessel found interfering with United States merchant shipping would be treated under the laws of piracy. This was bitterly resented in the South, and Davis later forced the North to modify its position by threatening comparable treatment of Northern prisoners of war if Southern privateersmen were punished as pirates. A blockade of Southern ports probably would have been forced upon the Union by the course of events, but Davis's call for privateers brought on the proclamation at the very outset of the war.

Gideon Welles had only a minor part in the preparation of Lincoln's proclamation, but he saw at once a flaw in it. As he pointed out to his colleagues in the cabinet and to the President, a country does not blockade its rebellious ports—it closes them. Proclaiming a blockade had the effect of recognizing a state of belligerency with the Confederacy, a condition which deeply affected the rights and duties of neutrals. The implied recognition was seized upon in the South. When Captain Adams at Pensacola informed General Bragg on May 13 that the port was blockaded, Bragg replied the next day: "Your communication . . . announcing . . . the blockade of this port, I accept and consider it a virtual acknowledgement of our national existence and independence." [1]

Welles's objection was overruled for good reason. Well before the proclamation was drafted, Seward sounded out Lord Lyons, the British Minister in Washington, on probable British

---

[1] ORN, Vol. 4, p. 168.

reaction to three alternatives. They were: to close the Southern ports; to station cruisers off the ports to collect customs dues; or to maintain a strict blockade of them. Lord Lyons made it clear that either of the first two might force British recognition of the Confederacy in order to protect the legitimate rights of British trade. Blockade was an accepted form of naval warfare which the British had used in their own wars. Lincoln and Seward concluded that the only safe course, to forestall formal recognition of the Confederacy as an independent nation, was the blockade.

Northern leaders were anxious to avoid having European countries, especially England and France, grant formal recognition to the Confederacy, insisting that the war was an internal disturbance. Southern leaders were equally anxious to secure such recognition. The diplomatic correspondence clearly reveals the strong effort made by the South to obtain this recognition and the even stronger effort by the Union to prevent it. By recognizing a state of belligerency through the proclamation of the blockade, on the other hand, the Union could not deny the right of European countries to recognize the same condition, but it was critical and resentful when they did so. Welles felt so strongly upon this point that at his insistence Congress passed a law closing Southern ports to trade, but the law had little significance since it came after the blockade had already been announced. Northern leaders, Lincoln excepted, tried to ignore the implications of recognized belligerency by consistently referring to Southerners as rebels and to Confederate warships as "rebel pirates."

The three related Presidential proclamations established the naval strategies of both the North and the South, but since they were the result of purely political decisions, they did not take into account the capabilities of either navy to carry them out. For the Union Navy, the main task was to establish and maintain the blockade. The Confederate Navy had as its main task to break, circumvent, or discredit the Union blockade.

Secretary Mallory saw this clearly and was steadfast in his effort to accomplish it.

In organizing his Navy Department Mallory followed the
pattern of the Federal Navy Department but with only a
skeleton staff. The first requirement was to obtain warships to
operate against Union commerce, and it was soon obvious
that, except for the few craft seized in Southern ports, they
would have to be bought elsewhere. Shortly after the department was organized, Mallory sent Commander Raphael
Semmes, who was to become the South's leading corsair, on a
fruitless trip to New York to obtain ships and other needed
naval equipment. Undaunted, Mallory decided that the real
answer to the South's naval needs was the ironclads. With just
one of the new ironclads of European design he believed that
he could break the blockade and engage successfully the entire
Union fleet of wooden vessels. In May, therefore, he sent
Commander James D. Bulloch to England to secure warships, including ironclads, and he even hoped to buy one of
the *Gloire* class from France. That hope may have been optimistic, but of the vicissitudes and successes of Commander
Bulloch we shall hear much more.

Gideon Welles also recognized the blockade as his main task
and set out to meet the challenge with vigor, but for him there
were other immediate problems.

Lincoln's proclamations created crises in the slave states
that had not yet seceded. Their governors refused indignantly
to call for any volunteers. Virginia as a whole was reluctant to
join the secession movement, for her people correctly foresaw
that their state would become a major battleground in a civil
war. But the high feeling aroused by the Lincoln proclamation tipped the scales and Virginia seceded on April 17. North
Carolina, Tennessee, and Arkansas followed. Maryland and
Missouri were saved to the Union by military coups, and Kentucky declared herself "neutral." Delaware, with few slaves,
had strong ties with the North and posed no serious problem.

After their secession, Lincoln extended the blockade to include Virginia and North Carolina ports.

Welles, noting the possibility in early April that Virginia might secede, became alarmed about the security of the Norfolk Navy Yard, the largest and best equipped in the country. Not only did it have extensive shops, warehouses, and a drydock, but also a number of ships were there, including the almost new steam frigate *Merrimack*. That ship, in particular, must not fall into the hands of the Confederates. Welles sent a special representative to Norfolk to get the *Merrimack* out of danger posthaste, but the Navy Yard was commanded by a superannuated officer who either could not or would not do anything to arouse local Confederates to action.

After Virginia seceded and Virginians moved toward the yard, loyal officers and men made a halfhearted effort at demolishing the yard, making their escape in *Cumberland*. Numerous fires were set, some damage was done to the drydock, but most of the shops were undamaged. *Merrimack* was set on fire but burned only to the water line and was easily salvaged. In addition, about 1,200 naval guns of all calibers and a large supply of gunpowder fell to the Confederates, the richest prize they obtained from the North, and Gideon Welles was understandably incensed by the losses.

FOREIGN REACTION

ON THE HEELS of the proclamation of the Northern blockade came a spontaneous movement in the South to stop the flow of Southern cotton to Europe—the best way, it was believed, to bring about European intervention in favor of the South. The "Cotton is King" doctrine was being put to the supreme test.

As it happened, most of the cotton already sold to European buyers was shipped out before the blockade was physically established. British and other neutral ships in Southern ports were given a limited time to clear those ports, and at New Orleans the time was extended because of the difficulty in getting the laden ships out of the passes of the Mississippi. By midsummer brokers in New Orleans had sent word to the back country to hold cotton and not send it to that port. A golden opportunity to export large quantities of cotton before the blockade could be made effective, thus building up substantial credits abroad, was thereby lost. However commendable the high patriotic spirit behind this self-imposed embargo, it was certainly one of the major blunders committed by the infant Confederacy.

Not all Southerners approved of the embargo. Judah P. Benjamin, Attorney General and the "Brains of the Confederacy," saw the need for foreign credits and urged that large quantities of cotton be shipped as fast as possible. His voice was not heard. Several efforts were made in the Confederate Congress to legalize the embargo, efforts that Jefferson Davis was able to forestall since he realized that such a law would make it appear that the South was trying to blackmail European countries into intervening in the war. As it was, most ships in Southern harbors that were free to sail did so with good cargoes. Aside from the heavy financial loss to the South, the cotton embargo played directly into the hands of the North. When Southern agents later argued before European leaders that the Union blockade was only a paper affair and not really effective, they were silenced by the simple question: "Where is your cotton?"

The principal European countries watched the events on the other side of the Atlantic with deep interest. In England Lord Palmerston, the Prime Minister, and Earl Russell, the Foreign Minister, were concerned with conditions on the Continent and especially with the ambitious schemes of Napoleon III in France. As war clouds were forming in the United States, England joined with France in a show of force in Mexico, where foreign debts were in default as a result of civil war. Most of the United States Home Squadron was also there keeping a close watch on developments. Early in 1862, when it became apparent that Napoleon III was intent on the occupation of Mexico, England withdrew rather than risk a clash with the United States over the Monroe Doctrine. Napoleon, on the other hand, saw in the Civil War an opportunity to extend his empire to North America. From the beginning he was sympathetic to the South, in contrast to most of the French people, who condemned slavery.

On May 14, less than a month after Lincoln's proclamation of the blockade, England issued a proclamation which recognized that a state of belligerency existed between the North and the South and declared its own neutrality in the struggle. France, Spain, and other European countries followed with similar proclamations within a few weeks. England's action was denounced by Seward as being taken with undue haste, and was interpreted in the North as an indication of English sympathy for the South. It was hailed in the South as the first step toward general European recognition of the independence of the Confederacy. Both reactions were badly in error for the British simply acted in self-interest. There were some thirty English ships in New Orleans and several million dollars' worth of English-owned goods in Southern ports. It was considered urgent that these receive the protection that a declaration of formal neutrality would give them.

The diplomatic correspondence between the United States and England during the Civil War was often heated and belligerent in tone. At times the situation seemed to present a very real threat of war to the Civil War leaders. But from the perspective of a century it is clear that neither Palmerston nor Earl Russell, while quick to assert and defend forcefully what they conceived to be British rights, had any intention of becoming embroiled in the Civil War.

England's formal neutrality actually played into the hands

of the North and struck a heavy blow at the South. By recognizing the Union blockade, the government in effect warned British shipping that it could trade with the South only at its own peril. In the event that legitimate shipping interests should attempt to trade with the South despite the blockade, they would be denied the protection of the government and would find it difficult to get insurance and other perquisites of normal trade. This decision forced all British maritime trade with the blockaded states into clandestine channels. The resulting profits proved so alluring that adventurers were able to develop many ways to evade the blockade and such trade with the South became substantial. But the very existence and recognition of the blockade disrupted the normal channels of trade to such an extent that the clandestine channels could never completely replace them.

Chapter III

The Offensive Begins

FIRST STEPS

Wᴵᵀʜ ᴛʜᴇ ꜰᴀʟʟ of Fort Sumter several cabinet officers in Washington turned to the aged General in Chief of the Army, Winfield Scott, for advice on recovering the South. Scott felt that the job could not be done by a citizen army enlisted for only three months but that it would take at least three years. It would be a mistake, he said, to rush an army headlong into the South as some hotheads were clamoring for. In conjunction with a naval blockade of the Southern coast, he suggested sending a column down the Mississippi. This would serve a triple purpose. It would split the Confederacy and, with the blockade, it would establish a cordon around most of the South. Finally, it would reopen the Mississippi as an outlet for the farming regions of the West. While this broad plan was not followed in detail, it proved to be a fairly accurate outline of how the war was fought on the Union side. It was General Winfield Scott, therefore, who suggested the basis of the naval strategy of the North, for it was he who specifically recommended the naval blockade, although it was not a new idea. Politicians had been talking about it for years.

When Scott's ideas became public, as they soon did, they were attacked bitterly by those who favored quick and direct action. He was accused of wanting to avoid fighting and of unnecessarily prolonging the coming conflict. His ideas were derisively dubbed the "Anaconda Plan," since the victim was to be strangled in the manner of the South American reptile. In the heated and united mood that then existed in the North the plan was doomed to popular rejection. Gideon Welles himself recorded that he disapproved of Scott's plan as being purely defensive.

As the costly, prolonged, and bloody campaigns in Virginia and the Mississippi Valley were to show, militarily the South could take care of itself until it was seriously weakened economically by the Union naval blockade and was split and isolated along the Mississippi River. In the end Scott proved to be a far wiser prophet than his critics. But within a few months after war began the gouty old general was to find the burden of directing the Army too much for him and he stepped aside.

The conduct of a naval blockade was subject to international law. It had to be formally proclaimed and the country proclaiming it had to be able to enforce it. Gideon Welles knew that Lincoln's proclamation had given him an almost hopeless task. If the blockade was to be accepted and respected abroad, it had to be established promptly and, according to an elementary rule of international law, it had to be effective. Just what "effective" meant was open to argument, but one recognized essential was that the blockading nation must keep ships constantly patrolling off the blockaded ports.

In the British blockade during the Napoleonic Wars the United States had insisted on the observance of this rule of "effectiveness." Now that her role vis-à-vis England was reversed she could expect England to hold her to the same standard. It is ironic that in the Civil War the United States was to find herself defending practices as a belligerent that she had vigorously denounced as a neutral. England, as a neutral, just as vigorously argued for neutral rights that earlier she had rejected as a belligerent.

Welles's problem, therefore, was to find the necessary ships to get the blockade established. Initially there were only three naval vessels in Northern ports that could be used. All but three ships in foreign stations were recalled, but it would be weeks and even months before they could return home and be made ready for blockade duty.

In Washington the security of the capital itself was in danger. When mobs in Baltimore tore up railroad tracks and bridges and clashed with Massachusetts troops en route to Washington, that city was isolated. During this crisis Welles received a recommendation from the Superintendent of the Naval Academy that the Academy be evacuated from nearby Annapolis, as that city was a hotbed of secessionist sentiment. Welles thereupon sent an officer to Captain Samuel F. Du Pont, commandant of the Philadelphia Navy Yard, with instructions for him to rush a ship to Chesapeake Bay to cover the evacuation of the Academy to Newport, Rhode Island, in the old frigate *Constitution*, then at Annapolis. Du Pont did so, and shortly afterward showed commendable initiative by assisting Brigadier General Benjamin F. Butler, a Massachusetts politician turned soldier, to set up a water route in Chesapeake Bay which bypassed troublesome Baltimore.

Welles sent another officer, via the western route through Wheeling, to Du Pont and the commandants of the Navy Yards at New York and Boston with instructions to buy or charter and arm suitable ships for blockade duty. At about the same time Welles was offered some voluntary assistance in ship procurement by the Chairman of the Senate Naval Affairs Committee, Senator John P. Hale of New Hampshire, who told him of two ships that the Navy should purchase. Welles investigated and found that neither was suitable. There was also a sharp difference of opinion between the Navy and the shipowners as to their ships' value. When the Senator returned to Washington for the special session of Congress and learned that Welles had refused to buy the ships, it was apparent that the Secretary had made an enemy.

In mid-May, when Welles learned that the Navy had been defrauded in a ship purchase in New York, he decided that naval officers were not well equipped for such work. Although knowing that he would have to defend himself from charges of nepotism, he appointed his brother-in-law, George D. Morgan, a New York businessman, as the sole purchasing agent for the Navy in New York. Months later, when this appointment was under fire, he was able to show his critics that Morgan had saved the government $73,000 in renegotiating contracts for five ships. Before the year was out the Secretary of War was forced to resign over Army contract scandals, but Welles, under repeated attack as he was, was able to defend his actions in every case. In doing so he also demonstrated that he was a master politician. Even before the President's message had been read to the special session of Congress on July 4, Senator Hale introduced a resolution calling for a complete report on the Navy's ship procurement contracts. Welles confounded his critic by submitting the required report along with the President's message.

Next to ship procurement, Welles's most urgent task was to get the ships stationed off the principal Southern ports to perform blockade duty. Hampton Roads was easy to cover, for the Home Squadron was based there. Flag Officer Pendergast, commanding that squadron, issued a notice on April 30 that he had sufficient ships to enforce the blockade for the Chesapeake Capes and warned all affected by the blockade to comply with its terms. On the next day he seized a schooner bound from Alexandria, Virginia, to Norfolk.

On May 1 Captain W. W. McKean, in *Niagara* at New York, was ordered to Charleston, South Carolina, to establish the blockade of that port. Two days later, after receipt of a report that a large shipment of European arms was on its way to New Orleans, the Navy ordered him to proceed to the Gulf of Mexico. Captain McKean arrived off Charleston on May 9 and gave notice of the blockade. During the next five days, until he received the change in his orders, he boarded several ships bound for Charleston and Savannah and warned them off. One square-rigger was so persistent in its effort to enter Charleston that it was seized as a prize and sent north under the command of Midshipman Winfield S. Schley, who was to become a well-known naval commander in the Spanish-American War.

Even before receiving the formal order to establish the blockade, Captain Adams, senior officer off Pensacola, notified Confederate officials ashore on May 13 that the blockade of that port was being enforced. Before the end of May blockading ships were also off Mobile and the mouths of the Mississippi. After the blockade was established off Mobile, Fort Morgan, the principal fort guarding the entrance to Mobile Bay, displayed a United States flag with its union jack down, below the Confederate flag.

Early in May, Flag Officer S. H. Stringham was appointed to command the Atlantic Blockading Squadron, charged with covering the Southern coast from Key West to Hampton Roads. As ships reported to him, he fitted them into the blockade where most needed. Within a month of Lincoln's proclamation the principal Southern ports were under a blockade of sorts. Curiously, in view of its subsequent importance as a haven for blockade runners, Wilmington was not blockaded until July.

This period also produced the beginning of another type of naval operation that was to become common as the war progressed. On May 7, Flag Officer Pendergast, senior officer in Hampton Roads, ordered Lieutenant Selfridge, in the armed steamer *Yankee*, to reconnoiter reported fortifications at Gloucester Point, in the York River in Virginia. As *Yankee* approached the fort a shot from a shore battery was fired across *Yankee*'s bow. When a second shot landed closer to the ship, Selfridge stopped, listed his ship to starboard to get increased gun range, and fired a few rounds in reply, but all fell short. The battery fired two more shots close aboard *Yankee* and Selfridge, realizing that he was outranged by heavier guns, withdrew. This little exchange, harmless to the participants, was the modest beginning of what was to become a characteristic feature of the naval side of the Civil War. For the next four years Union ships and gunboats would slug it out repeatedly with Southern forts and shore batteries.

It took time for the blockade to get into high gear, but by the middle of July Flag Officer Stringham could report that he had eleven ships off Savannah, Charleston, and the North Carolina coast, with others watching the mouths of the James, Rappahannock, and York Rivers in Virginia. From that time on his squadron built up steadily and the blockade began to take on a semblance of that "effectiveness" required by international law. An English observer noted that by June 1861 the blockade was already causing "some inconvenience" in New Orleans.

It became apparent early that directing the blockade from Hampton Roads would not be satisfactory. If they had to return there for coal and supplies, the ships off Savannah and Charleston would be off their stations too long and there were not enough ships available to cover for them in maintaining a continuous blockade of those ports. To meet this problem Welles took a characteristic action. Late in June he appointed a board to study the conduct of the blockade and to devise ways and means for improving its efficiency. His order convening the board specifically mentioned the desirability of seizing at least two points on the Southern Atlantic coast with Fernandina, Florida, as one of them. No general principles of naval strategy had been developed at this time, and the board had no formal title, but as its reports were actually strategic studies, the board will be referred to here as the Board of Strategy.

It was headed by Captain Samuel F. Du Pont, who had already shown his initiative as commandant of the Philadelphia Navy Yard. The second member, chosen for his specialized knowledge, was Professor A. D. Bache, superintendent of the Coast Survey. The third member was an Army engineer, Major J. C. Barnard, and Commander C. H. Davis served as secretary. The board made a thorough study of its problems and made its first report early in July. This was concerned primarily with the seizure of Fernandina. The depth of water off the port, at the Florida-Georgia border, was such that all but the largest ships of the Navy could use it. If it could be seized secretly, the docks and buildings of the unfinished Florida Railroad would provide ready facilities for the storage of coal and repair shops. It was a healthy spot and had ample wood and fresh water. It was estimated that 3,000 men could take and hold it.

The second and third reports, submitted later in the month, recommended that the blockading force be divided into two squadrons, with the dividing line between them in North Carolina near the South Carolina border. The nature of the coast north and south of the recommended line differed widely. With the use of supplementary measures it would be necessary to watch closely only ten to twelve harbors and inlets on the entire Atlantic coast. Unwatched inlets, especially those through the outer fringe of islands in the northern sector, could be blocked by sinking old hulks, loaded with ballast. In this sector the board recommended the seizure of Hatteras Inlet, a few miles southwestward of Cape Hatteras. Flag Officer Stringham earlier had reported that this inlet, so recently formed by storms that it did not appear on most charts, was a favorite passage for privateers and blockade runners. It had an easy entrance, provided a safe anchorage, and he recommended that it be seized. In the southern sector the board narrowed the number of suitable harbors that might be seized to five, of which Port Royal, about midway between Charleston and Savannah, was considered the most desirable.

The board next turned to the Gulf of Mexico and the special problems it presented. Key West remained in Union possession and provided one base, but it was too far from the Gulf's major ports—New Orleans, Mobile, and Galveston. Most of the board's report of August 9 was devoted to the delta of the Mississippi River and the approaches to New Orleans. It recommended that Ship Island, off Biloxi, Mississippi, which the Confederates conveniently evacuated in September, be occupied. In addition, the report suggested that Head of the Passes, where the three main channels from the Mississippi to the sea converged about ten miles from the Gulf, should be fortified and Barataria Bay, through which some minor channels led to New Orleans, should be occupied.

The significance of the work of this board was that its reports were the basis for a broad strategic plan to maintain the blockade. It provided for the seizure of ports in the South, intended as bases for the blockading ships, and this in itself was a severe blow to the Southern cause. Although its recommendations were not carried out to the letter, mainly due to inability to get the Army to provide troops needed to occupy key locations, it gave the Navy a solid foundation on which to build for the task at hand. That was something the Union Army did not achieve until late in the war.

Gideon Welles promptly presented these proposals to the President and cabinet, and early in August he informed Du Pont that they were approved. Du Pont would be the naval commander of the expedition to seize Port Royal and the War Department would order an officer to command the troops. The seizure of Hatteras Inlet was assigned to Flag Officer Stringham.

THE RIVER GUNBOATS

IN HIS PLAN for regaining control of the Mississippi River Winfield Scott estimated that from twelve to twenty gunboats and transports for 60,000 men would be required. At first Gideon Welles assumed that this would be purely an Army project. Early in May he received a letter from James B. Eads, a St. Louis engineer, suggesting the establishment of a protected base at Cairo, Illinois, at the mouth of the Ohio River. He also suggested the use of a river snagboat, a sturdy steamboat designed to remove obstructions from the rivers, to patrol the two rivers. She would be protected by cotton bales and be armed with 32-pounder guns. Welles merely passed these important suggestions on to the War Department.

A few days later, at the request of the War Department, he sent Commander John Rodgers to Cincinnati to report to General McClellan to help in developing a naval force to blockade the Ohio and Mississippi Rivers. Naval Constructor S. M. Pook was also sent out at Rodgers's request. The latter entered into his new duties with such zeal that by the end of May an irate citizen of Pittsburgh complained to the Secretary of War that Rodgers was purchasing steamers in that city, claiming that he had charge of all water movement, although, the writer asserted, the inland waters were obviously under the jurisdiction of the Army and the Navy had no business being there. Welles at the time agreed with this position. When Rodgers reported that he had obtained three steamers and asked for armament for them, Welles censured him for his action, telling him that McClellan would arrange for all such purchases. Rodgers replied that the general had already approved the purchases. To make his position quite clear, Welles then told Rodgers that all movements on the Ohio and Mississippi Rivers were under the control of the

Army. The effect of this was that unwittingly Welles established what became known in World War II as a unified command. For the next year and a half naval officers on the Western rivers operated under the orders of the Army commanders.

The three steamers purchased by Rodgers became the protected gunboats *Lexington*, *Conestoga*, and *Tyler*. The vital spaces were protected against rifle fire by a heavy sheathing of oak. They were manned by the Navy, and before the middle of August Rodgers was able to report that all three were assembled at Cairo. They were soon prowling the river below that town and reporting on the activities of the Confederate forces in the vicinity. On August 22, Commander R. N. Stembel, in *Lexington*, seized a steamer at Paducah, Kentucky, and turned it over to the Army at Cairo. That was the beginning of what would become a characteristic aspect of operations in the Mississippi Basin—the capture or destruction of every river craft that could be useful to the Confederates.

In getting his little force started and operating, Rodgers apparently stepped on some Army toes, for General John C. Fremont, commanding at St. Louis, asked for his removal, also requesting that a naval officer be placed in command of the naval operations on the rivers, with orders to report to him. Welles thereupon sent Captain Andrew H. Foote to take command of naval operations on the Western rivers under the direction of the War Department, thus formally setting up the unified command.

The War Department contracted with Eads in St. Louis to construct seven ironclad gunboats, to be completed by October 10. Naval Constructor Pook helped with the design and construction of these gunboats. When Captain Foote assumed command early in September, only the three naval gunboats at Cairo were actively operating. The seven Eads ironclads were coming along and two other steamboats, purchased by Fremont, were being converted to gunboats. It would be several months before their sting would be felt, but a good start toward a river fleet had been made.

In his early operations Rodgers co-operated closely at Cairo with a receptive brigadier general named Ulysses S. Grant, and the gunboats had several brushes with Confederate troops. When Rodgers reported that Confederate movements in southern Missouri were threatening Cairo and Paducah, Kentucky, Grant, who had similar reports from a scout, occupied Paducah with the help of the gunboats. Since Confederate forces had occupied Columbus, Kentucky, only two days before, that state's effort to remain "neutral" was brushed aside. For added insurance, Grant also occupied Smithland, at the mouth of the Cumberland River.

THE CONFEDERATE NAVY IS BORN

CONFEDERATE SECRETARY of the Navy Mallory concentrated his efforts on the building of ironclads, although he realized that it would be months before any of them could be ready for service. Not only was there a shortage of building yards; there was also a shortage of skilled workmen and above all of material. Mallory tackled this problem with vigor and early in May he outlined his plans to the Confederate Congress. In addition to converting the hull of *Merrimack* at the Norfolk Navy Yard, he proposed to build two powerful ironclads at Memphis, Tennessee, and two even more powerful at New Orleans.

The commissioning of privateers was not the responsibility of the Navy Department, but Mallory was interested in getting them to sea, for they would be the first to get at Union shipping and thus strike the first blow for the Confederacy at sea. However, before Jefferson Davis would issue any letters of marque he asked the Confederate Congress for a law authorizing and regulating privateering. The law went into effect on May 6, by which time there was a backlog of applications. The first letter of marque was granted on May 10, and in the next few months several more were granted.

The Confederate privateers were successful in varying degrees during the opening phase of the war, with some of them having profitable cruises. New Orleans and Charleston became the centers of privateering but two developments later doomed them. For a privateer to be successful it had to make a profit from the prizes it captured. Thus the first blow to privateering was a British proclamation of June 1 closing the ports of England and its possessions to prizes brought in by either of the belligerents and forbidding British subjects to become privateers. Similar proclamations by other European countries followed, leaving the privateers with no alternative but to try to send their prizes into Confederate ports. During the first few months several prizes did get into Southern ports, but as the Union blockade became tighter, fewer and fewer got through; most were recaptured and restored to their owners. The combination of the blockade and the inability to use neutral ports sealed the fate of the Confederate privateers. By the end of the first year of the war, for all practical purposes, the privateers had disappeared.

The privateers did have one effect that was out of all proportion to the damage they did. The American merchant marine was, in 1861, second only to the British merchant marine and was its close rival. Following Davis's call for volunteers to take out letters of marque, a near panic gripped the Northern coastal states. Wild rumors were rampant and there was a clamor for the government in Washington to do something about the threat. As the privateers began to take prizes, marine insurance rates began to move upward. In the highly competitive field of maritime commerce Northern shipping began to suffer, for the British could and did offer lower freight rates. This in turn initiated what has aptly been called "The Flight from the Flag"—the sale of Northern-owned ships to neutrals. Such transfers of ownership were greatly accelerated when the Confederate naval commerce raiding cruisers, obtained by Commander Bulloch and other agents, began to operate, but the initial impetus came from the privateers.

The operations of the privateers also caused a revision of the ill-conceived Union policy of treating them as pirates. This can best be exemplified by the short-lived cruise of the privateer *Savannah*, which slipped past the blockading ship off Charleston at dark on June 2. The next morning she captured a Northern brig with a cargo of sugar, got the brig into Georgetown, South Carolina, but then ran afoul of the Union warship *Perry* that afternoon and was captured. Her crew was removed and placed in irons. The men were sent to New York where in due course they were put on trial for piracy. Jefferson Davis pleaded with Lincoln to consider the men as legitimate operators, entitled to the treatment accorded prisoners of war, but to no avail. As the trials of *Savannah*'s crew got under way, Davis acted. He directed that an equal number of high-ranking Union officer prisoners of war be held as hostages, to be given the same treatment as the privateer's men. This had the desired effect, for while the hearings were over, the jury failed to agree on a verdict and the piracy charges were dropped.

Although the privateers were the first Confederate vessels to get to sea, a more lasting development began to take shape with Commander Raphael Semmes's return from his fruitless buying trip to New York early in April. He was placed in charge of the Lighthouse Bureau, the same post he formerly held in the United States Navy, but when Fort Sumter brought on open hostilities, he asked for service afloat. He did not want to go to sea as a privateer but in a commissioned vessel of the Confederate Navy, with himself as a commissioned officer in that Navy. Mallory showed him a report on the passenger steamer *Habana*—then at New Orleans—

which had been on a regular run between Havana and that city. Semmes decided that she could be converted to a cruiser and on April 18 he was appointed to command her. She had a complement of eighteen officers of the Confederate Navy.

Semmes rushed her conversion to an armed cruiser and re-named her *Sumter*. She had serious limitations, such as coal capacity for only eight days of steaming, but in two months she was formally commissioned as a Confederate man-of-war. On June 21 Semmes took her to Head of Passes, from where he could select the most favorable pass for a dash into the Gulf through the blockade. Union blockading ships were keeping close watch on the two principal passes, and it was not until the end of June that a chance came to get out. Early one morning *Brooklyn* was drawn well off her station while investigating a strange sail; she was returning when Semmes cleared the pass. By skillful seamanship and maneuvering he evaded the blockader and headed for the south coast of Cuba. There he began, as his orders directed, to do as much damage to Union commerce as he could. He did this so well that he be-came the best-known and most successful of Confederate naval officers.

His first capture was a schooner from Maine, in ballast, which he burned. By July 4 he had captured seven Union ships all laden with sugar. Six of them he took into Cienfuegos, Cuba, where he asked the governor general to give him haven for his prizes. He had studied law and practiced it in civil courts, and this knowledge stood him in good stead through-out his career as a corsair. In a long legalistic letter to the governor general he argued his right to haven, but that official referred the whole matter to Madrid. Spain followed Eng-land in proclaiming its neutrality and denying its ports to belligerent prizes. When news of this reached Cuba, Semmes's prizes were released to their crews.

Semmes felt sure that Union cruisers would be searching for him, but he had developed a plan to evade them. He would stay in one area only until he estimated that his presence there was known to the searchers, then change his area of operation, making the shift via ports where he could get coal. Using these tactics, he left Cienfuegos within two days and headed for the narrows off Brazil, a focal point where he expected to find many Northern ships. His first stop was at the Dutch island of Curaçao, and there he met with an enemy tactic that was to plague him in every neutral port henceforth. Seward had instructed all United States consuls to place every conceivable obstacle in the way of Southern privateers and cruisers in any neutral port they entered. At Curaçao the consul showed great ingenuity in putting obstacles in Semmes's way. He demanded that Semmes be treated as a "rebel pirate" and did his best to prevent his getting provisions, supplies, and coal. But Semmes was no ordinary antagonist. He engaged in a long legal correspondence with the Dutch governor, arguing that his vessel was a legitimate man-of-war, demanding that it be treated as such, and denouncing the "dirty Yankee tricks" used by the Union consul. In the end he got what he wanted.

For the time being we may leave him at the beginning of a mission that was to be successful beyond all expectation—the first of what would prove to be the most fruitful of Confederate naval operations. He and his fellow commerce raiders succeeded in disrupting the Northern merchant marine, yet this did not have the effect the Confederate leaders desired and expected. Instead of inflicting a severe economic blow, only a small segment of the North was hurt by the commerce raiders and Union trade with Europe flourished throughout the Civil War. Goods were merely shifted to neutral ships in which they were immune to interference by the Southern raiders.

Chapter IV

The Birth of Joint Action

HATTERAS INLET

THE UNION DEFEAT at Bull Run, in July 1861 burst the bubble of overconfidence and impatience that had swept over the North after Fort Sumter. Replacing it was a wave of bitterness and grim realization that this would be no easy and short war. Major General George B. McClellan, who had already cleared Confederate troops from the western part of Virginia, thus bringing into being the new state of West Virginia, was named to command the Union field army.

In the wake of Bull Run Gideon Welles approached the War Department for troops to be used in the seizure of Hatteras Inlet. On August 13 General Wool, at Fort Monroe, was ordered to provide the necessary troops and to confer with Flag Officer Stringham, the naval commander of the expedition. Two weeks later Wool ordered Major General Ben Butler to prepare 860 troops for the expedition and be ready to embark them the next day. The troops were to be supplied with only ten days' rations, suggesting that the Army commander did not attach much importance to the expedition.

There was no special training for these troops nor even time allowed to plan for an orderly landing of them. They were simply embarked in two transports. With five warships under Flag Officer Stringham, the expedition sailed on August 26 and on the afternoon of the 27th arrived off Hatteras Inlet, where it anchored for the night.

The larger and stronger of the two log and sand forts protecting Hatteras Inlet was Fort Hatteras,[1] near the inlet itself. It had ten guns mounted and five more, one of which was of ten-inch caliber, not yet mounted. Fort Clark was smaller, with five guns, and it was about one half mile northeast of Fort Hatteras. These defenses were manned by about 350 Confederate troops. When the local commander noted the presence of Stringham's squadron on the afternoon of August 27, he suspected that the forts were about to be attacked and sent a pilot boat to Portsmouth, North Carolina, to ask for more troops. About 365 reinforcements reached Fort Hatteras the next day.

That morning there was a southerly wind and a heavy surf running on the beach selected for landing the troops, about two miles northeast of Fort Clark. Disregarding the unfavorable conditions, Stringham ordered the troops to be landed and detailed three warships to cover and assist them. The troops commenced landing just before noon. Boats swamped and were smashed in the surf and only about 315 men could be brought ashore. They were soaked to the shoulders, their ammunition was wet, and they had no food.

Meanwhile Stringham, in the flagship *Wabash*, towing the sailing frigate *Cumberland* and followed by *Minnesota*, stood in toward Fort Clark and at 10:00 a.m. opened fire. The fort answered but it was outranged, making it a one-sided bombardment. *Susquehanna*, from the blockading squadron, joined the attack an hour later. At 12:25 the flags were down on both forts and men could be seen running from Fort Clark to Fort Hatteras. Fort Clark had expended all of its ammunition and its commander had decided to withdraw his troops

---

[1] Only the site remains and is not readily accessible.

to Fort Hatteras. Union troops already ashore occupied the abandoned fort.

Offshore the ships moved toward Fort Hatteras, and at 4:00 p.m. the shallow draft *Monticello* was ordered to reconnoiter the inlet past the fort, which suddenly came alive and opened fire on her. Colonel Martin, in command of the fort, had withheld fire while the attacking ships were out of range. Upon seeing *Monticello* under fire, Stringham made the signal "engage the batteries" and all ships opened fire on Fort Hatteras. *Monticello* was hit several times but was not seriously damaged and she made her way out of the inlet. After about two hours the ships ceased fire and, except for those left to cover the troops ashore, hauled off for the night.

The next morning the bombardment was resumed by the squadron and continued until a white flag was raised over the fort. General Butler boarded a tug and went into the inlet to take possession of the fort. On the way, the tug fired at some craft bringing reinforcements to the forts and drove them off. Once inside the inlet, Butler sent an aide to ask the meaning of the white flag. The aide returned with a note from Flag Officer Barron—the same man whom Porter had tried to have made Chief of Detail in April—offering to surrender under certain conditions. Butler's reply was blunt and to the point: "The terms offered are these: Full capitulation; the officers and men to be treated as prisoners of war. No other terms admissable." [2]

In the formal surrender on board *Minnesota*, signed by Stringham, Butler, and three Confederate commanders, are these words: "It is stipulated . . . that . . . all munitions of war, arms, men, and property . . . be unconditionally surrendered to the Government of the United States in terms of full capitulation." [3]

Flag Officer Stringham's report makes it clear that this

---

[2] ORA, Vol. 6, p. 583.
[3] ORN, Vol. 6, p. 120.

formula was agreed upon beforehand, but whether it was General Butler's or his own idea is not indicated. What is certain is that it was used at Fort Hatteras nearly six months before Grant, who is usually given credit for originating "unconditional surrender," first used it in the West.

It may seem strange that two forts should surrender after only a few hours of naval bombardment in which the troops that had been landed played no part. This was due partly to the disorganized state of the defenses. Along with the reinforcing troops on August 28 came Flag Officer Barron, commanding the North Carolina Navy. He was asked by the local Army commanders to take full command and did so. Fort Hatteras's guns were outranged by the ships' guns, and about all the fort's defenders could do was take cover in its bombproof shelter while nine, ten, and eleven-inch shells "rained down" accurately into the fort. As many as twenty-eight per minute were counted. With four men killed, twenty-five to thirty badly wounded, and the rest in a state of shock, Barron called a council in which it was decided that there was no choice but surrender.

Both Stringham and Butler rushed north the day after the battle with each claiming credit for the victory. Disgusted officers remaining behind believed that they raced each other back in order to be the first to make the claim. Since Bull Run was still fresh in memory, such a desire is at least understandable, but for the two commanders to leave the scene so soon after the action calls into question their sense of responsibility.

Hatteras Inlet was a striking demonstration of the strength of naval gunfire against shore positions. Although these forts were not nearly so strong as others successfully engaged later in the war, this was an important action if only because it was the first of its kind. Tactically, the Hatteras Inlet operation was poorly planned and executed, except for the bombardments. Strategically, it was a key operation, for it showed that an amphibious type of operation was not only feasible but also could be conducted with light losses. In addition, Hatteras Inlet provided a Union base which sealed off the sounds of North Carolina to privateers and blockade runners. Flag Officer Stringham, in a supplementary report, called Hatteras Inlet ". . . the key to all ports south of Hatteras . . ." and urged its retention and use.

Its loss caused a near panic in North Carolina, for it was realized that with the Inlet as a Union base, the entire inner coast and river system was open to Union attack. Demands were made to Richmond for troops and guns to build up the state's defenses. The Confederate Navy Department and its Secretary were severely criticized for being unable to stop the landing—the critics ignored the fact that the Confederate Navy had nothing to match the Union warships.

That Union naval officers were well aware of the possibilities offered by such coastal operations was recognized by the correspondent of the London *Times*, William H. Russell, who had ready access to every leader from the President down, on both sides. In Washington about the time of the Hatteras Inlet operation, he had dinner with Captains Dahlgren and Foote. He was impressed by Foote's description of using naval guns to batter down a six-foot granite wall in China a few years before. Russell's impression was that:

> It will run hard against the Confederates when they get such men at work on the rivers and coasts, for they seem to understand their business thoroughly, and all they are not sure of is the readiness of the land forces to cooperate with their expeditionary movements.[4]

PORT ROYAL

WITHIN A WEEK after the approval of the third report of Gideon Welles's Board of Strategy, the War Department or-

---

[4] *My Diary North and South* (New York; 1863), p. 517.

dered Brigadier General Thomas W. Sherman, "the other Sherman" as he was known later, to New York to organize an expeditionary force of 12,000 men. At the same time the Navy Department ordered Captain Du Pont to New York to organize and assemble the naval part of the expedition to seize Port Royal on the South Carolina coast. Each was to co-operate with the other.

All might have gone well and the expedition might have embarked in September as planned but for Bull Run. Following that Union setback, fear was felt for the safety of Washington. On September 14 General Sherman was ordered to proceed at once to Washington with his entire force. Concerned that this move might be misinterpreted, Lincoln sent identical letters to the Secretaries of War and Navy ordering that the Port Royal expedition was in no way to be abandoned and that it must be ready to move by October 1 or very early in the month at the latest.

But delays in arming the troops and in getting the necessary shipping assembled forced a postponement, and the expedition was not ready to leave Hampton Roads until the end of October. Formal orders to Captain Du Pont, designating him flag officer, and to General Sherman were issued on October 14. Both orders show how concerned Washington was about command relationships between the two. Each was told that Army officers could not command naval forces and that naval officers could not command Army forces except when embarked in naval vessels. Each was enjoined to co-operate fully with the other.

Welles was very anxious to preserve the secrecy of the objective and in the formal orders to Du Pont four places were named, which were to be considered for seizure. Sherman's orders were equally vague as to the target of the expedition. But each knew, from his conferences in Washington, that Port Royal was the real objective. Bad leaks occurred, however, for on October 4 the ever-present William H. Russell of the London *Times* recorded in his diary that when he asked to go along with the Port Royal expedition, he was told that McClellan was about to move in Virginia. On November 1 Judah P. Benjamin, by then Confederate Secretary of War, telegraphed to the governor of South Carolina and to General Drayton at Port Royal that he had reliable information that the expedition was headed for that port.

Foul weather prevented the sailing of the expedition until October 29. Off Cape Hatteras it ran into a severe storm and was scattered. Two transports were driven aground and one foundered, but the heroic efforts of Captain Cadwalader Ringgold, commanding the frigate *Sabine*, resulted in the rescue of all but six of the marines on the sinking ship. That Du Pont had assembled and trained a well-indoctrinated squadron is shown by the fact that, although badly scattered by the storm, most of it arrived off Port Royal early on November 4. By that date he already had twenty-five of the nearly 100 ships in company, and the others joined rapidly.

It was known that the Confederates had erected forts on either side of the entrance, but their strength was unknown. For working in inshore shoal water, Du Pont had six shallow draft gunboats. Professor Bache, of the Coast Survey, had also loaned him a survey vessel. On the day of arrival Commander Davis, now Du Pont's fleet captain (chief of staff), and an expert from the Coast Survey located and buoyed a channel through the outer bar. That afternoon the lighter draft vessels anchored inside the bar. Three Confederate gunboats, under Commodore Josiah Tattnall, came out to investigate, but were chased back to protected waters by the Union gunboats.

The next day Commander John Rodgers, temporarily on Du Pont's staff, made a reconnaissance and drew the fire of the forts on either side of the entrance, which was about two miles wide. The forts were found to be strong and well constructed, with Fort Walker,[5] on Hilton Head on the southern side of the entrance, much the stronger. That same morning Du Pont risked bringing his flagship, *Wabash*, over the bar with only a foot or two of water to spare. Assembling the squadron inside the bar, he prepared to attack Fort Walker that afternoon, intending to slug it out at close range. But there was a delay in getting a buoy on a dangerous shoal ahead, Fishing Rip, and *Wabash* grounded on it. By the time she was clear it was too late to attack. Du Pont anchored his ships out of range of the forts, chafing at the delay which proved to be a fortunate one for him. The next day was clear but strong winds were unfavorable for an attack.

Early in the morning of November 7 Commander Davis awakened with an inspiration which Du Pont approved at once. Instead of attacking Fort Walker only, the squadron should steam past Fort Beauregard, on the northern side of the entrance, bombarding it in passing. When about two miles inside Port Royal the squadron should turn left and steam past Fort Walker, engaging that fort in turn. This had the advantage of opening fire on the inland and weaker side of the fort and of enfilading the main battery before coming abreast of it. High tide was at 11:35 a.m., which would enable the squadron to steam past Fort Walker very slowly against the incoming flood current. It was a brilliant plan, but it was not executed exactly as planned.

The order of sailing was the flagship *Wabash*, followed by the frigate *Susquehanna* and the sloops *Unadilla*, *Ottawa*, and *Pembina*, with the sailing sloop *Vandalia*, in tow of *Isaac Smith*, bringing up the rear. On the flank and intended to keep Tattnall's force from interfering were the five shallow draft gunboats—*Bienville*, commanded by Commander Steed-

---

[5] Only the site remains; it is accessible over a two-mile sand track.

man, in the lead, followed by *Seneca*, *Curlew*, *Penguin*, and *Augusta*.

The squadron got under way at 9:00 a.m. and the action opened at 9:26 when Fort Walker, followed closely by Fort Beauregard, opened fire. This was immediately returned by the ships. At first the fire of the forts was accurate, but as the hail of shells, of up to ten-inch caliber, rained down on them their fire slackened. On the first pass by Fort Beauregard most of the ships were hit and suffered casualties. At 10:00 the column swung to the left and started to pass by Fort Walker at a range of 800 yards. Only three ships made the pass, *Wabash*, *Susquehanna*, and *Bienville*. Du Pont signaled to the other ships to close up, but they remained inside the harbor where they could enfilade the fort. The three ships completed the second loop and were about to start a third when, at about 1:15 p.m., the gunboat *Ottawa*, which was anchored inside, reported that Fort Walker was being abandoned. Du Pont then sent Commander Rodgers to the fort with a flag of truce, and shortly after 2:00 Rodgers hoisted the Union flag over the fort, an act that sent cheering crews into the rigging of the ships. Du Pont next sent a party of marines to occupy the fort until troops arrived.

The transports moved up and by nightfall the troops were ashore and had taken over. About noon the sloop *Pocahontas*, delayed by the storm, the gunboat *R. B. Forbes*, which was towing a transport, and the tug *Mercury*, with one gun, joined in the final part of the action. As soon as Fort Walker was secured, Du Pont sent a detachment to investigate Fort Beauregard. By sunset that fort appeared to be abandoned, and the next morning one of the gunboats sent a party ashore to occupy it until the troops could take it over.

The forts fell entirely as a result of naval gunfire, which was well controlled and accurate. At the height of the action, John Rodgers later wrote to a friend, the shells fell into the forts "not 28 per minute [as at Hatteras Inlet] but as fast as a horse's feet beat the ground in a gallop." [6] It was an intense bombardment which unnerved the defenders who were, it should be noted, but partly trained militiamen. *Wabash* alone fired 880 rounds into the forts, mostly at a range of about 600 yards. Most of the ships were hit by fire from the forts, but there were only six killed and twenty wounded in the squadron.

The Confederate accounts indicate that the defenders put up a gallant defense against overwhelming odds. General Drayton reported that:

> Not a ripple upon the broad expanse of water to disturb the accuracy of fire from the broad decks of that magnificent armada . . . advancing in battle array to vomit forth its iron hail with all the spiteful energy of long-suppressed rage and conscious strength.[7]

Shortly after noon General Drayton told the commander at Fort Walker to hold out as long as he could fire effectively. At about 1:00 p.m., with ammunition running low, it was decided to withdraw from the fort. A detachment of German-manned artillery was to cover the withdrawal and the Germans were ordered from their guns about 2:00. The Union accounts indicate that the withdrawal was made in haste and disorder. A large quantity of personal belongings was left behind, the guns of the fort were abandoned, and other personal belongings were found strewn along the line of retreat all the way to the opposite end of the island. Casualties in the fort were light—only ten killed and twenty wounded.

Through his bold and determined action Du Pont obtained an excellent base deep within the South. The capture of the two forts, located between Charleston and Savannah, threatened both of those major ports and created panic among the local population. Port Royal was in the center of

---

[6] B. J. Lossing: *Pictorial History of the Civil War* (New York; 1866), Vol. II, p. 120.
[7] ORN, Vol. 12, p. 302.

rich rice- and cotton-growing plantations on the offshore islands. Du Pont's gunboats, ranging the inland waters, found
the plantations abandoned by their owners. The day after the
capture of the forts he sent three gunboats to reconnoiter as
far as the town of Beaufort. Only one white man could be
found; the Negroes were running wild and looting the town.
He stationed a gunboat there to restore order. These reconnaissances determined that the nearest Confederate troops
were at Port Royal Ferry, ten miles from Beaufort.

The gunboats found that the whole coastal area, from
North Edisto, a few miles south of Charleston, to Ossabaw
Sound, south of Savannah, had been abandoned. Charleston itself was protected by its harbor forts and Savannah by Fort
Pulaski, on an island near the mouth of the Savannah River. As
soon as Port Royal was secured it was expected that Fernandina, Florida, would be occupied, but General Sherman
felt that first he had to consolidate and exploit the new
gains. Although he asked for more troops to expand his operations, few were sent to him. In the first broad outline of his
proposed conduct of the war to President Lincoln, McClellan suggested that an inland campaign from captured
Southern ports would be desirable. There is no evidence,
however, that the Union Army ever seriously considered any
major operation using Port Royal as a base.

Such an invasion would have presented the South with the
prospect of a three-front war. This threat was recognized by
Jefferson Davis. On the last day of October Robert E. Lee
reached Richmond from his earlier command in western Virginia. His prestige was then at its lowest, for he had failed to
hold what was to become West Virginia. On November 4,
after receipt of reports that Du Pont's squadron was off Port
Royal, Davis sent Lee to organize the defenses in South Carolina, assigning him the rank of full general in the Confederate
Army. Lee reached Coosawhatchie, the rail station nearest

Port Royal Sound, on the 7th, only to learn that the forts had been overwhelmed and lost that very day.

He made a hurried survey of the situation and found that his forces were small, scattered, and, being from both South Carolina and Georgia, unco-ordinated. He was deeply impressed by the power of the ships' batteries, as shown by the defensive measures which he took. It may be noted also that his later offensive campaigns were made in regions where the Union Navy was unable to support the Army. Early in January 1862, Lee's feeling was expressed to the adjutant general in Richmond in these words:

> Wherever his fleet can be brought no opposition to his landing can be made except within range of our fixed batteries. We have nothing to oppose its heavy guns which sweep over the low banks of this country with irresistible force. The farther he can be withdrawn from his floating batteries the weaker he will become, and lines of defense, covering objects of attack, have been selected with this in view.[8]

Lee's first emergency steps were to strengthen the defenses of Fort Pulaski, guarding Savannah, and the defenses of Savannah itself and of Charleston. He then obstructed the waterways which could be used by the gunboats and assembled his forces at the most probably points of attack by the Union Army—points carefully selected to be out of range of the gunboats. Later he put into effect a longer-range plan. He ordered the withdrawal inland of garrisons and guns on outlying positions. His idea was to hold only such key points as Charleston. Finally, at Savannah and along the southern part of the Charleston and Savannah Railroad, he built a strong defense line upon which he could concentrate his forces and compel the Union Army to fight without the help of the Navy. He was assisted in developing this plan by the in-

---

[8] ORA, Vol. 6, p. 367.

activity of the Union Army forces at Port Royal, which from the outset showed a strong inclination to follow rather than get in front of Du Pont's gunboats. Lee remained in command in the southeast until the following March. During that time there had been no serious fighting, but the entire coast south of Charleston and into Florida had come under the occupation or control of Du Pont's squadron.

While his gunboats were ranging freely along the coast, Du Pont planned to seal the entrance to Charleston harbor, as recommended by the Board of Strategy. Twenty-five old whaling hulks filled with stone arrived from New York in the middle of December, and he entrusted their emplacement to Commander Davis. With warships covering the operation, sixteen of the hulks were towed into the main channel and sunk on the first anniversary of the secession of South Carolina. Another channel was choked with similar blockships later on, but neither operation succeeded in actually blocking the harbor. Through misplacement of some of the hulks and the action of tidal currents the channels were never completely closed.

This action was bitterly resented and condemned in the city, although South Carolinians had themselves sunk hulks in January to block the channel and Lee had already ordered obstructions placed in the rivers to deny their use to Union gunboats. Nonetheless, he also denounced the blockships. He wrote to Secretary Benjamin in this vein: "This achievement, so unworthy any nation, is the abortive expression of the malice and revenge of a people which it wishes to perpetuate by rendering more memorable a day hateful in their calendar." [9]

Du Pont's ships roved far and wide within the limits of his command, which extended to Cape Canaveral, Florida, now well known for its place in the space age. An ingenious Con-

---

[9] ORN, Vol. 12, p. 423.

federate device, which had appeared earlier in the Potomac and was to plague the Union Navy in the future, was discovered in Wright's River, a tributary of the Savannah. It consisted of a row of anchored mines, called torpedoes in the Civil War. One of them was recovered and a full description of it was sent to Washington.

Early in March 1862, Fernandina, Florida, originally planned to be taken shortly after Port Royal, was occupied. St. Augustine and Jacksonville were taken later in the month. Earlier, Brunswick, Georgia had been occupied, and Fort Pulaski was captured in mid-April. Thus the entire coast within the limits of Du Pont's command, with the exception of Charleston, was sealed off. Charleston was to hold out for nearly three years, but it was to suffer severely for its resistance.

Du Pont had done his part well and the war might have taken an entirely different course if the Army had chosen to exploit its opportunities in that region.

ROANOKE ISLAND

THE PLAN for an expedition to capture Roanoke Island and adjacent positions in North Carolina originated with the Army. Shortly after McClellan took command of the Union Armies Brigadier General Ambrose E. Burnside, himself an adopted Rhode Islander, suggested the desirability of raising a division of three brigades of troops in New England, composed of men experienced in boating and working around the water. McClellan approved, and with the authority of the Secretary of War, Burnside was ordered to recruit and train the division. McClellan felt that such a division would be useful along the Potomac and in Chesapeake Bay, as well as along the coast. By early December he had developed the plan for his Peninsula campaign and had then realized that the

Burnside's division would be a strong threat to Confederate lines of communication if it had Roanoke Island as a base and could operate in North Carolina. In proposing the seizure of Roanoke Island to the Navy, he pointed out that it would assist in maintaining the blockade, although if his purpose in mentioning this was to gain more ready assent from the Navy, it was unnecessary, for Flag Officer L. M. Goldsborough, who replaced Stringham, had proposed the same thing in November. Welles agreed with McClellan and the Navy offered hearty co-operation.

Command of the naval part of the expedition was given to Goldsborough and for it he assembled a squadron of seventeen shallow draft gunboats.

Because of almost inevitable delays the expedition was not ready to sail from Hampton Roads until January 11, 1862. Flag Officer Goldsborough arrived at Hatteras Inlet on the 13th. Next followed the slow and tedious process of getting each gunboat over a shoal into the inlet. The boats had to be lightened by the temporary removal of as much weight as possible. Storms caused further delay, and it was not until February 5 that the expedition was ready to move to Roanoke Island.

On the west side of the island the Confederates had erected two fortified points overlooking the channel from Pamlico Sound to Albemarle Sound. Across the channel there were obstructions in the form of piling and sunken vessels, covered by a fort on the mainland. Thick and stormy weather on the 6th delayed the attack until the next day when, shortly before noon, the gunboats began bombarding the forts. By 1:30 p.m. the nearest fort had several fires burning. Five or six Confederate gunboats joined the battle above the obstructions, but they were driven off. By 4:30 the forts were silenced and the troops began landing about three miles south of the nearest fort. At 5:00 the forts came back to life and the Confederate gunboats returned to the scene. The Union gunboats rejoined the action promptly, but an hour later the firing died out.

By midnight 10,000 troops had been landed safely. Here, for the first time, the landing of troops was organized in a pattern suggestive of the typical landing plan of World War II. A clever scheme was used to get the first "waves" of boats ashore. Each brigade of General Burnside's division had a light draft steamer which towed twenty surfboats in tandem, each filled with soldiers. The steamers headed for the preselected landing point, and when sufficient speed was reached to carry the surfboats to the shore, they were cast off. Well handled by their helmsmen, the leading boats reached the beach in good order. There was no opposition and no attempt was made to advance inland during the night.

Commander Stephen C. Rowan, second in command of the naval force, was in the gunboat *Delaware*, stationed nearest the landing point. When he saw that the troops were about to land, he moved in to support and cover the landing. *Delaware* lobbed nine-inch shells into trees back of the landing point, where it was suspected Confederate troops were concealed. A most revealing description of what happened then was given by the captain of a North Carolina company which had been ordered to the threatened landing point shortly after the bombardment began. His company was halted by an order before it reached that point, and it was about that time that he ". . . saw two or three companies retreating from the landing last mentioned in double quick time." [1]

General Burnside planned to attack at daylight the next day, and because the troops would be moving north and into the line of naval gunfire, Goldsborough arranged that his ships would not resume firing until requested to do so from ashore. But at 9:00 a.m. heavy firing on the island located the lines and the gunboats returned to pounding the forts. By this time

---

[1] ORA, Vol. 9, p. 174.

the nearest one had only one gun left. Then it quieted down on the island and Goldsborough ceased fire. He was about to resume firing when he received word from Burnside asking him not to fire. Goldsborough then ordered the gunboats to breach the obstacles that barred ingress into Albemarle Sound. One of them succeeded in breaking through about 4:00 p.m., and in a short time the breach was widened enough for the whole squadron to pass through. About the same time the Union flag was raised over the principal fort and the island was taken.

This operation was an excellent example of the co-ordination that could be achieved by competent commanders. The naval bombardment was not heavy enough to do the job alone, but it made a material contribution to the success of the landing. While the gunboats were hit a number of times, there were only four killed or missing and seventeen wounded in the squadron. At a cost of fifty killed or missing and 214 wounded, Burnside's division captured forty guns and took over 2,000 prisoners out of a total garrison of about 4,000.

Goldsborough lost no time in capitalizing on the success at Roanoke Island. Early on February 10, Rowan, with eleven gunboats, appeared off Elizabeth City, at the southern end of the Dismal Swamp Canal, which connects that city with Norfolk. After a short fight a small fort below the city was captured, four Confederate gunboats were sunk or burned, and one was captured. Two others were driven up the canal, which was then obstructed by blowing up a canal lock about thirty miles above Elizabeth City.

With Goldsborough's squadron having complete control of the waterways, Burnside spread out to the mainland. On March 14 he moved against New Bern, covered by Rowan's gunboats in the Neuse River. The troops were landed near the mouth of the river. Gunboats shelled the road and Confederate strongpoints ahead of the advancing troops. The Confederates retreated in confusion and set fire to parts of the town as they evacuated it. The gunboats, arriving at the town ahead of the troops, fought the fires as they entered. There was some sharp fighting at times and Burnside suffered 470 casualties, but he gained an important base and captured large quantities of cotton and supplies. This victory gained Burnside a promotion to major general.

After New Bern he moved against Beaufort and Morehead City, the possession of which would give him good port facilities. Beaufort was protected by Fort Macon, which fought sharply for a few days, but by the end of April the town had fallen. Burnside had asked for cavalry, railroad equipment, and other necessary transportation, which would enable him to operate along the railroads into the interior. There he could threaten the important rail connections between Virginia and the rest of the South. But McClellan was then about to launch his Peninsula campaign, with all of the troops he could muster, and Burnside got no help. Thus still another opportunity for the Army to exploit gains made possible by Union naval control of water transportation was lost.

With the occupation of Beaufort and Morehead City the only important Atlantic ports left in Confederate hands were Charleston, within the geographical limits of the South Atlantic Blockading Squadron, and Wilmington, North Carolina, within the limits of the North Atlantic Blockading Squadron. Wilmington was protected by Fort Caswell, at the mouth of the Cape Fear River. Both cities attained fame and importance as centers for blockade running and Wilmington became the actual focal point of this traffic. One reason for this was that there were two channels of approach to the Cape Fear River, separated by an island and the Frying Pan Shoals. In effect, this meant that two blockading forces were required to close off that entrance.

In any case, just one year after the outbreak of the Civil War a firm blockade was established along the Atlantic coast of the Confederacy and all but two of its ports were either occupied or sealed off by Union forces. This had been accomplished by a promising, if at times somewhat crude, display of co-operation between the Army and the Navy. Unfortunately for the Union cause, the Army, committed to what were probably more costly and bloody plans, either was unable to appreciate the strategic significance of this accomplishment or was unwilling to exploit it.

Chapter V

Monitor *and* Merrimack

WELLES'S IRONCLAD BOARD

SOME NAVAL HISTORIANS, writing soon after the Civil War, were very critical of Gideon Welles and his attitude toward ironclad ships for the Navy. He was accused of ignoring the possibilities of ironclads, but such was not the case; he acted cautiously yet with his usual political acumen.

In his first report to Congress, on July 4, 1861, he referred to the importance of ironclad steamers and acknowledged that they would be costly. At the time, he merely asked for authority to appoint a board to study the subject, although by then Secretary Mallory had already authorized the conversion of *Merrimack* without waiting for the approval of the Confederate Congress. But Welles knew that Congressional minds were very conscious of the fact that since 1842 $500,000 had been spent on the construction by Robert L. Stevens of an ironclad warship and nothing had come of it. Nevertheless, just one month after Welles made his report Congress authorized not only the special board he had requested but also appropriated $1,500,000 for the construction of one or more ironclads. This last pleased Welles greatly, for he had not dared to go so far in his request. That his cautious approach to the subject was justified is indicated by the fact that the

Senate approved the authorization only by the narrow margin of 18 to 16.

Welles appointed Commodore (by courtesy) Joseph Smith, head of the Bureau of Yards and Docks, Captain Hiram Paulding, and Commander C. H. Davis, who had served on the Board of Strategy with Du Pont, to comprise the new board. The board, which in its report of September 16 admitted having "no experience, and but scant knowledge in this branch of naval architecture," [1] considered numerous proposed plans for ironclads, of which eighteen were mentioned by name. Three of these were selected and recommended for construction contracts. One, designed by Naval Constructor Pook, was awarded to C. H. Bushnell, of New Haven, Connecticut. Its novelty was that the armor consisted of two thicknesses of iron plate separated by iron bars; it became *Galena*. The second, *New Ironsides*, designed along the conventional ship lines of European ironclads, was assigned to Merrick and Sons, Philadelphia. The third and most radical design was almost not built at all.

Early in September Welles was in Hartford preparing to move his family to Washington. While there he was visited by his old friend Bushnell, who was to build *Galena* but who was now pushing another design by that genius of naval architecture, John Ericsson. Welles was so impressed by a cardboard model of *Monitor*, as she was to be named, and by Bushnell's enthusiasm, that he sent him to Washington to present the design to the board. Wise to the ways of Washington, Bushnell got an introduction to the President, to whom he first presented the plan. Lincoln was impressed and arranged a meeting with the board for the next day, which Lincoln himself attended. A long discussion followed in which the board members showed considerable skepticism. The clincher probably came when Lincoln closed the meeting with one of his quips:

[1] *Annual Report of the Secretary of the Navy for 1861,* p. 249.

"All I have to say is what the girl said when she stuck her foot into the stocking, 'It strikes me there's something in it.' " [2]

Bushnell was worried by the cool reception of his ideas and realized that it would be necessary to get Ericsson himself to Washington to explain the novel craft to the board. He went to New York and induced the inventor—who was still miffed at the Navy for its shabby treatment of him in the *Princeton* matter—to go to Washington. Appearing before the board on September 14, Ericsson first found an atmosphere of hostility, but his detailed explanation of his design largely convinced the members that he understood the problems involved and could solve them.

Monitor, the name he later suggested for the ship, was a unique design which he had developed during the Crimean War and offered to the French, who had rejected it. It consisted of a more or less conventional but simplified hull, designed to be built by ordinary mechanics and riveters, 172 feet long and with a beam of 41½ feet. The deck was very low and covered with iron plate. The sides were protected by a belt of armor which extended below the water line. The heaviest armor, which was to be built up to eleven inches in thickness, was in a revolving gun turret, mounted near the center of the hull. The concentration of the heaviest armor into this relatively small space saved much weight and made the craft seaworthy.

Ericsson's most appealing arguments were that her draft would be but eleven feet, thus permitting her to operate in Southern coastal waters and rivers, and that she could be built in ninety days. The next morning Welles sat in with the board to hear Ericsson resubmit his proposal. After a short session with the board alone, Welles called in the designer and told him that the board approved his plan, on which he was to start at once. A contract would be prepared and sent along

---

[2] William C. Church: *The Life of John Ericsson* (New York; 1890), Vol. I, p. 249.

later. Ironically, when this contract arrived early in October, it contained a stipulation requiring a guarantee of performance for the vessel, with a penalty of forfeiting all money paid in case of failure. Ericsson was angered by this, but it was probably inserted to placate members of the board who were not entirely convinced that the craft had stability.

The genius of Ericsson, already displayed in the novelty of the design, was now put into the construction of the ironclad. In New York he formed a syndicate consisting of himself, Bushnell, and two others, to underwrite the construction. The hull was built at Howland's Shipyard, Greenpoint, Long Island. Subcontracts were let to other firms to build the engine and turret, and their construction went on simultaneously with the hull. With Ericsson overseeing every detail, the work went on around the clock. The production schedule of the ship was impressive; keel laid October 25; engine installed and tested December 30; launched January 30, 1862; and the ship completed February 15. Her first trial developed engine trouble, which Ericsson corrected. More serious was a defect in the steering gear, and at first it was thought that a new rudder would be necessary, but Ericsson reworked the existing gear and corrected the defect.

Lieutenant John L. Worden, who was arrested and had an enforced stay in a Southern prison after delivering his message to Fort Pickens in April 1861, was ordered to command *Monitor* in January 1862. She was commissioned February 25 and on March 6, after only three short trials under power, *Monitor* left New York in tow of a tug, escorted by two naval craft, bound for Hampton Roads and Washington. The original intention was to send her to Farragut, to be used at New Orleans, but as alarming news came out of Norfolk about progress on *Merrimack*, her destination was changed.

Seldom, if ever, did a new ship design receive as much public attention as did *Monitor*. Early in November 1861, the *Scientific American* had a description of the craft. The New

York *World*, at the end of January 1862, published a complete description of the ship, giving all of her principal dimensions. Sneering remarks about "Ericsson's folly" and the "cheese box on a raft" were bandied about, but Ericsson ignored the criticism and concentrated on getting his ship out on time. *Monitor* was to do her part gallantly and to justify the inventor's confidence in her.

MERRIMACK STRIKES, MARCH 8, 1862

IN LINE with Secretary Mallory's conviction that the only way the South could overcome the superiority of the Union Navy was by the use of ironclads, he had authorized the conversion of *Merrimack* to an ironclad on May 11, 1861. It was found that, though burned to the water line, her hull was intact and her engine could be repaired. She was raised and work began on covering the central part of her hull with an iron citadel, flat on top and with sloping sides. The citadel consisted of two layers of two-inch iron plates, with the inner layer laid horizontally and the outer layer vertically. Both were laid over and bolted to a 24-inch shell of pine and oak. The armor was pierced for ten guns: six nine-inch, two seven-inch, and two six-inch rifles. An iron ram was fitted to her bow.

The conversion was plagued by delays and shortages, especially of iron, which was in heavy demand by other Southern agencies. Mallory tried unsuccessfully to get railroad branch lines abandoned, so that he could have the rails rerolled into armor. But in spite of the delays, those in charge of the work reported in early winter that she would be ready for service in March. Early in 1862 tension on both sides increased as both *Merrimack* [3] and *Monitor* neared completion. So great was

---

[3] Renamed *Virginia* by the Confederates, but this name has fallen into disuse.

the pressure to get *Merrimack* into action before *Monitor* appeared that when she got under way for the first time on March 8, her crew thought that she was merely going on a trial run.

It was no trial run, for Flag Officer Franklin Buchanan, in command, was heading directly into action. It was only while steaming toward Hampton Roads that it was found that she could make no more than five knots speed, that she steered very poorly, and that her deep draft of twenty-two feet limited her to using only a small part of Hampton Roads. She left the Norfolk Navy Yard at 11:00 a.m. and shortly after 1:00 p.m. Union Army observers at Newport News and alert lookouts on naval vessels there sighted her rounding Craney Island, at the mouth of the Elizabeth River. The alarm spread quickly, but there was little that the wooden sailing ships in Hampton Roads could do to cope with her attack. *Merrimack* was accompanied by the gunboats *Beaufort* and *Raleigh*. Three other gunboats of the James River flotilla were ordered down that river to assist her.

As soon as she was clear of the river, *Merrimack* headed for Newport News, where she intended to engage the sloop *Cumberland* and the frigate *Congress*, both at anchor blockading the James River. It was also Buchanan's intention to ram *Cumberland*. At 2:00 p.m., when less than a mile away, *Merrimack* opened fire on hapless *Cumberland* and the action became general when that ship, *Congress*, and shore batteries at Newport News returned a spirited fire. *Merrimack* bore in and rammed *Cumberland*, whose captain was at Fort Monroe when the action started. He obtained a horse and reached Newport News only to watch *Cumberland* sink. She fought gallantly until rising water within her hull silenced her guns.

The ramming of *Cumberland* almost resulted in the destruction of *Merrimack* at the same time. Rear Admiral T. O. Selfridge, who was a lieutenant in *Cumberland* during this action, later described what happened. After *Merrimack*'s ram had penetrated the side of *Cumberland:*

> She could not extricate herself; and as the Cumberland commenced to sink she bore the Merrimac [sic] down with her, until the water was over the forward deck. Had the officer forward on the spar deck on the Cumberland had the presence of mind to let go the starboard anchor, it would have fallen on the Merrimac's deck, and the latter have been carried down in the iron embrace of the Cumberland. But the opportunity was lost; the weight upon the ram broke it off in the Cumberland's side and the Merrimac swung around broadside to the Cumberland.[4]

Since *Merrimack*'s stability was very poor after her conversion to an ironclad, and she did take some water as a result of ramming *Cumberland*, there is little doubt that Selfridge's observations were correct. Captain William H. Parker, who commanded the Confederate gunboat *Beaufort* in this action, in his later *Recollections of a Naval Officer* also expressed the belief that *Merrimack* would have been sunk if her ram had not broken off.

Seeing *Cumberland*, which lost 121 officers and men, being rammed, *Congress* slipped her cable to get clear but ran aground. *Merrimack* and the gunboats next concentrated on her. Taking a position about 150 yards astern of the grounded vessel, *Merrimack* raked her with salvo after salvo. At about 4:30 p.m., with not a gun operating, with her captain dead, the executive officer surrendered the vessel to stop the carnage.

When *Merrimack* was first sighted, *Minnesota* got under way from the vicinity of Fort Monroe to assist the threatened ships, but she too ran hard aground and was unable to help.

Now, with the surrender of *Congress*, firing ceased tem-

---

[4] *Papers of the Military Historical Society of Massachusetts* (Boston; 1902), Vol. XII, p. 121.

porarily and Flag Officer Buchanan hailed *Beaufort* and ordered Lieutenant Parker to go alongside *Congress* and accept her surrender, taking off the officers. After the wounded had been removed, he was to allow the remainder of the crew to escape to the shore and then burn the ship. In keeping with the code of the times, Parker insisted on receiving Lieutenant Pendergast's ceremonial sword instead of an ordinary cutlass which was offered. While this was going on, a party of troops on shore opened fire on *Beaufort*, causing a number of casualties. Parker permitted Pendergast and a Commander Davis— who had been relieved of command of *Congress* only the day before but was still on board—to return to the ship to care for the wounded until they could be removed. Then Parker hauled away to bring his lone gun to bear on the offenders onshore. When Buchanan learned of the shore-based attack, he ordered *Congress* set on fire with incendiary shells. The burning ship exploded about midnight. She lost 120 officers and men.

Meanwhile some heavy fire was exchanged between *Merrimack* and the grounded *Minnesota*, during which Buchanan was wounded and had to turn over command to his executive officer, Lieutenant Catesby Ap R. Jones. With nightfall approaching, *Merrimack* withdrew to Sewell's Point, across the Roads from the scene of the battle, intending to finish off *Minnesota* the next day. As a result of the day's action *Merrimack* had ten killed and wounded, *Minnesota* twenty-two, *Patrick Henry*, of the James River flotilla, fourteen, *Beaufort* eight, and a few other casualties occurred in the smaller Confederate craft.

That night and the next day there was deep gloom and near panic in the North and great rejoicing in the South over the results of the day's battle. As luck would have it, a telegraph line had been opened that day between Washington and Fort Monroe, by way of Maryland and Cape Charles. After getting a short message off to Washington reporting the results of the battle, the telegraph line broke down. If we accept Gideon Welles's account of what happened at a cabinet meeting, the next day was a very hectic one. The President rushed off to the Navy Yard to consult with Captain Dahlgren. Stanton was the most excited of the cabinet officers and had visions of *Merrimack* appearing off Washington at any moment. He even sent telegrams to the governors of three states advising them to close their harbors with booms.

Welles knew the characteristics of the Confederate ironclad and he reassured the President and several cabinet members that it was impossible for *Merrimack* to come up the Potomac because of her deep draft. Most of the tension disappeared that evening when the telegraph line was back in operation and a welcome message from Assistant Secretary Fox, who had gone to Hampton Roads to meet *Monitor*, reported the meeting that day between that ship and *Merrimack*.

THE BATTLE, MARCH 9

As IF GUIDED by an Act of Providence, at 9:00 p.m., March 8, *Monitor* arrived in Hampton Roads after a rough and trying passage from New York. She received orders from Captain Marston, the senior officer present, to proceed immediately to the assistance of *Minnesota*. Lieutenant S. D. Greene, the gunnery officer, who assumed command when Worden was wounded during the next day's battle, described that action in only one short but vivid paragraph. In view of the volumes of romantic balderdash that have been written since about this battle, his brief description tells an eloquent story.

Monitor lay at anchor near *Minnesota* during the night, and at about 8:00 a.m. the next morning, when *Merrimack* was observed to be under way, Greene reported:

> Hove up the anchor and went to quarters. At 8:45 a.m. we opened fire upon the *Merrimack* and con-

tinued the action until 11:30 a.m., when Captain Worden was injured in the eyes by the explosion of a shell from the *Merrimack* upon the outside of the eyehole in the pilot house, exactly opposite his eye. Captain Worden then sent for me and told me to take charge of the vessel. We continued the action until 12:15 p.m., when the *Merrimack* retreated to Sewell's Point and we went to the *Minnesota* and remained by her until she was afloat.[5]

What Greene did not report was that when Worden sent for him to take command, he told him to break off the action and retire toward Fort Monroe. On his own responsibility Greene turned her about and renewed the action.

Most eyewitness accounts agree that *Merrimack* broke off the action, but later Confederate accounts insisted that *Monitor* did so. What really happened is readily deduced. In her maneuvering during the battle, *Monitor* proved to be much the nimbler of the two. *Merrimack* tried to ram the smaller ship but she was too clumsy and failed. At one time she ran aground. Most of the action was fought at very close range, sometimes with the ships touching each other. *Merrimack* was struck at least twenty times by *Monitor*'s eleven-inch shot. Lieutenant John T. Wood, who served in *Merrimack* in this action, later criticized *Monitor*'s gunnery for not concentrating her fire at one point, for that would have broken *Merrimack*'s armor. That was probably true, for another ship of *Monitor* type did just that later at Mobile Bay and succeeded in disabling her opponent.

In *Monitor*'s defense was the fact that the ship had been in commission less than two weeks and her crew was not yet shaken down when this action took place. It barely had enough training to operate the ship. Her shots struck *Merrimack* and dented her armor but, more important, they cracked and splintered her inner structure. Each hit caused concussion within the citadel and one shot severed her anchor chain, open-

[5] ORN, Vol. 7, p. 25.

ing a leak from the day before when she lost her ram. In this battle *Merrimack* lost two killed and nineteen wounded. Captain Worden was the only one seriously injured in *Monitor*, although she was struck twenty-four times by shot from *Merrimack*. Several others were knocked down or slightly injured from the concussion caused by shots hitting her turret. She fired a total of fifty-five rounds in two-gun salvos, loading and firing every six to eight minutes.

What happened in this battle was simply that the crews of both ships fought to the point of physical exhaustion. The breaking off of the action after three and one half hours of close in-fighting was equally welcomed by both crews.

The battle between *Monitor* and *Merrimack* did not revolutionize naval warfare, as so often has been asserted. The revolution occurred when France built *Gloire* in 1860. But the unique and distinguishing feature of this battle was that it was the first meeting of ironclad ships in action.

STRATEGIC CONSEQUENCES

TACTICALLY the battle between *Monitor* and *Merrimack* was a standoff, but it had far-reaching strategic consequences. On March 10 Welles sent a telegram to Fox, who was still at Hampton Roads, ordering that *Monitor* not be unduly exposed and under no circumstances was she to go to Norfolk unattended. That was symptomatic of the alarm created in the North by the appearance of *Merrimack*. *Monitor* was the only thing that stood between *Merrimack* and the devastating destruction which she was believed able to inflict. Amplifying instructions were that *Monitor* was not to seek battle with *Merrimack* unless the latter attacked the wooden ships present. *Merrimack* poked her nose into Hampton Roads several times during the next two months as if to challenge *Monitor* to a fight. Each time *Monitor*, now commanded by Lieutenant William M. Jeffers, bristled and made ready, but her apparent unwillingness to duel it out was misinterpreted by the Confederates. She was merely carrying out her orders—since *Merrimack* did not attack the other ships, *Monitor* declined the bait.

Fox was deeply impressed by the failure of *Monitor*'s eleven-inch shots to penetrate *Merrimack*'s armor. At Fort Monroe he saw a discarded fifteen-inch gun that the Army had experimented with before the war. To him that provided the answer—future *Monitors* should be armed with fifteen-inch guns! Long before this battle he and Welles became convinced that the design of *Monitor* was sound. In his first annual report, in December 1861, Welles asked for the immediate construction of twenty-one ironclads. The House passed the necessary legislation, the Senate approved it in February 1862, and construction commenced at once. After *Monitor* had proved her worth, Welles reported to Congress that the Navy would build more ironclads of the same type. These low-freeboard turreted ironclads soon became known as monitors, after the prototype, and they became a distinct class of ironclads. The Navy would also build guns of fifteen-inch caliber, and would attempt to build them as large as twenty-inch caliber. We will see later that the monitors were not capable of all that their champions claimed for them, but the impact of *Monitor* itself was so great that monitors for coast defense were still active into the 1920s, and the last one was not stricken from the Navy List until 1937, although it had been out of commission for eleven years.

The battle between the ironclads occurred as McClellan was completing the assembly of troops to launch his Peninsula Campaign. To that general, who in many ways brings to mind that controversial leader of World War II, Field Marshal Montgomery, the only way to attack Richmond was along the peninsulas formed by the James, York, and Rappahannock Rivers. He had a sound reason for this. A drive directly from the vicinity of Washington toward Richmond had several rivers in the path of advance. By using the channels of the main rivers he could depend upon water transportation for supplies and equipment, and naval gunboats could support his movements.

When McClellan reached Fort Monroe early in April, Flag Officer Goldsborough told him that the threat of *Merrimack* was so great that he could not send ships up the James, as McClellan had planned to do. This restriction forced him to shift his main effort to the York River. Federal gunboats supported him in the capture of Yorktown and he established his main supply base at West Point, the head of navigation on the York.

After capturing Yorktown McClellan advanced steadily as the Confederates fell back on Richmond. The position of Norfolk became precarious, with its communications with Richmond threatened and with Burnside in position to attack it from the south. Anticipating a great victory, Lincoln himself went to Hampton Roads to be closer to events. On May 8 a report was received that Norfolk was being abandoned. On May 9, on Lincoln's order, Union ships bombarded the Confederate batteries on Sewell's Point in an effort to draw *Merrimack* out to where heavy, specially rigged ships could ram her. Under cover of this diversion, troops from Fort Monroe were landed on Ocean Beach and they advanced rapidly toward Norfolk.

The evacuation of Norfolk had been ordered on May 1 by General Joseph E. Johnston, then the Confederate commander. Two Confederate gunboats came down the James River during the night of May 5 and towed the unfinished ironclad *Richmond* and two gunboats from Norfolk up the James the following night. This was undetected by and unknown to Union forces. The Navy Yard was ordered destroyed and *Merrimack* was to move up the James as far as she could go. Flag Officer Josiah Tattnall, who had replaced

79

the wounded Buchanan, lightened her to the extent that she drew only eighteen feet of water. Even so, her pilots reported that she could go only a few miles up the river, where she would be at the mercy of Union batteries. As Federal troops approached her anchorage off Craney Island on May 11, Tattnall set her on fire to prevent her capture. The explosion of her magazine made a total wreck of what had been the Confederacy's most powerful ship.

Her destruction changed the strategic situation radically, for the James could then be used freely by the Federal forces. McClellan's campaign was going well and on May 7, while *Merrimack* still posed a threat, Welles ordered Goldsborough to render every assistance to the general and to harass the Confederate retreat. On the same date Lincoln sent a personal note to Goldsborough stating that McClellan had again asked for gunboats on the James and suggested that *Galena* and two gunboats be sent up that river. There was a note of urgency in Lincoln's order as it was his desire that *Galena* should proceed at once, that same night. Goldsborough then ordered *Galena*, with the gunboats *Aroostook* and *Port Royal*, to move up the James and assist McClellan's troops. Lincoln's personal intervention in the naval dispositions at this time reflected the current belief that a major victory was imminent and his own desire to make it decisive.

Galena, under Commander John Rodgers, was the second of the ironclads to be built and had arrived at Hampton Roads only a few days before. She had been built by Bushnell and was designed so that the two one-inch plates of armor on her sides were separated by an air space in which there were iron bars. In a private letter Rodgers expressed doubt that she could stand up to a shore battery, but since so much was expected of her, he intended to give her a fair trial at the first opportunity.

Moving upriver on May 8, *Galena* silenced one Confederate battery on the right bank. A second one, farther up, proved tougher, so *Galena* ranged in as close as possible to the battery and heavily engaged it while the wooden gunboats ran by. There were no casualties, but later in the day *Galena* ran aground and it was May 11 before she reached Jamestown. From there Rodgers asked for more gunboats, as he had learned that there were five Confederate gunboats in the river and he doubted that he could get *Galena* above Harrison's Landing. With *Merrimack* then out of the way Goldsborough sent *Monitor* and the semi-armored gunboat *Naugatuck* up the James with orders to proceed to Richmond and shell that city into surrender. As soon as that was accomplished, Goldsborough reported to Welles, he would take the ironclads to the Cape Fear River with the object of capturing Fort Caswell and Wilmington. Farragut's capture of New Orleans was fresh in his mind and here was a comparable situation. Welles, with Charleston in mind, told him to defer Wilmington for the time being. Events frustrated these schemes but they reflect the wave of Union optimism that existed in May 1862.

Monitor and *Naugatuck* reached Jamestown on May 12, and Rodgers moved up the river that night. After grounding several times, *Galena*, with *Monitor* and the three gunboats in company, reached a series of obstructions in the river and discovered hastily built but strong fortifications (called Fort Darling) on Drewry's Bluff, only about eight miles below Richmond. Commander Rodgers anchored *Galena* about 800 yards below the fort and turned her around with a stern anchor so that her entire broadside would bear on the fort. At 7:45 a.m. she opened fire on Fort Darling, which replied in kind. *Monitor* anchored nearby to join the battle. As the exchange continued she moved inside *Galena*, but *Monitor*'s guns could not be elevated enough to reach the fort, so she dropped down the river to fire at longer range. The gunboats also joined the fight, but *Naugatuck*'s gun burst, putting her out of action. By 11:15 *Galena* had expended nearly all of her ammunition and Rodgers made the signal to discontinue the action. As she withdrew, defenders in the fort, which included the crew of *Merrimack*, moved onto the parapets and gave her a rousing cheer for her gallant performance.

Galena was badly battered, being hit twenty-eight times with eighteen shots penetrating her armor and with one passing completely through the ship. She had thirteen killed and eleven wounded. *Monitor* was hit three times but suffered no damage or casualties. The gunboats had a few casualties and slight damage.

This action might be dismissed as merely showing that a ship of *Galena*'s construction could not stand up to a duel with shore fortifications, except for one important fact. The attempt to reach Richmond and shell the city into surrender was entirely a naval operation in which the Army had no part. Apparently instigated by Lincoln himself, it lacked the one feature that might have caused the fall of Richmond. As Confederate officers who were in Fort Darling observed, had a few thousand troops attacked in concert with the ironclads, they could have captured the fort. The road to Richmond would then have been wide open, for there were no defenses between that fort and the city.

McClellan's requests for gunboats and ironclads were linked with his appeals for reinforcements, which he planned to move up the James. He maintained close liaison with Rodgers and promised to provide assistance to the gunboats, but on May 17 he reported to Secretary Stanton that he had received only meager accounts of the action at Drewry's Bluff. He complained that he had no official information of its objectives. This indicates that his own superiors, who probably were equally uninformed had not told him in advance of Rodgers's orders from his naval commander. McClellan was, however, kept informed of the movements of the gunboats. When *Galena* ran aground he offered to send troops to cover her until she was refloated.

A few days after the action Goldsborough called at McClellan's headquarters to ask him to throw a force across the James and unite with the ironclads and gunboats to seize the fort at Drewry's Bluff. McClellan was unwilling to do so at that time. He wanted to wait until his army was across the Chickahominy and then decide whether Drewry's Bluff was worth while.

No one can say how the Peninsula Campaign might have ended had this opportunity to capture Drewry's Bluff been seized. It would have had to be done promptly, for the Confederates realized the weakness of their position, strengthened the fort itself, and stationed troops to counter any move from that direction toward Richmond. Yet it does appear that McClellan, by adhering to his set plan, passed up an opportunity to remove the one obstacle that would have permitted *Monitor* and the gunboats to support his troops and open the way to the city via the James River.

While McClellan was fighting what appeared to be a successful battle for Richmond, Welles was urging Goldsborough to be ready to take the ironclads and other ships to the mouth of the Cape Fear River and capture Fort Caswell as soon as possible. Charleston, for the moment, was in the background, for the fall of Richmond seemed imminent and Caswell should be easy to take in the confusion following the loss of Richmond. While the general's lines were within sight of the city, the ironclads and gunboats patrolled the river, heckled from time to time by snipers and artillery from the right bank. The gunboats silenced them and drove the Confederate parties away by shelling their positions. Late in June McClellan began sending ships up the James with forage and supplies for his army.

On June 25 began the series of actions known as the Seven Days Battle, in which McClellan was driven back from Richmond. He notified Goldsborough that he was being forced to fall back between the Chickahominy and the James. He asked for shallow draft gunboats to be sent up the Chicka-

83

hominy, while the ironclads and gunboats in the James covered his left flank. Goldsborough ordered Commander Rodgers, who was still in the James, to render all possible support. Lincoln showed his own concern for McClellan's position by ordering Goldsborough to do all that he could in support on the York and James Rivers. On June 30 Rodgers reported privately to Goldsborough that much of McClellan's army was safely under the protection of his guns on the bank of the James. The next day the Union Army fell back again and the gunboats actively shelled the Confederate Army in direct support. Rodgers took McClellan on a personal reconnaissance down the river to show him Harrison's Landing as a site for a military base on the river. It was a natural peninsula a few miles below the existing front. Throughout these hectic days McClellan himself kept appealing for more gunboats.

On July 2 McClellan reported to Lincoln that his army was at Harrison's Landing and was in good spirits. He did not mention that Rodgers's gunboats had covered his withdrawal nor that they were then protecting his position. On July 5 General Lee, who commanded the Confederate Army after June 1, reported to Jefferson Davis that he was unwilling to expose his troops to the fire of the Union gunboats and thereby confirmed the security of McClellan's position. Davis approved, and that marked the end of the Peninsula Campaign. McClellan and his army remained in place until August, when it was decided to withdraw it to positions around Washington. The ironclads and gunboats, which had been strengthened by a third ironclad, *New Ironsides*, were then withdrawn from the river.

The Union Navy saved McClellan's army from probable destruction on the bank of the James, but it got no thanks or credit for that job from Army leaders. They were too much involved in acrimonious debate over who was to blame for the failure of what became the most controversial campaign of the Civil War.

Chapter VI

The Mississippi Valley

September 1861–February 1862

THE RIVER GUNBOATS

THE BEGINNING of a Federal gunboat squadron on the Western rivers was described in Chapter III. While Gideon Welles at first treated this as an Army project, he soon took an increasing interest in it. When Fremont asked that Commander Rodgers be relieved, Welles sent a more senior officer to take over. In September 1861 Captain Andrew H. Foote assumed command of the gunboats then operating under the over-all command of the Army, under General Fremont at St. Louis. Since his command was under the War Department and his gunboats were procured by that department, Foote got much sympathy but little real help from the Navy Department. His problem was to organize, man, and arm the squadron that was being built. Man power was his biggest headache. He was assigned sufficient regular naval officers to provide commanding officers for the gunboats and to take over other key positions. The rest of his officers were former river steamboat officers who proved, on the whole, to be quite capable and efficient.

Enlisted men were the most difficult to recruit. Experienced river boatmen enlisted in disappointingly few numbers because of the relatively low pay. Foote appealed to the Navy Department for men and some were assigned, but most of the men were obtained through his own efforts. He sent recruiters to the Great Lakes and managed to sign on a substantial number of men with sailing or steamboat experience in that region. His appeals to the War Department brought orders to Fremont that the Army would supply him with qualified men. Many soldiers volunteered for service in the gunboats but Foote had trouble getting them released by their local officers. By the time he was ready to begin active operations, early in 1862, he still needed almost 1,000 men to fully man the gunboats.

Another troublesome problem was his relationship with the Army. Foote had been sent to the Mississippi with the rank of captain, and a fairly junior one at that. He found that Army officers of the same, or even junior rank in some cases, "pulled rank" on him. In October he appealed to General Fremont to clarify his status by specifically assigning him to command the gunboats, instead of leaving him in the somewhat nebulous status that Commander Rodgers had had before him. Fremont not only did this but in his order to Foote he placed under his command all craft and shipping ". . . belonging to the entire floated expedition down the Mississippi River; and you will also consider yourself in charge of, and commanding, this expedition." [1] Foote was wise enough not to take this sweeping order too literally, for the Army officers with whom he would have to work locally would be apt to challenge his authority.

In any case, Fremont's order still did not fully establish his status, and in November Foote asked Welles to give him the designation of flag officer, which was done. That gave him the relative rank of major general and did much to clear up his command relationships. In December Assistant Secretary

---

[1] ORN, Vol. 22, p. 336.

Fox asked for his opinion on the desirability of transferring the river squadron to the Navy Department. He answered that while he wished that that had been done in the beginning, it was not politic to make the change at this time.

The contract date for the delivery of the seven ironclad gunboats that Eads was building for the War Department was October 10. Four of the boats were built at Carondelet, a suburb of St. Louis, and three at Mound City, a few miles up the Ohio from Cairo. That date came and passed with none of them yet completed. That was not entirely Eads's fault, for he had trouble collecting promised payments on his contract. But the gunboats did begin to come out in November, and as they did, Foote sent them to Cairo where they received their guns, equipment, supplies, and crews. In October a protected gunboat, *New Era*, later changed to *Essex*, was added to the squadron. She was commanded by Commander William D. Porter, brother of David D. Porter, whom we have already met in the Fort Pickens affair.

For the next two months Cairo was the center of activity for Foote's squadron. The ironclads, which he named for cities and towns on the Mississippi and Ohio Rivers, were quite formidable craft. Covered with a partially armored casemate similar to that of *Merrimack*, they were 175 feet long, 51½ feet in beam, and they drew only six feet of water. They were protected by two and one half inches of iron across the bow and on the sides over the machinery. The stern paddle wheel was also enclosed in the casemate. The armament consisted of thirteen guns, the three largest in the bow being nine- and ten-inch guns. Four smaller guns were mounted on each side and two in the stern. Designed for a speed of nine miles per hour, the ironclad gunboats proved to be slower in service and sometimes had trouble bucking the currents when the river water was high.

While the new boats were being fitted and manned, the three gunboats already in commission provided yeoman service. In the middle of September *Conestoga*, under Lieutenant Ledyard Phelps, was assigned to work with Brigadier General C. F. Smith, commanding the troops at Paducah, Kentucky. Phelps made regular patrols up the Tennessee and Cumberland Rivers. His reports kept his commanders advised of the condition of the rivers and of Confederate developments in the region. In October those rivers were too low for him to ascend them and he operated on the Ohio, with a close eye on points where Confederates had shown signs of activity. Phelps was a very aggressive officer who was alert to the problems of his command. From Evansville, Indiana, for example, he reported that he could enlist 100 men along the river, something that Foote's recruiters were unable to do.

When the water rose again he returned to the Tennessee River as far as Fort Henry, which the Confederates were building in Tennessee, just across the Kentucky border. There he learned that they were converting three river steamers to gunboats and would plate them with iron. Two days later he ran up the Cumberland sixty miles and anchored overnight at Eddyville, where he learned that Union sympathizers had been driven from their homes. "I found it necessary to use strong language to the citizens in regard to the persecution of Union people. The more active secessionists fled." [2] On October 20 he reached the Tennessee border in the Cumberland where he found that the Confederates were also building a fort near Dover—this was Fort Donelson. A week later he escorted a transport with troops to Eddyville, where a Confederate detachment was encamped. The troops were landed below the town at night and at daylight made a surprise attack, taking a number of prisoners as well as mules, horses, and military equipment and supplies. Such raids were unimportant in themselves but they illustrate the aggressiveness that the Union gunboat was showing.

---

[2] ORN, Vol. 22, p. 371.

The other two gunboats, *Tyler*, under Commander Henry Walke, and *Lexington*, under Commander Roger N. Stembel, were keeping a watchful eye on the Mississippi below Cairo. They reported regularly on the buildup of the Confederate fortifications near Columbus, Kentucky, eighteen miles below Cairo, which became known briefly as the Gibraltar of the West. By the end of October this had become a formidable fort with about 10,000 troops under the Louisiana bishop-turned-soldier, Major General Leonidas Polk.

On November 1 Fremont ordered Grant at Cairo and Davis at Paducah to be prepared for a demonstration against Columbus in an effort to drive Confederate troops out of southeastern Missouri and to prevent reinforcements from being sent into that state. Following this order, he sent columns of troops into the region. Grant embarked his troops in transports ont he 6th and dropped seven miles below Cairo to await developments. Early on November 7 he received a report from one of the columns that, on the day before, the Confederates had sent troops across the river from Columbus to cut off the Union soldiers. Grant acted quickly and at 6:00 a.m. he moved out, escorted by *Tyler* and *Lexington*. His plan was to land on the Missouri side, out of range of the forts at Columbus, and attack the Confederate camp at Belmont, opposite Columbus. After clearing it out, he would re-embark his 3,500 troops and return to Cairo.

The troops were landed about three miles above Belmont at 8:00 a.m. and moved off toward the Confederate camp, which then contained about 2,500 troops. When the landing was completed Walke took the two gunboats down river to bombard the forts at Columbus.

After some sharp fighting Grant drove the Confederates out of their camp and they retired to the river bank. Grant's troops fell to looting and he had the camp set on fire in order to regain control of the men. Meanwhile, General Polk sent reinforcements across the river, and the Confederates rallied in an attempt to cut off Grant's force from its transports. However, Grant succeeded in getting most of his troops re-embarked before the Confederates were able to attack the transports in strength. The gunboats then closed in on the Confederates and broke up their attack. Later, while covering the withdrawal of the troops, the gunboats picked up some stragglers. It was not much of a battle but Grant was to profit by his mistakes in it. More important, he had been given an impressive demonstration of what gunboats could do in support of troops.

While the gunboats were actively patrolling the rivers and supporting these minor troop operations, Foote was trying to solve another troublesome problem. In the summer of 1861 Assistant Secretary Fox suggested to Fremont that Army thirteen-inch mortars be mounted in boats for use in offensive operations on the rivers. Fremont was impressed and ordered a number of these craft to be built. Foote found that they were little more than scows that had to be towed into position, and at first he doubted their effectiveness. Since they were to carry an Army weapon he wanted the Army to man them. In any event, by November the mortars had not yet arrived from the arsenal at Pittsburgh.

In the middle of November Fremont issued an unauthorized edict emancipating slaves in Missouri. For doing so, Lincoln removed him from command and he was replaced by Major General Harry W. Halleck. Shortly after Foote found an artillery officer, Captain A. G. A. Constable, who was familiar with the mortars and who volunteered to command them under Foote. It was some time before Halleck would approve of the transfer.

In December McClellan became seriously ill and Lincoln decided to check personally on affairs in the West. Thus in January 1862, when Foote sent in one of his periodic reports, a telegram arrived from Washington saying that the President wanted a complete accounting of Foote's command, including the status of the mortar boats. Lincoln's direct intervention resulted in orders to the Pittsburgh arsenal to provide the mortars at once. The delay in producing them cost the Army's Chief of Ordnance his job. Foote was also required to make daily progress reports on the mortar boats for the information of the President.

By the time Foote was ready for his first offensive operation with the ironclads, the mortar-boat program was moving fast.

FORTS HENRY AND DONELSON

AT ABOUT the time that Halleck took command at St. Louis there was a reorganization of the Union Army. McClellan, in over-all command of the Union field army, developed a strategic plan for the employment of that army. A Department of Kansas was established to recover the Indian Territory and to operate in Texas. This was a minor command, as was the smaller Department of New Mexico. Halleck's command became the Department of the Missouri, embracing the upper Mississippi Valley, Missouri, Arkansas, and that part of Kentucky west of the Cumberland River. Brigadier General Don Carlos Buell, with headquarters at Louisville, had the Department of the Ohio. McClellan commanded the Army of the Potomac and his plan was to make a concerted drive into the South—southward from Kansas, down the Mississippi River, through Kentucky into Tennessee, but with the main thrust through Virginia.

At this time the Confederate line of defense in the West ran from Columbus, Kentucky, on the Mississippi, through Bowling Green to Mill Spring, Kentucky. Fort Henry on the Tennessee River and Fort Donelson on the Cumberland River were on this line and they were intended to protect the two rivers, the main highways into their watersheds.

Credit for the idea of capturing Forts Henry and Donelson has been claimed by and given to several individuals. On the day after Halleck had assumed command, an engineer on Halleck's staff had pointed out in a short memorandum the advantages of capturing the two forts. Then, early in November Commander W. D. Porter, after a patrol in the Tennessee River, reported to Foote that he could take Fort Henry with the ironclad *New Era* but that General Smith, at Paducah, would not permit him to go up that far. On several occasions Buell urged Halleck to attack the forts. Foote also proposed the idea to Grant, using his gunboats to support the attack.

Early in January 1862 Halleck ordered Grant and Smith to make demonstrations toward Columbus and Fort Henry. This was to prevent reinforcements being sent from Columbus against Buell, who was launching a movement in his department. On his return to Paducah, Smith told Grant that he thought the fort could be taken. Grant then wired to Halleck in St. Louis asking for permission to go there to present a plan for the capture of Fort Henry, but this was refused. Grant did not give up, and after another request later in the month he did get permission for a personal visit to St. Louis. He returned to Cairo much discouraged, for Halleck had rejected his ideas in a very unpleasant meeting.

This series of developments shows that the idea of capturing Forts Henry and Donelson evolved gradually, but there is much substance in the observation of Confederate Colonel William P. Johnston, writing about his father's experience at Shiloh. Commenting that there has been much discussion about who originated the move up the Tennessee and Cumberland Rivers, he concluded that: "Grant *made* it and it made Grant." [3]

On January 28 Grant and Foote sent similar telegrams to Halleck stating that they felt that Fort Henry could be taken

---

[3] *Battles and Leaders*, Vol. I, p. 547.

with the help of four ironclad gunboats and asking for permission to make the attack. These messages arrived at about the same time that Halleck received a report from McClellan that Beauregard and fifteen regiments of Confederate troops were being ordered from Virginia to the West. The report was only partly true—Beauregard himself had been ordered to report to General Albert Sidney Johnston, who commanded all Confederate forces west of the Alleghenies. Halleck, alarmed that Columbus would soon be heavily reinforced, now ordered the two commanders to go ahead. Halleck's change of mind was also influenced by Lincoln's personal intervention in an effort to get military action started. Disturbed by McClellan's inaction in the field, Lincoln issued an order on January 31 that a general attack must be launched by February 22. Grant and Foote needed no urging.

Foote had four ironclads ready for the expedition, three of them Eads gunboats: *Cincinnati*, the flagship, *Carondelet*, and *St. Louis*. The fourth ironclad was *New Era*, renamed *Essex*. The three older gunboats, *Conestoga*, *Tyler*, and *Lexington*, were also in the expedition. Owing to a shortage of steamboats for transports, Grant's troops were moved up the Tennessee in two stages, but they were ready to jump off from a point about four miles below Fort Henry early on February 6. General Smith and his troops were landed on the left bank and moved up to occupy the high ground opposite Fort Henry. The plan was for Grant to cut off the fort in the rear while the fort was being bombarded by the gunboats.

At about 10:00 a.m. Brigadier General Lloyd Tighlman, who commanded the fort, realized that it was about to be attacked in overwhelming force and sent all of his troops (about 2,500), except the heavy artillery crews, to Fort Donelson. They made it successfully because Grant's advance was delayed by muddy roads and high water in the streams.

Foote planned to have the four ironclads approach the fort slowly in line abreast, with the three unarmored gunboats joining the action from astern at longer ranges. Following this plan, at about 12:30, when some 1,700 yards from the fort, the gunboats opened fire, which the fort returned promptly. When the range was reduced to 600 yards the volume and accuracy of fire increased on both sides. About this time *Essex* received a hit in her boiler and was disabled. She drifted down the river and out of the fight, with ten men killed or disabled and twenty-six, including Commander Porter, wounded by scalding. The fort was taking heavy punishment and by 1:10 p.m. only four of its seventeen guns were serviceable. At 1:50, after a battle which lasted less than two hours, General Tighlman ordered his colors hauled down and surrendered the fort to Flag Officer Foote. A total of seventy-eight officers and men were surrendered. Half an hour later Grant arrived to take over the fort. In this spirited action *Cincinnati* was hit thirty-one times and had one killed and nine wounded. *St. Louis* was hit seven times and *Carondelet* six, but neither gunboat had any casualties. Within the fort casualties were also light: five killed and sixteen wounded.

Foote and Grant were elated at the ease with which the fort had fallen. In fairness to the defenders it should be noted that its site was poorly chosen. It was subject to flooding at high water and water was beginning to enter it from the river even as it was surrendered.

Immediately after the surrender of Fort Henry, Foote sent *Conestoga*, commanded by Lieutenant Phelps, and the other two wooden gunboats up the river to destroy a railroad bridge about twenty-five miles above the fort. Held up briefly at the bridge by a jammed draw, Phelps left one gunboat to destroy the track and continued on up the river in pursuit of some Confederate gunboats. He steamed all the way to Florence, Alabama, where he was stopped by Mussel Shoals. By then he had captured three steamers and forced the Confederates to burn six others. Only one steamer escaped him by hiding up a small stream. One of the captured steamers was *Eastport*, one of the fastest and finest river steamers of the time. She was being converted to an ironclad and with her Phelps collected the timber and iron that had been assembled for her conversion. At Florence he found and gathered more iron intended for her.

Leaving *Carondelet* at Fort Henry to support Grant, Foote returned to Cairo with his damaged ironclads. Grant had reported to Halleck that he expected to attack Fort Donelson, about twelve miles overland from Fort Henry, on the 8th. He did not move against that fort until the 12th, however, for the intervening time was needed for *Carondelet* to go down the Tennessee and up the Cumberland and appear before the fort. When he learned that only one ironclad was being sent up the Cumberland, Halleck intervened and ordered Foote to send more ironclads at once. Even two would be satisfactory, but they must precede the transports which were to ferry some of the troops up that river.

By shifting crews around, Foote managed to fit out three Eads ironclads, *St. Louis* as flagship, and the newly reported *Louisville* and *Pittsburgh*. He also recalled two of the three wooden gunboats in the Tennessee. At Grant's urgent insistence that the presence of the ironclads was a matter of military necessity, Foote set out, although he felt that he was not properly prepared for another fight with a fort. He reached the vicinity of Fort Donelson on the 14th.

Meanwhile Commander Henry Walke, now in *Carondelet*, arrived below the fort on the 12th, and seeing or hearing nothing of Grant's troops, he fired a few shots into Fort Donelson as a signal that he had arrived. This fort was in a much better selected and prepared position than Fort Henry. It was located on a bluff with batteries on three levels, including a ten-inch gun in the lower battery.

The next morning, at Grant's request, Walke attacked the fort until *Carondelet* was hit by a ten-inch shot which penetrated her armor. This caused some slight damage as the shot bounced around inside the casemate and finally settled in the engine room, wounding ten men slightly. After that mishap Walke dropped down the river to his anchorage, but when he heard distant firing in back of the fort he returned and again shelled it.

After Foote arrived on the 14th he attacked the fort at about 3:00 p.m., using the same pattern that he had used against Fort Henry. Ordering the four ironclads to disregard the upper batteries, he headed for the fort in line abreast, changing speed from time to time to diminish the accuracy of the fort's fire at them. This is how the ensuing battle appeared to that famed Tennessee cavalryman, Nathan B. Forrest:

> Of this attack I was an eyewitness, and have never seen a description which did anything like justice to the attack or defense. More determination could not have been exhibited by the attacking party, while more coolness and bravery never was manifested than was seen in our artillerists. Never was there greater anxiety depicted in the faces of brave men than during the terrific roar of cannon, relieved ever and anon by the slow but regular report of our one single 10-inch gun. Never were men more jubilant than when the victory crowned the steady bravery of our little fort; old men wept; shout after shout went up; the gunboats driven back; the army was in the best possible spirits, feeling that, relieved of their greatest terror, they could whip any land force that could be brought against them.[4]

Foote reported that after a very severe fight of an hour and a half, when within 400 yards of the fort, *St. Louis* and *Louisville* received hits that disabled their steering gear and drifted helplessly downstream. The fort then concentrated on *Carondelet* and *Pittsburgh*, and they too were heavily hit and had to drop out of the battle. Each of the four ironclads was hit thirty times or more, but their casualties were light.

---

[4] ORA, Vol. 8, p. 384.

Gideon Welles
Lincoln's Secretary of the Navy

Gustavus V. Fox
Welles's Assistant Secretary of the Navy

Stephen R. Mallory
Confederate Secretary of the Navy

Rear Admiral David G. Farragut, U. S. Navy

Rear Admiral David D. Porter, U. S. Navy

Rear Admiral Samuel F. Du Pont, U. S. Navy

Rear Admiral Andrew H. Foote, U. S. Navy

Rear Admiral John A. Dahlgren, U. S. Navy

Monitor *and* Merrimack
from an original drawing by Samuel Ward Stanton

U.S.S. Carondelet
from an original drawing by Samuel Ward Stanton

U.S.S. Kearsarge
from an original drawing by Samuel Ward Stanton

U.S.S. Onondaga *in the James River*

River Tinclad, U.S.S. Cricket

Deck Scene, U.S.S. Pawnee *off Charleston, S.C.*

River Ironclad, U.S.S. Osage

U.S.S. Fort Donelson
ex-Blockade Runner Robert E. Lee

Ironclad Ram, ex-C.S.S. Stonewall
in the Potomac River, 1865

Union Mortar Schooner in the Mississippi

Blockade Runner A. D. Vance *also known as* Advance

Wreck of a Blockade Runner near Charleston, S.C., 1865

Foote himself was wounded. The rugged ships certainly took a bad mauling in this action, but Foote was undismayed. He conferred with Grant the next day, and leaving the least damaged ironclad at the fort, he returned to Cairo determined to return with the repaired gunboats and with mortar boats to lay siege to the fort.

Foote was a deeply religious man; "He could preach, fight or pray with equal facility," was the observation of an officer who had served under him. An incident that occurred between the battles at Forts Henry and Donelson illustrates this. When he went to church on Sunday morning the minister failed to appear and Foote volunteered to conduct the service. He preached what was reported to be a very fine sermon. This incident suggests that a sharper contrast between this deeply religious teetotaler and the cigar-chomping and reportedly tippling Grant would be hard to imagine. Yet they worked together closely and in harmony. One quality they had in common—neither hesitated to attack when in the presence of the enemy.

General Johnston, the Confederate commander, was much concerned over the loss of Fort Henry and worried about the security of Fort Donelson, which was under the command of Brigadier General Gideon J. Pillow. Johnston ordered Brigadier General Simon B. Buckner, whose son and namesake gave his life on Okinawa in World War II, to reinforce the garrison at Fort Donelson. Johnston also decided to withdraw from Bowling Green to Nashville with about half of his total force, sending Brigadier General John B. Floyd with more troops to Donelson. That raised the total strength at Fort Donelson to about 17,000, more than the 15,000 Grant attacked with on the 14th. Buckner arrived there on the 12th and Floyd early the next morning.

After the defeat of the gunboats the three Confederate generals, of whom Floyd was the senior, held a conference during the following night. They decided that the fort could not be held against Grant and that an attack on his right flank should be launched the next day in order to open an escape route up the river. This attack was made and Grant's right flank was turned temporarily. When Grant himself returned from a conference with Foote on his flagship, he surveyed the field and ordered the lost positions to be retaken at once. Most of the ground was regained by nightfall.

That night another conference was held in the fort at which the Confederate generals agreed to surrender it, although Floyd had good reason for not wanting to surrender himself, for he had been Buchanan's Secretary of War and was wanted in Washington for mishandling of funds, among other charges. He announced that he would attempt to get away from the fort. Floyd passed the command to Pillow, who was the next senior, but Pillow felt that he was too valuable to the South to surrender himself and immediately passed the command to Buckner, the only professional soldier of the three, who elected to remain and share the fate of his troops. Pillow escaped across the river and Floyd got away by steamer during the night, taking some of his troops with him. A thoroughly disgusted Forrest, who was present, announced that he could not and would not surrender his cavalry. He rounded up his men during the night and made his way up the river close to the shore and got through without being seen by Union pickets.

Foote left *Carondelet* at Fort Donelson when he returned to Cairo on the 15th. That gallant ironclad arrived at Cairo two days later to announce the fall of the fort. Foote then sent *Cairo* and six mortar boats up the Cumberland, and the next day went to Fort Donelson in *Conestoga* to confer with Grant. On the 19th, with *Cairo* accompanying, he went up the river above the fort for a reconnaissance. There the reputation of the Union gunboats was well illustrated by an incident that occurred at a small fort near Clarksville, Tennessee, about midway between Fort Donelson and Nashville.

Reporting the gunboats in sight down the river, the commander of the fort wired to General Floyd asking for instructions within ten minutes, "as I will have to go in a hurry when I go." [5] When the gunboats reached the fort they found a white flag flying over it, no troops were to be seen, and Lieutenant Phelps and Grant's chief of staff landed to take possession of the fort.

Foote was preparing to proceed against Nashville with a force of gunboats and mortar boats when he saw a telegram from Halleck to Grant ordering him not to allow any gunboats to move above Clarksville. By then Nashville was being evacuated by Johnston, and Foote believed that the city would be an easy prey for his gunboats.

What appears to have happened is that Halleck had a report that Beauregard was reinforcing Columbus in preparation for an attack against either Paducah or Fort Henry and he wanted the gunboats handy for their defense. His order stopping Foote enabled Johnston to evacuate a large quantity of supplies from Nashville before it was occupied by Union forces. A few days later, either on learning that Clarksville had been abandoned or that the earlier reports of Beauregard's movements were not correct, Halleck reversed himself and ordered all of the gunboats concentrated at Clarksville. By then a disappointed Foote had returned to Cairo. He attributed Halleck's order to stop at Clarksville to jealousy of the successes of the gunboats on the part of Halleck and McClellan. Having been ordered against Fort Donelson when not fully prepared, he then determined to undertake no further offensive operations until his damaged ironclads were repaired and once again ready for action.

Forts Henry and Donelson were among the most significant battles of the Civil War. Brilliant victories for Foote and Grant, they marked a turning point in the war and opened the

---

[5] ORN, Vol. 22, p. 619.

way to the geographical heart of the South. For the next year the main course of the war in the West would be directed up the Tennessee and Cumberland Rivers, to the neglect of the Mississippi. But at one stage during the Battle of Shiloh, or Pittsburg Landing, fought on April 6 and 7, 1862, Grant's left flank, on the Tennessee River, was about to be turned. The gunboats *Tyler* and *Lexington*, the only ones present, pitched in and helped to drive back the Confederates. That was the only significant naval action in support of the troops in that campaign.

Chapter VII

The Middle Mississippi

March–June 1862

ISLAND NUMBER 10

WHILE THE damaged gunboats were being repaired and readied for further operations Foote, with Halleck's chief of staff, General Cullum, who was then in Cairo on an inspection trip, reconnoitered Columbus on February 23. Accompanied by four ironclads and two mortar boats, 1,000 troops were sent as a reconnaissance in force. But just as the gunboats were coming within range of the fortifications at Columbus a steamer bearing a flag of truce approached them. It carried a request from General Polk that the families of some of the senior officers captured at Forts Henry and Donelson be permitted to proceed north in order to be with those officers. Foote and General Cullum protested to General Polk that this visit was a violation of a flag of truce and a thinly veiled attempt to learn the strength and intentions of the gunboats. The Confederate general disavowed any such motive, but if his intention had been to create a diversion he succeeded completely, for when the reconnaissance force returned to Cairo it had no inkling of Polk's preparations to evacuate Columbus, on orders from Generals Johnston and Beauregard. Seriously threatened by the Union successes on the Tennessee and Cumberland Rivers, they had decided to evacuate Columbus before it too was assaulted. Most of the guns and military supplies from the fort were sent down the river to Island No. 10, so named because it was the tenth island below the mouth of the Ohio River.

Another flag of truce on March 1 informed Foote of the evacuation of Columbus. Brigadier General William T. Sherman, who was then in command at Paducah, sent a cavalry reconnaissance overland from Paducah, and on the 4th Foote appeared off Columbus with six gunboats, four mortar boats, and three transports with embarked troops. Seeing no signs of activity, a party was landed to raise the flag over the fort, only to find Sherman's cavalrymen already in possession.

Foote's experience at Fort Donelson had a sobering effect on him and he decided that he would not try again to get within point-blank range of forts with his gunboats. At Forts Henry and Donelson the gunboats had moved upstream and when they were disabled they had drifted downriver and out of range. From now on, on the Mississippi, he would be forced to attack from upstream, and any damaged gunboat would then drift toward the forts and almost certainly be destroyed or, if captured, it might be repaired and subsequently used against him.

The battle between *Monitor* and *Merrimack* and the latter's earlier ramming of *Cumberland* were fresh in men's minds, and the Union Navy suddenly became very ram conscious. The Confederates had a squadron of six to eight gunboats in the middle Mississippi, some of which were rigged with rams. They had been fitted out and manned under the direction of the Confederate Army and were only nominally under the command of Commodore Hollins, the Confederate naval commander on the river. Even so, they were a threat to be reckoned with in any Union advance down the river. The Confederates were also known to be building two or three ironclad rams, one of them at Memphis. In view of the potential threat of these Confederate craft, Foote believed that the security of the entire upper Mississippi Valley depended upon his squadron. As a result he approached his downriver operations with some caution instead of the dash that he had shown at Forts Henry and Donelson.

These considerations help to provide an understanding of Foote's decisions at Island No. 10.

Moving down through Missouri to drive the Confederates out of that state, Major General John Pope appeared at New Madrid, Missouri, on March 1. The town, which had a Confederate garrison, was on the river a few miles below the island. Island No. 10 lay near the Kentucky-Tennessee border in the upper part of a double hairpin turn in the river. There were five batteries on the island itself and there were five more on the Tennessee bank of the river. There was also a naval floating battery moored to the island. More than fifty guns, the largest of which was eight-inch caliber, covered the river over a three-mile stretch of mainland and island.

While Pope was closing in on New Madrid, Foote at Cairo was showing a stubborn streak. Under pressure from Halleck to move against Island No. 10, he insisted on taking the time needed to get the gunboats fully ready for the operation, which he expected to be a very difficult one. He had learned by experiment that the Eads ironclads could not be anchored by the stern due to defects in their design, and that they probably could not hold a fixed position in flood-stage currents.

He was ready to move by March 12 and on the 14th he left Cairo with seven ironclads, including the newly converted *Benton* as his flagship, and eleven mortar boats. He was accompanied by a regiment of troops which would occupy any point captured by the squadron. Arriving above Island No. 10 the next day, he was unable to station his craft for an immediate bombardment owing to rain and dense fog.

Early on the 16th the mortar boats were emplaced along the Missouri bank of the river and they opened what was to become a prolonged bombardment. Shortly after daylight the gunboats joined in the action. Foote had *Benton* lashed between *St. Louis* and *Cincinnati*, and these three engaged the upper battery on the Tennessee bank while the remaining gunboats shelled other batteries. The *Benton* group had a lively time that day. *Benton* was hit four times, *St. Louis* had a gun burst which killed two and wounded thirteen, and *Cincinnati* had her engine damaged. In his first report Foote noted that this place was far stronger and more difficult to take than Columbus ever would have been. After a second try at intense bombardment without any apparent success, he had the mortars and gunboats maintain merely a harassing fire on the network of batteries.

Below the forts General Pope was faced with problems of his own. He occupied New Madrid on the 13th but he could not cross the river to get at the Confederates for lack of transports. Furthermore, Commodore Hollins's squadron of gunboats was operating below New Madrid. Pope placed batteries below his main position opposite Tiptonville, Tennessee, and they served to keep the Confederate gunboats below that town.

Pope sent his engineer over a roundabout route to reach Foote and appealed to the naval commander for two or three ironclads to run past Island No. 10 and join him. Foote called a council of his skippers to get their ideas on the feasibility of making such a run. Lieutenant Phelps, now shifted from *Conestoga* to command *Benton*, and Commander Walke of *Carondelet* believed that the run could be made and volunteered to make it. The others were opposed, believing that such an attempt would result in disaster. This was also Foote's view and he refused to approve the attempt. It is of interest to note that the lieutenant commanding the Confederate naval floating battery expressed the same opinion in a report made after eleven days of the bombardment. In this case Foote also had to think beyond Island No. 10 to his future operations. He was fortified in his beliefs by instructions from Halleck not to submit the gunboats to undue risks and there was no need for hurry in reducing the fortifications.

The river was in flood stage and much of the surrounding country was under water. In this situation, the army engineers found at least a partial solution to the lack of progress that threatened to create a prolonged stalemate. By linking the river with a natural bayou a few miles above the gunboats' position, a canal was formed through which shallow draft transports could be sent down for Pope's use in crossing the river. The remarkable feature of this canal was that part of it had to be cut through flooded woods. The trees were cut off four and one half feet below the water surface and dragged clear of the channel. The project was completed in only two weeks.

During this time the gunboats and mortars continued their slow bombardment without noticeable effect on the fortifications. Pope became increasingly annoyed at Foote's refusal to risk a gunboat to run past the batteries and repeatedly pleaded with him to do so. In desperation some of his troops undertook to improvise gunboats by mounting artillery pieces on reinforced coal barges. Foote finally realized that something must be done to end the stalemate. He called another council of his commanders to reconsider the idea of running a gunboat past the batteries. Walke remained convinced that it could be done and again volunteered to try it. On March 30 Foote sent written orders confirming Walke's offer but imposing strong precautions on the attempt.

Walke carefully prepared *Carondelet* for the run against expected heavy gunfire. The roof of the casemate was reinforced with timbers to protect against plunging fire from the batteries. The vulnerable stern was protected by bales of hay, and lashed on the port side, the one which would be exposed, was a barge partly loaded with coal and partly with baled hay. This was intended to protect the magazine from shot and shell. Anchor chains and heavy ropes were wound around exposed and weak spots such as the pilot house.

Once the gunboat was ready it was necessary to wait for a favorable night in which to make the run. The moon set early on April 4 and in the late afternoon storm clouds appeared; Walke decided to make the try that night. As *Carondelet* started slowly down the river about 10:00 p.m., with not a light showing, a violent thunderstorm erupted. Each lightning flash illuminated the gunboat, but it was not seen from the shore until after it had passed the first two batteries. To muffle the characteristic chugging sound of exhaust steam from the engine through the stack, the exhaust line was modified and piped into the paddle-wheel house. Suddenly there was a flash of flame from the stack, caused by dry soot becoming ignited. Even this was not observed from the batteries. But a second flash of flame from the same source was seen on shore and every gun that could bear opened fire on the gunboat. Walke immediately rang up full speed in order to complete the run as quickly as possible. At one point the barge alongside bumped the embankment under the batteries but it did not run aground. The gunboat got by the land batteries without a scratch and only the naval battery now remained as a threat. It had been cut loose from its mooring in one of the bombardments and was grounded below the batteries. This obstacle was also passed without *Carondelet* being hit once, and at about 1:00 a.m. she arrived at New Madrid. Following that success, *Pittsburgh*, commanded by Lieutenant Thompson, also ran past Island No. 10 during the night of April 6 with equal success.

On April 6 *Carondelet* embarked an Army staff party and made an extensive reconnaissance of the Tennessee shore below New Madrid, seeking out Confederate batteries and a suitable landing point for the troops. Several batteries were silenced and their guns spiked. General Pope, losing no time, announced his intention of crossing the river the next day.

Preceding the crossing, the two ironclads were to silence the Confederate batteries and then cover the landing of the troops. This was done and the Confederate forces on the mainland surrendered to Pope the same day. Finding itself completely cut off, Island No. 10 surrendered to Foote that afternoon.

The gunboats were the key to the capture of one of the Confederacy's strong networks of fortifications. By themselves they could not reduce the batteries by bombardment. Yet Pope could not, or thought he could not, get at his enemy without the support of the gunboats. When Walke broke the deadlock by successfully running past Island No. 10, Pope captured the Confederate force opposite him without the loss of a man. This action, which ended so suddenly, provides an excellent illustration of what Foote meant when asked later which was the more important in this type of operation, the Army or Navy. His reply was that the blades of a shears, when properly joined, made an efficient and useful instrument; separated neither blade was of much use.

At Island No. 10 the Union losses were only seventeen killed and thirty-four wounded, including the fifteen casualties from the gunburst on *St. Louis*. Confederate losses are not known accurately but they were also small and estimated to be about thirty in all. Some 23,000 Union troops were present and more than 6,000 Confederates were captured. At Shiloh, which was fought at the same time, there were far more troops involved and each side had more than 10,000 casualties.

FORT PILLOW AND MEMPHIS

WITH THE OBSTACLE at Island No. 10 removed, Flag Officer Foote was ready to move his squadron to the next Confederate strongpoint and he arrived at New Madrid on April 11. The new target was to be Fort Pillow, at the head of a hairpin bend in the river about midway between

Island No. 10, and Memphis, near the Mississippi border. This fort had about forty heavy guns, including several ten-inchers. They were placed along the top and near the base of a steep bluff—another formidable obstacle. Foote wanted to take a detachment of troops with him, but when he learned that Pope was also planning to move against Fort Pillow with most of his army, Foote started ahead with the gunboats on April 12. They anchored for the night about fifty miles above the fort. Early the next morning he was joined by Pope's transports and the combined fleet moved down to a point just above the fort but out of range of its guns. Five Confederate gunboats appeared steaming up the river and Foote went after them with his gunboats. Only a few long-range shots were exchanged as the Confederates were chased back under the protection of Fort Pillow.

During the day Foote arranged with Pope for a concerted attack on the fort. The mortar boats would be placed along the Arkansas shore within range of the fort early the next day. Pope would land about five miles above the fort and endeavor to work around behind it. When he was in position to make his attack, Foote would concentrate with everything he had on the river side of the fort. But on the afternoon of the 14th Pope returned to Foote's anchorage to report that he had been unable to carry out his plan, the way being barred by a swamp. Pope then proposed to cut a canal across the base of the peninsula on the Arkansas side, through which his transports and some of the gunboats could travel, coming out on the Mississippi below the fort. There they could cross the river and attack from the southward.

Covering Pope's operations, the mortar boats would continue their bombardment and force the Confederate gunboats to move farther down the river, well out of their range. But on April 16 the new scheme of attack was frustrated by orders from Halleck. He was then preparing for his own attack on Beauregard at Corinth, Mississippi, and he ordered

Pope to join him, leaving only enough troops with Foote to occupy the fort should it be evacuated.

Pope's withdrawal resulted in a long period of relative inactivity while the mortars lobbed shells into the fort. This was no more than a harassing fire, having only nuisance value. In his periodic reports to Welles, Foote showed some concern about a flotilla of ten or eleven gunboats that the Confederates were assembling below the fort. He also had a report that the Confederate naval commander, Commodore Hollins, had gone to New Orleans to bring up the new ironclad *Louisiana*, but the report proved to be unfounded. Hollins had gone to New Orleans, but it was because that city was threatened by Farragut's squadron, which had appeared in the river below the city. The gunboat flotilla below Fort Pillow was an improvised and a motley group. Some of the gunboats had light iron protection around vital parts, but for the most part they were protected by cotton bales, hence the term "cotton clads."

Foote's foot wound, received at Fort Donelson, refused to respond to treatment, and while at Island No. 10 he asked to be relieved so that he could go north for a rest. As a mark of confidence in him Welles did not send an officer to relieve him. Instead he ordered Captain Charles H. Davis, Du Pont's chief of staff at Port Royal, to report to Foote for such duty as the latter might assign him. Davis was already earmarked to head a bureau in the Navy Department and this was only a loan of his services so that Foote could get away for proper treatment and rest. As events developed, Foote never returned to the command, and Davis was later designated flag officer in his own right. Davis took over the command on May 9. The next morning the Confederates chose to attack with their gunboats.

By this time it was daily practice to keep the squadron moored to the banks upriver and out of range of the fort while a mortar boat or two was placed in position behind the point of the turn of the hairpin bend, which was within range of the fort. One of the Eads ironclads was sent down to cover and protect the mortars. On May 10 this was *Cincinnati* commanded by Commander Roger N. Stembel.

At Fort Pillow at this time was Brigadier General M. Jeff Thompson, a Missouri militiaman who had caused much trouble for Union troops in his native state until he was driven out. He now put his men aboard the gunboats as marines and sharpshooters and at a meeting with the gunboat captains in the evening of May 9, decided to try to capture the Union gunboat that habitually covered the mortars. Eight Confederate gunboats got under way at 6:00 a.m. the next morning, and shortly after 7:00 they rounded the point and headed for *Cincinnati* at full speed. The other Union gunboats were moored above the threatened craft, but they got under way on signal as rapidly as they could. The action lasted only about an hour and only a few of the Union gunboats got into it.

Cincinnati also got under way as soon as she sighted the Confederates and opened fire upon them. At the same time, the young officer in charge of the mortar boat turned his weapon on the attackers and fought his craft with spirit. The Confederates' leading rams meanwhile bored right in through the gunfire. The first one, *General Bragg,* rammed *Cincinnati* and one of her sharpshooters wounded Commander Stembel. *General Bragg* had her tiller ropes shot away and drifted down the river out of the action. A second gunboat, *General Sterling Price,* also rammed *Cincinnati* and pushed her stern around to a position that enabled *General Sumter* to ram her for the third time in the stern. Still another gunboat, *General Earl Van Dorn,* rammed *Mound City* as she closed in to assist *Cincinnati.* By that time other Union gunboats were getting within range and firing rapidly. Captain Montgomery, commanding the Confederate group, broke off the action and retired down the river. The Union gunboats attempted pursuit, but the ironclads were much slower, and the group was soon safely back at Fort Pillow. While Union gunboat commanders claimed to have disabled most of the Confederate gunboats, Montgomery reported that, even though all of his craft were hit repeatedly, there was no serious damage. His casualties, only two killed and one wounded, attest to that. The Union squadron had but five wounded.

Cincinnati was so badly holed underwater that she was run aground to save her from sinking, but in less than a week she was refloated and sent upriver for repairs. *Mound City* was also grounded for a short time, but the next day she too was afloat and sent up the river. Thus there were no outright losses. Yet the Confederate rams had seriously damaged Davis's squadron and the lesson of this action was not lost. The gunboats were reinforced against ramming by putting railroad iron around the stems and sterns and by suspending logs along the sides.

Nothing of interest occurred at Fort Pillow for the next two weeks, but it was about this time that another novel element of the naval war on the Mississippi appeared. During the summer of 1861 Charles Ellet, a civil engineer from Pittsburgh, had appeared at the Navy Department with a scheme for destroying the Confederate ironclad *Merrimack*. He would build or convert existing steamers into fast unarmed rams and depend entirely upon speed and surprise to ram and sink the ironclad. The Navy was unimpressed with the idea, but about a week after the battle between *Monitor* and *Merrimack*, Ellet had a meeting with Secretary of War Stanton, who responded to his scheme. Ellet was given a green light and returned to Pittsburgh, where he displayed commendable energy in putting his plan into operation. He bought nine of the fastest steamers that he could find on the Ohio, strengthened their bows, and ran several heavy longitudinal timbers the length of their hulls to absorb the shock of ramming. The striking feature of these boats was that they were entirely un-armed, although Ellet did provide some protection for the machinery against gunfire.

Stanton appointed him a colonel in the Army and Ellet in turn commissioned several other Ellets in the Ram Fleet, as it was called, presumably because he wanted men under him whose ideas conformed to his own. His original instructions made him independent of the naval forces, except that he was to get the concurrence of the naval commander for any of-fensive he wanted to make. Ellet objected to that proviso since he felt that the naval commander might not be sympathetic with his mode of warfare; the restriction was removed. He ar-rived at Fort Pillow with the first of his rams on May 26 and Davis soon learned that he had no control over Ellet and his craft. But a working arrangement was made between the two and there was surprisingly little friction between them. When Ellet proposed to run his rams past Fort Pillow to get at the Confederate gunboats lying below, Davis tactfully suggested that Ellet should consider himself in the nature of infantry. He should move forward to mop up after the artillery—in this case the gunboats—had softened up the target for him. Fortunately, before Ellet's restlessness could lead him into some rash act, there was a sudden change in the situation at Fort Pillow.

After the Battle of Shiloh Halleck took personal command in the field, leaving Grant with little to do, and launched an attack against Beauregard at Corinth, Mississippi. Halleck's advance from Shiloh was cautious and slow, but by the end of May Beauregard evacuated Corinth. That made Fort Pillow untenable and it was ordered evacuated at the same time. The evacuation was completed on June 3 and the fort was occu-pied by Union troops from Davis's squadron the next day. Leaving one gunboat to support the troops in the fort, Davis sailed the next day for Memphis with the rest of the gunboats.

En route he captured a Confederate transport and anchored that evening about a mile and a half above the city.

At daylight eight of Montgomery's gunboat flotilla were seen lying at the levees in Memphis. At first they moved down the river but soon returned and ranged themselves before the city. On signal *Benton, Louisville, Carondelet, Cairo,* and *St. Louis* got under way and stood down the river to engage the Confederate gunboats. The latter opened fire and a deliberate fire was returned by the Union gunboats, using care not to fire into the city. While this exchange was taking place and the range was being closed Colonel Ellet, with two of his rams, steamed rapidly through Davis's squadron and headed for the enemy. Ellet's own ram, *Queen of the West,* rammed and sank *Colonel Lovell* but sustained considerable damage to herself. Ellet himself was severely wounded in this action and died of his wounds several days later. Meanwhile the Union gunboats got into close range and disabled *General Beauregard* and *Little Rebel* when their boilers blew up. Ellet's second ram, *Monarch,* rammed *Beauregard* almost simultaneously and forced *Little Rebel* ashore, whereupon her crew fled. *Monarch* then took the sinking *General Beauregard* in tow to shallow water, where she sank.

Until this time the remaining Confederate gunboats maintained their positions in the battle, but upon seeing three of their number either sunk or disabled, the rest fled down the river at high speed. The Union gunboats and two Ellet rams followed and maintained a running fight for about ten miles. *Jeff Thompson* was set on fire and grounded on the Arkansas shore, where she was abandoned by her crew. *General Price,* which was damaged in a collision with one of her companions, was also hit by shells and run aground on the Arkansas shore. Only *General Earl Van Dorn,* the fastest Confederate gunboat, escaped.

Thousands of Memphis citizens lined the banks of the river

and with mixed feelings watched the destruction of the Confederate flotilla. General Jeff Thompson also watched the battle from the river bank and, seeing how it was going, discreetly rode out of town before the city was occupied. After the battle Davis sent a formal demand for the surrender of the city. Having no defenses, the mayor could only answer: ". . . the civil authorities have no resources of defense, and by the force of circumstances the city is in your power." [1] Davis sent Colonel Fitch, who came from Fort Pillow with him, to take military possession of the city. Although its capture was not as spectacular as that of New Orleans, Memphis was a very significant victory for the Union squadron and a severe loss to the Confederacy. It was the terminus of four railroads, three leading to the east and south and one a spur line into Arkansas. It soon became an important Union Army base, and a former naval facility located there was reoccupied. Several months later, when its equipment was restored, it became one of the principal repair centers for the Union river squadron.

The literature and lore of the Civil War is rich in anecdotes which show that the soldiers and sailors on both sides had a keen sense of humor. On this occasion Flag Officer Davis showed that he too possessed one. Three of the captured and sunk gunboats were later raised and put into Union service. The smallest of these, *General Sumter*, was renamed *General Pillow*, for the Confederate general who fled from Fort Donelson with Floyd to avoid capture. "The only objection to the name," Davis reported, "is that the little thing is sound in her hull, which can't be said of General Pillow. However, she resembles the general in another particular; she has a great capacity for blowing and making a noise altogether disproportionate to her dimensions." [2] In the months which followed she performed gallantly under her new name in the Tennessee

---

[1] ORN, Vol. 23, p. 121.
[2] ORN, Vol. 23, p. 210.

and Cumberland Rivers, where guerrillas were to become especially troublesome to the Union forces.

Guerrillas were also a problem on the Mississippi. As a result, except for a brief appearance off Vicksburg to join Farragut, Davis's squadron was engaged chiefly in patrolling that river and convoying steamers for the Army. But with no large Union Army forces on the Mississippi there was no opportunity to operate seriously against Vicksburg, the principal remaining Confederate strongpoint on the river.

Chapter VIII

New Orleans

PLANS AND PREPARATIONS

IN HIS *Incidents and Anecdotes of the Civil War* Admiral
David D. Porter gives a highly colored and dramatic account of how he conceived the idea and developed the plan
for the capture of New Orleans. His version contradicts the
more realistic account of Gideon Welles in the November and
December 1871 *Galaxy* magazine. Porter did have an important part in that operation and was consulted early in the
planning, for he had recently been blockading the Mississippi
River and had spent several years running in and out of New
Orleans. But the real author of the plan for taking New
Orleans was the Assistant Secretary of the Navy, Gustavus
Fox, who appreciated the importance of the city from the be-
ginning.

When Porter appeared in Washington in November 1861,
he had just returned to New York in *Powhatan*, the ship he
had taken over as part of the scheme of Seward and Meigs for
the relief of Fort Pickens. Gideon Welles had not forgotten
that incident and it was probably Porter's friendship with
Gustavus Fox that saved him from some disciplinary action.
The fact that Porter had at least shown personal initiative in
that venture was also in his favor, for Welles was constantly
on the lookout for that quality.

Broad plans for the capture of New Orleans were developed before Porter arrived on the scene. Even before the seizure of Port Royal, Welles and Fox believed that the city could be taken by naval forces.

New Orleans was the South's greatest seaport and the Mississippi River was the main highway over which Middle West grain and other products reached the sea, although Northern railroads were cutting into that traffic. Welles's Board of Strategy in August 1861 recommended that the Head of the Passes, at the junction of the three main passes from the river to the sea, be fortified but that the capture of the city be deferred until suitable ships were available. The main obstacle was two forts about twenty miles above the Head of the Passes. The one on the left bank, Fort St. Philip, was built by the Spaniards and it had successfully withstood a bombardment by a British squadron in January 1815. Fort Jackson, on the right bank, was of modern masonry construction and both were heavily armed.

Late in September 1861 four blockaders moved up to the Head of the Passes and sealed off the main river to blockade runners. On October 12 the turtlebacked Confederate ironclad ram *Manassas* came down from New Orleans and in the darkness rammed a schooner alongside *Richmond*. When burning fire rafts also appeared the blockaders fled from the river in panic. The incident was given full play by Southern newspapers and Welles was much embarrassed, fuming about the conduct of the blockaders.

Once the blockade had been established, the attack on New Orleans was delayed by difficulties in getting the necessary ships and in persuading the Army to co-operate. Welles and Fox pleaded with Winfield Scott for the necessary troops, but he was noncommittal. Shortly after McClellan took over he agreed to the plan and authorized General Ben Butler, then in New England recruiting troops for another Gulf project, to recruit 10,000 men for the New Orleans expedition.

One element of the plan was to bombard Forts Jackson and St. Philip into submission by the use of thirteen-inch Army mortars, mounted in schooners. It was hoped that they would soften the forts sufficiently for a fleet to be able to run past them. The use of the mortars was proposed by Porter, and McClellan thought that they would be essential for the task. Porter was given command of the mortar flotilla and placed in charge of procuring and equipping it.

Welles personally selected the commander of the expedition. For various reasons he ruled out most of the senior captains, choosing instead a fairly junior one, David Glasgow Farragut. He had a Southern background but Welles was impressed by the fact that he had left Norfolk and moved to New York when Virginia seceded. He also knew that Farragut had presented a daring but well-thought-out plan for the capture of a castle at Vera Cruz during the Mexican War. Careful inquiries among the senior officers revealed a general agreement that Farragut was a capable officer but there was considerable doubt that he could command a large force, mainly because he never had commanded one. Porter backed him strongly. Farragut had first gone to sea under Porter's father in the War of 1812 and had become, for all practical purposes, a member of the Porter family. Disregarding the doubts, Welles settled on him for the command, and he was formally notified of his selection on December 23. To preserve secrecy of the objective the Gulf Blockading Squadron was divided and Farragut's new command was named the West Gulf Blockading Squadron. The East Gulf Blockading Squadron, assigned the Florida coast from east of Pensacola to Cape Canaveral, was a minor command in which no significant naval events occurred.

Orders for the New Orleans operation were issued to Farragut late in January 1862. He was to wait until Porter's mortar flotilla had reported to him and then, when he was fully ready, he was to proceed up the Mississippi, reduce the forts below

New Orleans, and appear before that city to take possession of it until troops could arrive and take over. If the upper Mississippi expedition had not already descended the river, he was to take advantage of the expected panic and push a strong force up the river, attacking Confederate positions from the rear. Following that, he was to reduce the defenses of Mobile and hold it for the Army.

Farragut reached Ship Island off Biloxi, Mississippi, late in February and he plunged at once into preparations for the operation. Ship Island had been occupied by the Navy in September 1861, on recommendation of the Board of Strategy. The heavier ships of his squadron were sent to the passes of the Mississippi to begin the difficult task of getting over the bar and assembling at the Head of Passes. It was not until April 15 that this was completed and he was ready to move. By then Porter's mortar flotilla, consisting of twenty schooners and six shallow draft gunboats, had arrived and Butler's troops were at Ship Island.

Farragut's preparations for this operation were most thorough. He issued detailed instructions to each ship, covering such precautions as removing all unnecessary masts and spars, having howitzers in the tops, ladders ready for carpenters to go over the side to cover shot holes, and spare hawsers on hand to take the next ship astern in tow. Anchor chains were hung along the sides to give added protection against shot and shell. That he intended to go in but one direction is shown by his order for each ship to trim a few inches down by the bow, so that it would not be turned downriver in case of grounding. Surveyors from the Coast Survey made accurate surveys of the river and spotted Porter's mortar schooners precisely in their selected positions. Most of them were placed on the right bank below Fort Jackson, protected from direct observation by a woods on the river bank. Each had the top of its mast camouflaged by tree branches. Six of the schooners were lined up on the left bank to bombard Fort St. Philip.

APRIL 16–28 BELOW NEW ORLEANS

ON APRIL 16 Porter's gunboats began to feel out the forts by exposing themselves to their fire and firing a few shots in return. It was not until the 18th that all of the mortar schooners were emplaced and a deliberate bombardment of the forts began. Accurate fire from the forts caused those on the left bank to be withdrawn after the first day and thereafter Fort Jackson received the bulk of attention. Porter had boasted that his mortars would subdue the forts within forty-eight hours, but his bombardment continued for five days with no sign of submission from the forts. By then Farragut had decided that more drastic steps were necessary.

During the night of the 20th three gunboats succeeded in making a breach in a boom, formed of hulks chained together, that obstructed the river below the forts. On the 22nd Farragut called his captains on board the flagship *Hartford* and went over in detail his plan for running past the forts that night, but he later postponed the run for one day.

On the 23rd Brigadier General J. K. Duncan, commanding the defenses of the lower Mississippi in Fort Jackson, noted that the mortar fire had slackened materially and correctly surmised that the mortar crews were becoming fatigued and that Farragut would try something else to crack the forts. In the afternoon, when he saw small boats placing white flags at regular intervals on the left bank below Fort St. Philip, his suspicions were confirmed and he warned his command to expect an attack by the ships. This word also went to Commander John K. Mitchell, commanding the Confederate naval forces in the vicinity of the forts.

Mitchell was at New Orleans on April 20 when he was ordered to embark in the ironclad *Louisiana* and proceed to the assistance of the forts. The craft was not yet completed and a crew of mechanics was on board trying to get the propulsion machinery in operation. She had to be towed down the river to a mooring above Fort Jackson. General Duncan wanted Mitchell to place her below Fort St. Philip where she could drive off the mortars, a good sign that the mortar bombardment was hurting. Mitchell explained that to do so would expose her to certain destruction as, with her guns either poorly emplaced or not emplaced at all, she would be outranged by the mortars and the Union ships. However, he did shift her to the left bank opposite the fort in order to cover the approaches. The Confederate Army officers were very critical of Mitchell and his failure to co-operate—criticism that is not well justified when *Louisiana*'s unreadiness for action is considered.

In the vicinity of the forts were fourteen armed vessels of which six, *Louisiana*, the ram *Manassas*, two gunboats, and two armed steam launches belonged to the Confederate Navy. There were also two gunboats of the Louisiana State Navy and six so-called river defense craft. The latter, manned by rivermen and sponsored by the Confederate Army—as were the Confederate boats in the upper river—refused to place themselves under Mitchell's command and made a poor showing when exposed to danger.

At 2:00 a.m. on April 24 Farragut made the prearranged signal to get under way. Leading the procession through the breach in the boom were six gunboats and two sloops of war under the command of Captain Theodorus Bailey. These were to engage Fort St. Philip. Next came *Hartford* with the sloops *Brooklyn* and *Richmond*, followed by a third division of six gunboats. At 3:30 the ships were seen by the forts, which opened a heavy fire upon them; each ship opened fire in return as it came within range. Order was soon lost in the smoke and confusion of battle. Nonetheless, the ships charged on up the river. *Hartford* ran aground above Fort St. Philip and was set on fire by a fire raft, but her crew soon had everything under control and she pulled off. The Confederate

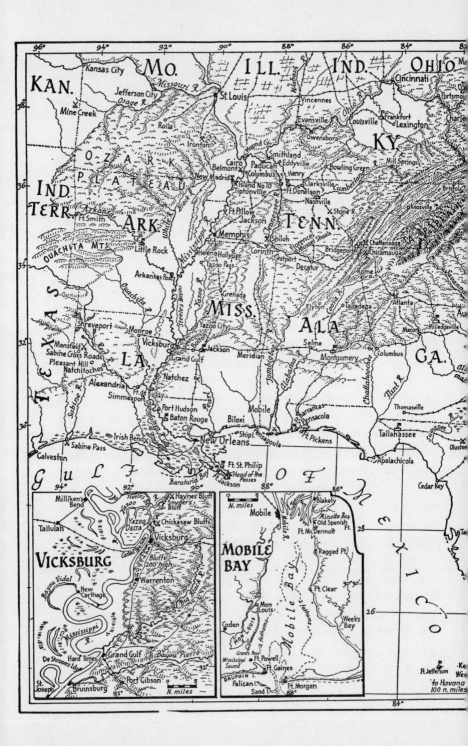

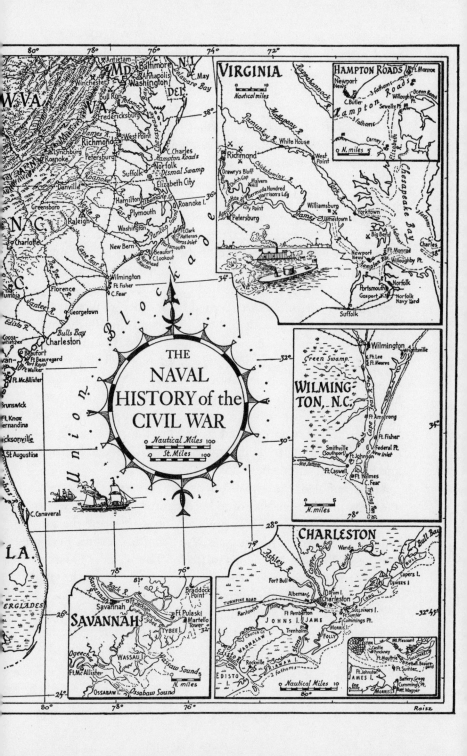

THE NAVAL HISTORY of the CIVIL WAR

Nautical Miles 100
St. Miles 100

VIRGINIA

Nautical miles

HAMPTON ROADS

WILMINGTON, N.C.

CHARLESTON

SAVANNAH

Raisz

naval craft made a brave but futile fight of it, and most of them were either sunk or set on fire to drift down the river. *Manassas* got so far down the river that she came under the fire of both forts. She tried to ram several ships and did strike *Brooklyn*, but was then driven ashore and sunk. Nearly every Union ship took a crack at *Louisiana* as it passed, and she replied with all the guns that could bear.

By 4:40 Farragut's squadron was safely above the forts. Three of his ships failed to get through by running aground, fouling the boom, or being overtaken by daylight. The gunboat *Varuna* got safely past the forts, but being faster than the rest, she pulled so far ahead of them that she was set upon and rammed by one of the Louisiana State gunboats and one of the river defense craft. She had to be run aground to keep from sinking; her crew was rescued by another gunboat coming to her relief. The cost to Farragut of making this daring run past the forts was this one gunboat. Every ship that made the run was hit at least once. *Hartford* received thirty-two hits but, thanks to the precautions taken, her casualties were light—three killed and ten wounded. Total casualties in the squadron were thirty-seven killed and 146 wounded. Some of his captains had been opposed to making the run, but Farragut's determination to do it showed his confidence in his ships and in his own judgment.

He assembled the squadron at the Quarantine Station, about six miles above the forts. He sent word of his success to Porter by a roundabout way and told him to demand the surrender of the forts. Word was also sent to General Butler that he could land his troops in Breton Sound, near Quarantine. Farragut's squadron then steamed up the river, leaving two gunboats at Quarantine to cover Butler's troops. It did not reach New Orleans until the next day, but burning cotton-laden ships drifting down the river revealed that panic had seized the city. At Jackson's old line of defense in 1815 there were fortifications on both sides of the river. The ships received heavy fire as they approached these positions, but as they got abreast of them their broadsides raked the Confederate lines and the troops fled from the ships' bombardment.

Nothing further hindered the squadron as it anchored off the city. The levees, shipping, cotton, and coal along the river bank were all ablaze and a hostile mob was milling about. Farragut sent his second in command, Captain Bailey, with Lieutenant G. H. Perkins to demand the surrender of the city. They had to make their way through the jeering, armed, and threatening mob, but they strode along ignoring the mob and looking straight ahead. "It was one of the bravest deeds I ever saw done," [1] a man who watched it as a youth described it later. The mayor told Bailey that the city was under martial law but that General Lovell, who commanded the local troops, had said he would withdraw from the city. Following Lovell's withdrawal, the mayor and the Council refused to co-operate on the grounds that Farragut had come among them as a conqueror and was free to impose his will upon the city. The mayor refused to haul down a Louisiana flag flying over the City Hall, and a Union flag which Farragut had hoisted over the mint was torn down by the mob and dragged through the streets. Farragut threatened to bombard the city after that act of defiance, but he was really helpless to gain control until Butler arrived on May 1 to occupy the city with his troops.

When Farragut passed above the forts, Porter remained below them with his mortar schooners, his own gunboats, and the three that had failed to make the run. On learning that Farragut was safely past, he sent a demand to the forts for surrender, which they refused. The next day he renewed the bombardment but got no response. Not knowing the condition of *Louisiana*, he then sent all but six of the mortars down

---

[1] *Battles and Leaders*, Vol. II, p. 21.

the river for safety. The six were sent into bayous back of Fort Jackson to cut off possible retreat. On the 27th, believing that Farragut was then in New Orleans, he sent another demand for surrender, offering very liberal terms. In his report he explained that he did not demand unconditional surrender as it was imperative that he get possession of the forts as soon as possible in order that Farragut could be supplied. On the 28th, under a flag of truce from Fort Jackson, a delegation came aboard Porter's flagship to accept his terms. The troops in Fort Jackson had mutinied the night before and had refused to continue to fight. While General Duncan and Colonel Higgins, who commanded Fort Jackson itself, were on board Porter's flagship negotiating the surrender, *Louisiana* was seen drifting down the river on fire. When off Fort St. Philip she exploded, killing one man in the fort.

Commander Mitchell, on learning that the forts were about to be surrendered, had decided that *Louisiana* would not be allowed to fall into Union hands. She was hastily prepared for demolition and set on fire. When her mooring lines burned through, she broke free to drift down the river. Porter was enraged over this and considered that cutting her loose while on fire was a threat to the safety of his own ships and a breach of the truce. Duncan and Higgins made it clear that they had no control over Mitchell and did not speak for the Navy, but Porter's mind was made up. When Mitchell and his officers surrendered, Porter put them into close confinement. They were sent to Fort Warren in Boston harbor, where they were also held in close confinement. It was only after an exchange of correspondence between Mitchell and Gideon Welles, explaining Mitchell's side of the incident, that they were released and treated as other prisoners of war.

Fort Jackson was a shambles after the bombardment but the casualties were light—only nine killed and thirty-three wounded. The troops in the fort had retired to bombproof shelters when they saw the mortar shells lobbing through the air toward them. All of the wooden buildings were set on fire the first day. The bombardment breached the levee and there was a great deal of flooding in the fort. Most of the guns were disabled for varying periods of time but only eleven were dismounted. Even the heavy masonry parapets were cracked.[2] General Duncan reported that 25,000 mortar shells were fired at the fort, with thousands landing inside it. Porter claimed to have fired 18,000 and Farragut's secretary gave the figure as 13,500. About half of the mortar schooners reported their ammunition expenditures and these indicate that the total was nearer 7,500, but even that was a remarkable performance and the effect within the fort was demoralizing. General Duncan reported his belief that one reason the men mutinied was that most of them were Germans and Irishmen who had no real interest in the Southern cause.

After Porter turned the forts over to the Army, on Farragut's order, he retired with the mortar flotilla to Ship Island. On May 7 he went to Mobile Bay bar to locate sites for the mortars and to buoy channels for Farragut's ships when they appeared. He was attracted to Pensacola by fires that he saw one night. Both Mobile and Pensacola had been stripped to reinforce Beauregard in northern Mississippi. It was believed that Mobile would be early on Farragut's timetable, and when Porter appeared off Mobile Bay, Pensacola was hastily evacuated after the Confederates had set fire to the Navy Yard and other public installations. Now Porter helped to reoccupy Pensacola and then used some of his mortar schooners on blockade duty.

FARRAGUT IN THE MISSISSIPPI

SHORTLY AFTER he reached New Orleans Farragut set his ships and gunboats to clearing the river above that city. On

---

[2] The fort is being partially restored by Plaquemines Parish, Louisiana.

May 3 *Richmond* was sent to Baton Rouge—above Baton Rouge Farragut thought only smaller gunboats could operate. *Richmond* ran aground and was delayed, but on May 7 *Iroquois*, commanded by Commander J. S. Palmer, arrived at Baton Rouge and Palmer sent for the mayor, who was reported to be out of town on that day. When the surrender of the city was demanded on the same terms as those given New Orleans, the mayor replied that the city was defenseless but that Baton Rouge would not surrender voluntarily to any power on earth. Commander Palmer, "determined to submit to no such nonsense," moved abreast the arsenal, landed a force, and took possession. He had the Union flag raised over the arsenal and warned the mayor that it must not be molested. Farragut arrived on the 10th and confirmed Palmer's action. He then sent Commander S. P. Lee, in *Oneida*, to Natchez on a similar mission and incidentally to be on the lookout for coal, which was in short supply on the river.

Before she reached Natchez *Oneida* was overtaken by *Iroquois*, which led the way into the town. Palmer's demand for Natchez's surrender was answered to the effect that since he came as a conqueror he did not need the help of city officials in occupying the place. On the 18th Commander Lee arrived at Vicksburg, which was already partially fortified, and demanded its surrender. The colonel commanding the military post there replied somewhat arrogantly: "I have to state that Mississippians don't know, and refuse to learn, how to surrender to an enemy. If Commodore Farragut or Brigadier General Butler can teach them, let them come and try." [3] The general commanding the defenses of Vicksburg said that he had been ordered to hold the city and intended to do so, and the mayor answered that neither the municipal authorities nor the citizens would ever consent to the surrender of the city. Lee's reaction to this defiant attitude was to

---

[3] ORN, Vol. 18, p. 492.

order the mayor to evacuate the women and children on the grounds that if he attacked the defenses of the city he could not avoid damaging the city itself.

Vicksburg is on a bluff over 200 feet high, some distance back from the river and near the head of a deep hairpin turn. It is midway between New Orleans and Memphis, about 400 miles from each. When Farragut arrived a few days after Lee's demand for its surrender, he found that eight to ten heavy guns had been mounted on the high bluff and these could not be reached by the ships' guns. A detachment of about 1,500 of Butler's troops were in transports with Farragut, who conferred with their commander, and it was decided that nothing could be done with that small a number of troops. Vicksburg was defended by an estimated 10,000 Confederate troops and 30,000 more were believed to be an hour's train trip away in Jackson, Mississippi. Both estimates were many times too high, but that does not affect the soundness of the decision. Leaving some gunboats to harass the place and to attempt to prevent its being strengthened, Farragut returned to New Orleans on May 30. Butler's troops occupied Baton Rouge, with two gunboats assigned to cover the occupation.

Farragut was discouraged by this experience and sent off a pessimistic report to the Navy Department. The hazards of the river itself, with four- to five-mile currents to buck, no pilots available, and the resultant frequent groundings made the ascent a most difficult one. Added to that hazard was the fact that two thirds of his ships were badly in need of repair and many of the one-year men were clamoring to be sent north for discharge. Considering that Farragut and his officers were deep-water sailors, that his ships were seagoing types, and that there were no aids to navigation in the river, the first ascent of 400 miles to Vicksburg was a remarkable performance, even though it was fruitless.

In Washington, Welles and Fox were annoyed that the Army had taken credit for opening the upper river as far as

Memphis, and they were anxious that the credit and honor of opening the rest of the river should be the Navy's. But New York papers of May 16 reported that Farragut had retired down the river with his squadron after nearing Vicksburg. The report was in error since he did not reach Vicksburg until the 20th and remained there six days before retiring. However, without waiting for Farragut's own report, orders were sent to him by three different ships to open the river, the most emphatic stating that the President himself assigned the highest priority to this task. These orders were waiting for him at New Orleans, and Farragut had no choice but to try to comply with them.

Butler offered to ascend the river with 7,000 men and take Vicksburg if some of Porter's mortar schooners were brought up to be used against the fortifications. The necessary orders were issued and by June 9 Porter was at New Orleans with all of his available mortars. In reply to Farragut's order to return to the river Porter expressed the pessimistic opinion that Butler had set his sights too high and that a falling river would strand the expedition. Had the mortars gone up with the first ships, he opined, they might have done the trick. Porter had a good point, for the alarmed Confederates were busy mounting batteries on bluffs along the river, and one at Grand Gulf, Mississippi, had already mauled two of the gunboats.

Upon completing arrangements for provisions and supplies to follow, Farragut headed back for Vicksburg in *Hartford*. As these preparations consumed the first week of June, it was also a remarkable performance that his squadron, including three big sloops of war, were assembled below Vicksburg by the 25th. Porter had seventeen mortar schooners in position in time to fire ranging shots at the Confederate batteries below the city on the 26th. By then there were four separate batteries covering the downriver approaches.

Butler had a second thought about sending a large force to

Vicksburg and sent only 3,000 men under Brigadier General Williams. He put the troops to work, with the help of Negro laborers, on cutting a ditch across the narrow neck of land formed by the hairpin turn in the river, in order that the river might cut a new channel that would bypass Vicksburg. This idea occurred to a number of people at about the same time. Farragut's chief of staff suggested it to Captain Craven of *Brooklyn*, who preceded Farragut up the river. Butler ordered General Williams to do it. From Washington Gideon Welles suggested it to Flag Officer Davis at Memphis. By the time the ditch was completed, the river level had fallen below that of the bottom of the channel. Grant was to try the same thing a year later and he too failed. Old Man River just refused to be harnessed.

Farragut's orders were to join Davis at Fort Pillow. When he learned that General Williams felt he had too few troops to take Vicksburg, then defended by an estimated 8,000, Farragut was impatient to run past the batteries and go on up the river. On June 27 he issued his order for making the run that night. It was to be made in three divisions in a pattern similar to that used at the forts below New Orleans. The larger ships would stay in the main channel while the smaller ones favored the Louisiana shore.

At 2:00 a.m. the squadron got under way. At 4:00, as the first ships were moving abreast the batteries, Porter's mortars opened up at the maximum rate of fire. The Confederate batteries bombarded the passing ships and they, in turn, replied with rapid fire. The combined attack of ships and mortars silenced the batteries momentarily but they resumed fire when the ships shifted targets. The most damage was done by a battery above the city which had a long clear range down the channel opposite the city. *Hartford* was hit by raking shots from this battery but was not seriously damaged. By 6:30 the run was over and the ships were anchored safely above the city. Three of the starters failed to make the run for various reasons. Casualties were light, with seven killed and thirty wounded. Porter's gunboats, which joined in the attack on the lower batteries, had two killed and six wounded.

Above the city, with three of his rams, was another Colonel Ellet, a brother of the one lost at Memphis. He had come down from Memphis to reconnoiter the Yazoo River for signs of the Confederate ironclad ram *Arkansas*, which was reported nearly ready for service. He had been in communication with Farragut across the neck of land since his arrival. Ellet sent one of the rams to Memphis with a message from Farragut asking Davis to join him and another to Halleck requesting troops with which to capture Vicksburg.

Part of Davis's squadron was then with an expedition moving up the White River in Arkansas. In capturing a Confederate battery at St. Charles, Arkansas, the Eads ironclad *Mound City* had her boiler exploded by a shell, causing 103 killed, drowned, or missing, and thirty-eight wounded. This was one of the heaviest losses to be suffered by a naval ship in the Civil War. When Davis received Farragut's message he left for Vicksburg at once with whatever boats he had immediately available.

He joined Farragut above the city on the 30th. Davis brought four mortar boats with him and these were set up to assist Porter's, which were shelling the works while Farragut waited for an answer from Halleck. The latter replied that he could send no troops at that time but held out the hope that he might be able to do so in a few weeks. Halleck had occupied Corinth nearly a month earlier and was currently inactive. Meanwhile the defenses of Vicksburg, begun only after Farragut had taken New Orleans, were being strengthened by guns sent from coastal positions at Mobile and Pensacola. A determined ground attack at this time, with the help of Farragut's and Davis's squadrons, might have been successful. Giving the Confederates another year in which to perfect

Vicksburg's defenses was to result in one of the longest and bloodiest campaigns of the war. Farragut reported to Welles that he could run past the forts any time he wanted to, but without sufficient troops to take the place, all that he would accomplish was to silence their guns temporarily.

On July 6 Welles telegraphed an order to Farragut to send Porter and twelve of his mortar schooners to Hampton Roads at once. Farragut linked this order to McClellan's defeat in the Peninsula campaign, but he was surprised that Welles would send so far for the mortars. In a report to the Secretary at this time he suggested that he could accomplish more down the river, noting that if he did not go down soon, his ships would have to wait for high water in the spring. Washington had already sent an order for him to retire down the river, but Farragut did not receive the order until several days after he sent his own report.

Before he moved there was one more incident of note. On July 15 a ram and a gunboat, covered by the ironclad *Carondelet*, went into the Yazoo River in search of the ironclad *Arkansas*. They met her coming down just above the mouth of the river and in the fight which followed both ironclads ran aground. *Arkansas* got off first and headed down the river. The gunboat steamed ahead to warn the fleet, which was at anchor under low steam. But *Arkansas* ran the gauntlet of the Union ships and reached Vicksburg safely.

Farragut was mortified by this affair and incensed. He told Davis that he was going after *Arkansas* as soon as he could get up steam. After passing below the ironclad, he would turn and make a run up the river, repeating the runs until she was destroyed. He wanted Davis to cover him by keeping the upper battery under bombardment. Davis, who seemed not very concerned by the incident, persuaded Farragut to postpone his run until late afternoon. In his order to his ships for the attack Farragut borrowed a Nelsonian axiom: ". . . no one will do wrong who lays his vessel alongside of the enemy or tackles the ram. The ram must be destroyed." [4]

Unfortunately, by the time the ships reached a position abreast *Arkansas* it was too dark to see her and they had to fire blindly. They ran on past the batteries successfully with very few casualties. In the morning Farragut asked Davis to join him for a concerted attack on the ram. Davis declined on the ground that his primary job was to keep the river open and that *Arkansas* was harmless in her present position. She could be destroyed easily if she came out from under the guns of Vicksburg. But Farragut persisted in his determination to destroy her at once, and got Davis to send down his most powerful ironclad, *Essex*. In making her run *Essex* tried to ram *Arkansas*, but the latter's skipper let go his bow line, drifting the bow clear. *Essex* struck only a glancing blow and went aground. She was under heavy gunfire before she got clear, although only two shots penetrated her armor. One of the Ellet rams also ran down past the batteries, but it was badly cut up by gunfire.

As usual, Confederate newspapers gloated over this incident in which Union ships had been caught off guard. Welles fired off letters to both flag officers expressing the department's "mortification" over the escape of *Arkansas* and instructing them to capture or destroy the ram as soon as possible. Farragut was told that he was not to leave Vicksburg until this was done.

On July 22, however, Farragut received the order from Welles for him to return down the river at his discretion. General Butler had already recalled General Williams to Baton Rouge, noting that at Vicksburg he was in Halleck's territory. With the withdrawal of the troops the line of communication across the neck of land was cut off. *Essex* and the Ellet ram, of Davis's squadron, were stranded below the

---

[4] ORN, Vol. 19, p. 8.

city and would have to get coal and supplies at Baton Rouge. For that reason they were assigned to patrol the river between Vicksburg and Baton Rouge.

Davis's prediction about the fate of *Arkansas* if she came out from under the protection of Vicksburg's guns was borne out shortly. On August 5 Confederate troops attacked Baton Rouge, but with the help of *Essex* and two of Farragut's gunboats the attack was repulsed. It was planned that *Arkansas* would run down from Vicksburg and make a co-ordinated attack on the Union gunboats. However, she had engine trouble en route and at a point only a few miles above Baton Rouge an engine breakdown caused her to run aground on the western bank. The next day *Essex* steamed up to attack her. When her commanding officer found that only her stern guns could bear, he had her guns loaded, set her on fire, and cut her loose. She became a total loss when her magazine exploded—the third Confederate ironclad to be destroyed by her own crew.

Essex's commander, William D. Porter, while not as flamboyant as his brother, had many of his characteristics. He wrote a glowing report of how he had blown up *Arkansas* in a fierce action. His statements were challenged by both Davis and Farragut after seeing the reports of the two gunboats in company, and this resulted in an investigation of Porter's conduct during this action. He was still defending himself when he died less than two years later.

Farragut, back at New Orleans, next planned to attack Mobile, and for that purpose he assembled most of his squadron at New Orleans. He did not entirely abandon the Mississippi and left some gunboats in the river to patrol it. Butler used this reduction of force as an excuse to evacuate Baton Rouge, which was done in August. Thus whatever gains Farragut's energetic operations in the Mississippi produced were largely wiped out by default through lack of co-operation by Butler. Confederate batteries on the bluffs between Baton Rouge and Vicksburg closed that part of the river to all but gunboats and convoyed shipping.

Even so, New Orleans was a most important Union gain and the South could not recover from its loss. It was one of the truly decisive actions of the Civil War. Cutting out the heart of the economy of the lower Mississippi Valley was a blow that was to increase in impact for the remainder of the war.

The rest of the year 1862 was one of frustration for Farragut. Butler promised to provide troops for the attack on Mobile but he could not be pinned down as to when he would actually do so. He even failed to provide sufficient troops for taking Galveston, Texas, which was considered a much easier target. Thus in October when Commander W. B. Renshaw, with four gunboats and a mortar schooner, captured the place after only feeble resistance and asked for troops to hold the city, Butler sent him only a small and inadequate token force. Farragut's hopes were raised late in the year by the arrival of Major General N. P. Banks with 20,000 troops. Banks had orders to relieve Butler, open the Mississippi, and capture Mobile, but he proved to be yet another political general of questionable initiative.

Under the circumstances, Farragut was forced to sit on his hands and devote his attention to his part of the blockade. In July Congress, at Welles's instigation, authorized the flag grades of rear admiral and commodore for the Navy. Farragut received the first appointment as a rear admiral—a well-deserved distinction, for he had shown himself to be one of the most aggressive and energetic leaders the war had so far produced.

Chapter IX

Operations in the Mississippi
July 1862–July 1863

THE UPPER RIVER

W HEN FARRAGUT RETIRED down the Mississippi from
Vicksburg in July 1862, Flag Officer Davis's river gunboat flotilla continued to patrol and keep open the upper parts
of the river and the Tennessee and Cumberland Rivers for the
support and supply of the Army. Increasing guerrilla activity
along the rivers kept his flotilla busy, but as there were only a
few troops available in the Mississippi, there could be no important offensive operations.

Back in Washington some very important developments
were in progress. The subordination of the Mississippi flotilla
to Army command had not worked out well in practice, and
Welles and Fox were anxious to have the command transferred to the jurisdiction of the Navy Department. Their efforts were successful and, under a law passed in August, October 1 was the date set for the formal transfer. Henceforth
the flotilla was to be known as the Mississippi Squadron. A
change of command was also in the making. Welles had long
planned to recall Davis to Washington to become Chief of the
Bureau of Navigation and had named him an acting rear admiral. David D. Porter was the surprise selection to relieve

Davis. Although Porter had Fox's most enthusiastic support, for Welles to reach down and pick a commander over the heads of all the captains was unprecedented. But Welles wanted a relatively young and energetic man for the job and he had been impressed with Porter's performance at New Orleans. Lincoln was skeptical about Porter's abilities but gave his assent. Porter was made an acting rear admiral, and he set out for his new command with his customary enthusiasm and energy.

When he took over the Mississippi Squadron on October 15, Porter began firing requests back to Washington for more gunboats, more guns, and more of just about everything. Before the fall of Vicksburg he could boast that he had increased his squadron by fifty-four vessels. Some of them were lightly armored against small arms fire and were dubbed "tinclads." One of the new craft was his flagship, the fabulous *Blackhawk*. She was a river steamer that had been given some protection and guns but which retained luxurious quarters for himself. Fond of riding, he carried his own horses on board, and the tales of him riding his horse over the gangplank for a gallop ashore became legendary on the river.

One of his first problems was the disposition of Colonel Ellet's ram fleet, which was not turned over to the Navy in the general transfer of gunboats. It was intolerable to Porter that an independent command should operate on the river. He recommended that the rams be placed under his command, with Ellet's officers and men organized into a marine brigade which would operate with his squadron. This would give him a mobile force which could be sent against guerrillas and on other semi-independent missions. Ellet himself favored this solution, but it was some time before Welles could get Stanton to agree to it.

Before he left Washington Porter had conferred with Major General John A. McClernand, a political general and friend of Lincoln. Lincoln had authorized McClernand to recruit an army to operate independently down the Mississippi. Porter supported this at first because he had an aversion to West Pointers and preferred not to work with them. But after assuming his new command he had a change of heart, for he realized that such an arrangement would be embarrassing to Grant, who was then in command in the West. One of Grant's corps, under General William T. Sherman, was then at Memphis. Porter, on hearing a rumor that his squadron would not be ready to move against Vicksburg until February, reported to Welles at the end of October that he was ready to support the Army at any time.

Grant, who had learned vaguely of McClernand's project, launched an overland attack early in November aimed at Vicksburg. It consisted of three columns, including Sherman's corps, and by the end of the month Grant himself was at Holly Springs, Mississippi, where he established a supply base. He was unable to get clear-cut instructions from Halleck, who by then was general in chief of the Army in Washington, but on December 7 he was told that he could move his troops as he thought best. Grant then changed his plan and sent Sherman back to Memphis to move down the river to attack Vicksburg with Porter's help. Grant would continue his move toward Grenada, Mississippi, in order to draw away from Vicksburg as many of General John C. Pemberton's defending forces as possible.

By the middle of November Porter was assembling most of his squadron at Helena, Arkansas, in preparation for McClernand's prospective move against the Yazoo River and Vicksburg. At this time he received orders from Welles to co-operate with McClernand, who should be ready to move in about three weeks. Porter ordered Captain Walke, in *Carondelet* at Helena, to take the ironclads down to the Yazoo and, if possible, to operate in that river to prevent the Confederates from erecting batteries.

Walke began his operations in the lower Yazoo near the

end of November. The Confederates had planted numerous mines in the river and clearing them became the first task. Most of the ironclads were in the Yazoo by early December. One of them, *Cairo*, was blown up by a mine, but this loss only increased Porter's determination to get at his enemy. Porter joined Sherman at Memphis on December 18, where final plans were made for a joint expedition to the Yazoo River. Sherman's plan was to capture the Confederate forts at Snyder's Bluff, usually referred to as Haynes Bluff, which was farther up the river, and to cut the railroad leading to the city, before attacking Vicksburg itself. This would clear the Yazoo for gunboats and transports and open a new line of communication with Grant inland.

By December 27 the mines were cleared from the river up to an obstruction near Snyder's Bluff. On the 26th Sherman disembarked his troops below that point and on the 28th they were in position to attack Chickasaw Bluffs, below Snyder's. For two days the attack continued, closely supported by the gunboats, but the defenses were too strong for Sherman's men. Meanwhile, Grant's attack from the direction of Grenada failed to materialize. A Confederate cavalry raid captured his base at Holly Springs and destroyed his supplies. With the loss of his base Grant had to withdraw, and with ample warning of the approach of Sherman's troops, General Pemberton was able to reinforce Vicksburg. Sherman broke off the fight and began to re-embark his troops on December 30.

Stung by this reverse and anxious to recoup his fortunes, Sherman proposed to Porter a joint expedition to take the Post of Arkansas, a Confederate fort on the Arkansas River about fifty miles above its mouth. Porter agreed but a new complication arose. McClernand arrived on the scene much concerned that Sherman had taken over the troops that he had recruited and sent to Memphis. Porter, who had developed an excellent relationship with Sherman, now formed an immediate dislike for McClernand and became even more favorably disposed toward Sherman. Together they persuaded Mc-Clernand, who was senior to Sherman, to approve the Arkansas Post expedition. To attack the fort by water Porter took three ironclads and seven light gunboats. Sherman's troops landed about four miles below the fort on January 9, and on the 10th, while the troops were surrounding the fort, Porter had the gunboats bombard to obtain accurate ranges. In a short fight on the 11th the fort was silenced as the gunboats closed to point-blank range. The fort itself surrendered to Porter and the troops fighting outside the fort surrendered to Sherman. Both made much of this diversion with the hope that it would help to remove the stigma of Sherman's defeat at Chickasaw Bluffs.

Grant, who did not relish having an independent command within his geographical area, at first took this action to be a wild goose chase initiated by McClernand. Later, when told the reason for the attack by Sherman, he withdrew his criticism. With McClernand on the scene Grant went to Memphis and took personal command of the campaign against Vicksburg. By the end of January 1863 his troops and Porter's squadron were again above the city. By then the fortifications around the city were so strong that a frontal assault was out of the question. At Lincoln's instigation a new effort was made to cut a canal across the neck of land near the base of the hairpin turn.

Porter's first move was an attempt to stop supplies from reaching Vicksburg from Texas and western Louisiana via the Red River and the Mississippi. Early in February the Ellet ram *Queen of the West* ran past the Vicksburg batteries and into the Red River, but there she ran aground near a shore battery, which had fired on her rupturing her steam pipe and disabling her. Most of the crew escaped in a river steamer, which had been captured earlier. It was chased up the river by four Confederate gunboats until it met the Union ironclad *Indianola*, which had run past the Vicksburg batteries during the night of February 12.

The life of that ironclad was to be a short one, for near the mouth of the Red River she received a report that a Confederate force, which now included *Queen of the West*, was preparing to attack her. She started up the Mississippi but about thirty-five miles below Vicksburg she was overtaken at night by two rams and two steamers filled with troops for boarding. She was rammed repeatedly and after a fight of an hour she surrendered in a sinking condition, the only Union ironclad to be surrendered in the entire war.

A few nights later Porter got a measure of revenge for her loss. To induce the Vicksburg batteries to waste ammunition he had constructed a dummy monitor on an old barge. It was set adrift in the river and floated past the batteries at night. Porter had the satisfaction of seeing a heavy bombardment as the dummy drifted by. The craft was sighted the next day by *Queen of the West*, which was standing by a party trying to salvage the gunboat *Indianola*. The ram took off down the river to spread the alarm and the salvage party, panicked when it saw her leave, blew up the gunboat and fled.

Porter's fertile mind now adopted some adventurous measures that were heartily endorsed if not originated by him. A few miles below Helena, Arkansas was a bayou that had been an old channel of the Yazoo River, now sealed off by a levee. Given the very high-water stage of the Mississippi, it was believed that by cutting the levee a route through the Yazoo Cut could be found that would allow a force of gunboats to get into the Yazoo well above Yazoo City.

On February 20 a group of two ironclads, including one Eads type, five shallow draft gunboats, and thirteen transports with about 4,500 troops embarked, entered this channel. Progress was very slow, for the overhanging trees along the banks had to be cleared so that the steamers could pass. Further obstacles developed when the Confederates found out what was going on. Large trees were felled across the channel ahead of the gunboats and these had to be cleared as the expedition moved along. By March 11 the group was in the Tallahatchie, one of the streams which form the Yazoo, when it came up against a Confederate fort and a raft obstruction across the stream. The river was only wide enough for two gunboats abreast and the two ironclads engaged the fort for several days. *Chillicothe*, a new shallow draft side-wheel ironclad, was heavily damaged in this exchange. The flooded country and a swamp prevented the troops from taking part in the attack. After a week's effort the attack was abandoned and the expedition returned to Vicksburg on April 12.

Porter himself led a similar expedition about the same time. In March he found a bayou in the Yazoo through which he hoped to find a route to get around Snyder's Bluff. On March 14, accompanied by Sherman with some of his troops, he started with some ironclads and worked his way about sixty miles into the bayou. He was within a few miles of a clear stream when he was stopped by the Confederates. When his presence was discovered they felled trees across the bayou. The gunboats succeeded in cutting these clear and were within about 800 yards of clear water when they were attacked by a large party of sharpshooters in a very narrow channel. Porter was frightened in this predicament, for there was a real danger of the gunboats being captured by boarders. Sherman, with his troops, was moving up by land, and a frantic message from Porter brought him on the double. Sherman dispersed the sharpshooters and the expedition made its way slowly back to Vicksburg without further incident. That adventure ended the effort to get behind Vicksburg by circuitous water routes.

THE LOWER RIVER

THE YEAR 1863 opened on a sour note for Farragut's command in the Gulf of Mexico. At Galveston were five Union gunboats and a garrison of about 250 troops. Shortly after midnight on New Year's Day two or three Confederate steamers approached the gunboats. Although detected in time for *Harriet Lane* to get under way, the steamers got close enough to put troops on board under the cover of heavy sharpshooter fire. *Harriet Lane* was surrendered after her captain was killed. *Westfield* was run aground and burned to avoid capture, and the other gunboats ran out of the harbor. After that, the small Union garrison was easily overrun. Investigation revealed that the affair was an easy Confederate success which should not have occurred if the defenders had been more alert. Farragut was furious when he learned the details and in Washington Gideon Welles was equally so. Welles was very sensitive to Confederate gloating over such events and his anger was greater than usual over this one.

Farragut sent a strong squadron to Galveston to recapture it, but disaster struck again. During the night of January 11 *Hatteras* was sunk while investigating a strange ship which proved to be the Confederate cruiser *Alabama*, under Raphael Semmes. Still another calamity occurred a few days later when the cruiser *Florida* ran through the blockading ships at Mobile and escaped to sea.

While Farragut was having his troubles with the blockade, General Banks was picking away at some operations aimed at cutting off the Red River country in Louisiana. Late in February Halleck, impatient at Banks's inaction, prodded him to push a drive up the Mississippi, aimed at co-operating with Grant before Vicksburg. Farragut also had this in mind and he felt that he should get above the forts at Fort Hudson, about thirteen miles upriver from Baton Rouge, in order to cut off Confederate supplies from the Red River. While he did this he wanted Banks to operate against the land defenses at Port Hudson. Banks demurred, claiming that it would take all of the force under his command to do so. By March 14, however, some of Banks's troops were in position to attack and Farragut decided to run past the batteries that night. In his order for the run was this often-quoted passage: ". . . the best protection against the enemy's fire is a well-directed fire from our own guns."

The batteries at Port Hudson were located on a bluff at the head of a hairpin bend in the river and were almost as formidable as those at Vicksburg. The order of passing was to be *Hartford*, *Richmond*, *Monongahela*, and the side-wheeler *Mississippi*. The first three, being screw steamers, each had a gunboat lashed to the off side. As the ships steamed by they were brought under heavy fire by the shore batteries and only *Hartford*, with the gunboat *Albatross*, succeeded in getting above the forts, losing only two killed and two wounded. *Richmond* almost got past but a shot ruptured her steam line, and being unable to breast the river's current with only the power of her companion gunboat, she had to drop back below the forts. *Monongahela* came under very heavy fire. One shot carried away her bridge and wounded her captain. Her engine was stalled by an overheated bearing. She also had to drop back down the river out of range, with six killed and twenty-one wounded.

Mississippi almost made it. She had passed the last battery and made her final turn in the channel when she ran aground. For thirty-five minutes she tried to back clear but remained hard aground while under the heavy and accurate fire of three batteries. The sick and wounded were brought up and with the rest of the crew were put into the boats. Captain Melancton Smith then had her set on fire in several places and abandoned her. She later came clear of the mud and drifted down the river still on fire. Her losses were severe—

sixty-one killed or missing. In his report Captain Smith felt it his duty to call attention to the coolness in action of his executive officer, Lieutenant George Dewey, who was to display some of Farragut's qualities in Manila Bay thirty-five years later.

After passing the batteries Farragut waited until morning and then moved down near the forts to try to communicate with the ships on the other side of the neck of land, but he was unable to do so. He then headed up the river to confer with Grant and Porter at Vicksburg. He arrived below that city on March 19 after having run a four-gun battery at Grand Gulf with the loss of two men. Porter was away on his expedition into the bayou, but Grant and Farragut agreed that Farragut should try to stop the supplying of Vicksburg via the Red River. Porter and Grant would provide him with coal. He asked for two of the Ellet rams to assist him in the action. One ran the batteries, sustaining some damage, but the second was sunk in the attempt.

After getting coal and provisions from Porter's squadron by the simple expedient of having them floated past the batteries in barges at night, Farragut returned down the river. He spent several days blockading the Red River, then returned to Port Hudson to confer with Banks, who still had troops there. Banks himself was clearing out the Teche country west of New Orleans. Some shallow draft gunboats under Farragut's command were supporting Banks in the Teche. By April 22 they had developed a water route through a series of waterways to the Atchafalaya River, which flows into the Red River a few miles above its mouth, thus opening a circuitous line of communication between New Orleans and the Mississippi above Port Hudson.

Early in May Porter, who had run some of his ironclads below Vicksburg's batteries to assist Grant's operations against that city, arrived at the Red River. He took over the blockade of that river and Farragut returned to New Orleans through the Atchafalaya route. Military events now began to develop rapidly. Banks had driven the Confederates beyond Alexandria, Louisiana, and was in communication with Grant as to how each could best support the other. At one time Banks was inclined to move the bulk of his troops to Vicksburg, but Farragut urged him to press an attack on Port Hudson, which appeared to be ripe for the taking. By May 20 Banks decided to launch an all-out attack on the place and took the field himself. Farragut's ships and mortar schooners were brought up to support the troops. *Hartford,* still above the batteries, would also support from that direction. The troops which had been at Alexandria were withdrawn to Bayou Sara, on the Mississippi above Port Hudson. There they crossed the river and invested the place from above. Thus, with other troops already below the batteries, Port Hudson was surrounded.

After one general attack was repulsed on May 27 Port Hudson was placed under regular siege. A second general attack on June 14 was also repulsed. Farragut's ships, gunboats, and mortars kept up a continuous bombardment of the batteries. On July 7 word was received from Grant that Vicksburg had surrendered and two days later Port Hudson followed suit.

During the siege the Confederates in western Louisiana returned to the river. Raiding parties reached the right bank of the Mississippi about the middle of June and began to attack outposts between Port Hudson and Baton Rouge in an effort to interfere with the supply traffic on the river. Farragut kept several gunboats in that part of the river, and they were near enough at hand to steam toward any threatened post and drive off the raiders. After the fall of Port Hudson this nuisance was quickly disposed of.

VICKSBURG

GRANT APPROVED of Porter's efforts to get into the Yazoo above the defenses of Vicksburg as this would give employment to some of his otherwise idle troops. Before he could conduct active operations against Vicksburg Grant had to wait until the heavy winter rains ceased and flood waters had subsided enough for his troops to move overland. These conditions obtained by the middle of April, by which time Grant had decided to move his army below Vicksburg, cross the river at a suitable point, and attack from below the city. Porter fell in with this plan but warned that once his ironclads were below Vicksburg they could not return until the batteries were taken. During the night of April 16 he ran past the batteries with seven of the ironclads, accompanied by three transports which Grant would need on the river below. The movement was subjected to a heavy shelling in which various minor mishaps occurred, but the run was successful. One of the transports was sunk and one was damaged but was repaired in a few days. There was no loss of life. A week later six more transports ran past the batteries, and one more was lost.

After Farragut had come up the river, General Pemberton in Vicksburg, knowing in general of Grant's plans, had the batteries reinforced at Grand Gulf at the head of a hairpin turn about fifty miles below Vicksburg. On April 29, in preparation for Grant's crossing, Porter attacked these batteries for five and one half hours before he withdrew up the river with his ironclads rather badly battered. His flagship *Benton* received forty-seven hits but her fighting efficiency was not impaired. The Eads ironclad *Pittsburgh* was hit thirty-five times. The ironclad gunboat *Tuscumbia*, a new type with a turret mounted forward, was hit numerous times, had one engine disabled, and had to drop below the batteries to anchor.

After withdrawing, Porter consulted with Grant, who had his troops already embarked in the transports, ready to be landed if Porter's attack was successful. Grant decided to march his troops across the neck of land, out of range of the batteries, and to re-embark them below. Porter would run past the batteries with the empty transports that night, after which a search would be made for a more suitable landing place below Grand Gulf. This was done successfully that evening. The next day Grant landed unopposed at Bruinsburg, nine miles below Grand Gulf.

Grant now made one of the boldest decisions of the Civil War. When he had lost his base and supplies at Holly Springs the preceding December he had found, during his withdrawal, that he could live off the country. Now he proposed to repeat that experience. At Bruinsburg he struck inland with a minimum supply train and only five days' rations, and he established no supply base on the river. His plan was to get between General Pemberton at Vicksburg and General Joseph Johnston at Jackson. With Grant's forces away from the river, Porter was free for a time to act independently. On May 3 he returned to Grand Gulf, intending to attack again, but he found the position abandoned. Grant's movements had threatened it from the rear. Porter then went to the Red River where he remained for some time, relieving Farragut of responsibility for that river.

To cover his movements and intentions Grant had Sherman's corps, with gunboat support, make a feint attack at Snyder's Bluff, up the Yazoo River. This was done on April 29–30 and a very convincing feint it was, for General Pemberton sent reinforcements to the forts there. On learning of Grant's landing at Bruinsburg, he also set out to attack what he presumed to be Grant's supply base there. Both moves played into Grant's hands.

On May 14, after some preliminary fighting, Grant attacked Johnston at Jackson, forcing him to retire from the city after a sharp fight. Grant intercepted an order sent by

Johnston the day before, directing Pemberton to attack Sherman's corps, which by then had joined Grant, as rapidly as possible and with all of the troops he could bring up. Grant ordered McPherson's corps back to Bolton, about twenty miles west of Jackson, to meet this expected attack. But Pemberton meanwhile had decided that Johnston's orders were impracticable and he moved south in order to get between Grant and his base. Leaving Sherman at Jackson to complete the destruction of factories, bridges, and other military facilities, Grant turned his army against Pemberton. On the 16th and 17th, in hard fighting, Pemberton was driven back toward Vicksburg. By the 19th the city was invested, the Confederate positions on the Yazoo were occupied, and Grant had a secure water supply route via the Yazoo River. Appropriately, it was Sherman's corps that occupied Chickasaw Bluffs, where they had been defeated the preceding December.

Porter returned to the Yazoo on May 15 to be ready to cooperate with Grant. When firing was heard on the 18th, Porter knew that Grant was approaching and he deployed his ironclads and gunboats to support him. As one of the ironclads approached Snyder's Bluff, which the Confederates had begun to evacuate the day before, those remaining fled, and the forts with their equipment were taken intact. Porter also ordered the gunboats below Vicksburg to engage the hill batteries below the city. On the 19th he put six mortar boats into position with orders to fire into the city at the maximum rate and around the clock. Porter was optimistic that the city would fall shortly but that was not to be.

The Confederates had a strong line of defenses on a ridge around the city. A general attack on May 22 was repulsed with heavy losses, whereupon Grant decided to make a regular siege. Porter supported this siege with all available gunboats shelling the various batteries within range.

Grant's problem was to make his own position as strong as

the one he was besieging, to bring up and emplace artillery, and to entrench his troops. He also had to be prepared for an attack on his rear by Johnston. He had no heavy siege artillery but Porter lent him a battery of heavy naval guns.

Vicksburg received the heaviest artillery pounding of any place in the entire Civil War, and from all sides. Porter had his mortars shelling regularly and the gunboats joined in whenever a target presented itself. The city itself, as well as its defenses, was under fire, and by June 9 no sign of life could be seen. The troops were in their trenches and the people were hiding out in caves and underground. It was brutal, but Pemberton held out stubbornly, hoping for relief from Johnston. The siege was not without loss to the Union naval squadron. On May 27 the ironclad *Cincinnati* moved down the river to shell some rifle pits that were being troublesome. She was raked by heavy fire from three batteries, whose presence and location were unknown. When they got the range she was hit repeatedly. Finding that she was about to sink, her captain moved up the river close to the shore, and about ten minutes before she sank a gangplank was put over to land the wounded.

Grant called up all of the troops he could muster and Halleck ordered reinforcements sent to him. Grant also put great faith and effort into a huge land mine which was laid in a shaft driven under a strongly held hill. The defenders learned what was going on and tried to countermine the work. Failing in this, they retired from the hill and dug in new defenses. When the mine was exploded on June 25 it blew off the top of the hill but it did not open a breach wide enough for an attack to be made. By that time, however, there were signs of weakening in the Vicksburg defenses. As early as June 21 there were reports that the garrison had a large number of boats and would attempt to escape by water. Porter alerted his squadron to be ready for such an attempt.

Finally, with Vicksburg reduced to rubble suggestive of

German and Japanese cities in World War II, and the food supply nearly exhausted, on July 3 General Pemberton asked Grant for terms. Early the next morning he accepted the terms offered and the surrender was signed at 10:00 a.m. on July 4. There is still some strong feeling in Vicksburg about the selection of that date, but Pemberton himself made it clear that it was deliberately chosen in order to get the best possible terms from Grant. The terms were liberal and there was no "unconditional surrender" here. Grant was later criticized for paroling the Confederate troops, after taking their arms, but his defense was that trying to send 30,000 prisoners north in steamers would have been an almost insuperable task.

An outstanding feature of the Vicksburg campaign was the full and close co-operation that the Navy gave the Army, and Porter deserves the credit for that. He was on especially cordial terms with Grant and Sherman. Grant later commented that:

> The navy, under Porter, was all that it could be, during the entire campaign. Without its assistance the campaign could not have been successfully made with twice the number of men engaged. It could not have been made at all, with any number of men, without such assistance. The most perfect harmony reigned between the two arms of the service. There never was a request made, that I am aware of, either of the flag officer or any of his subordinates, that was not promptly complied with.[1]

In a congratulatory letter on the day of the surrender Sherman wrote to Porter: "In so magnificent a result I stop not to count who did it; it is done, and the day of our nation's birth is consecrated and baptized anew in a victory won by the united Navy and Army of our country." [2]

In his own report of the siege of Vicksburg Porter, rather

---

[1] *Battles and Leaders*, Vol. III, p. 538.
[2] ORN, Vol. 25, p. 106.

modestly for him, said that his squadron had had a less conspicuous part than the Army but he felt that it performed highly creditably. For his part in the campaign Porter was given the thanks of Congress and he was made a permanent rear admiral.

One of the curious phenomena of the month-and-a-half siege of Vicksburg was the fraternization that took place between the opposing sides. The entrenchments were at no place more than 600 yards apart and in most places they were within easy hail of each other. As the long artillery exchange continued, unofficial truces were declared from time to time and men from each side would meet within the lines to swap tobacco and bread. After the Confederate troops marched out and stacked their arms in surrender, there was no cheering, and soon Union soldiers were rushing to share with their emaciated and half-starved countrymen their rations, with which they were amply supplied.

With the fall of Vicksburg it was only a matter of time before Port Hudson would also fall and, as we have seen shortly after the word of Vicksburg's surrender was received, it did so. As a result the entire length of the Mississippi was open to Union forces and the South was split in two. To dramatize this a steamer from St. Louis, with a commercial cargo, arrived at New Orleans on July 16.[3] The Union Navy retained control of the river to the end, although there was much harassment from guerrillas, requiring constant patrolling by gunboats to keep the river open.

Since the start of the war a great change had taken place on the Mississippi. In 1863 it was no longer the main highway from the Middle West to the sea. During the two and one half years that the river had been closed, poor crops in western

---

[3] Lincoln's oft-quoted letter in which he said "The father of waters again goes unvexed to the sea," was dated August 16, 1863, more than a month after the fall of Vicksburg and Port Hudson.

Europe had created a heavy demand for the grain of the Middle West, which enjoyed bumper crops. The pressures to meet this demand stimulated the railroads to expand, improve their facilities, and extend themselves across the Northern states. The water route through the Great Lakes and the Erie Canal was also improved and it carried much of the increased traffic. All of this benefited primarily the port of New York, at the expense of New Orleans, which has regained its position as one of our great ports only gradually and not until well into the twentieth century. To cite but one instance of the change that took place during the Civil War years, Chicago shipped more than twice as much wheat and wheat flour in each of these years than in any year before 1860. For this reason Vicksburg was strategically less important than it otherwise might have been. It did sever the Confederacy, however, and isolate that part of it west of the river.

While events were reaching their climax at Vicksburg, Confederate Brigadier General John H. Morgan began his famous raid into Kentucky, Indiana, and Ohio. On July 4 he attacked a small Union stockade at Green River, Kentucky, during which he demanded its immediate unconditional surrender. The colonel commanding replied that the "Fourth of July was no day for me to entertain such a proposition," and Morgan broke off the attack to continue his raiding.

At this time Porter had a number of shallow draft gunboats on the Cumberland, Tennessee, and Ohio Rivers, with those on the Ohio under the energetic and resourceful Lieutenant Commander Leroy Fitch. When Fitch learned that Morgan had captured two steamers below Louisville, he moved down to that point in an effort to intercept the raider, who had already crossed into Indiana. Then began a game of hide and seek, with Fitch keeping abreast of Morgan in the river while Union troops pursued him on land. By the time Fitch reached Cincinnati he had six gunboats patrolling the river and watching the fords that Morgan might use in trying to cross back into Kentucky. Morgan, pursued by every Union unit that could be mustered plus some hurriedly assembled militia, tried to ford the river at Twelve Mile Island, above Louisville, but two gunboats intercepted him and drove him back. Only a few of his men got across and some others were trapped on the island and later captured. After crossing Ohio, Morgan again tried to ford the river a few miles below Parkersburg, West Virginia, but Fitch was also waiting for him there and again drove him away from the river. Morgan was captured on July 19. Except for the alarm and consternation it caused, his raid was pointless, and the gunboats again showed how important it was to the Union cause to have control of the waterways.

Chapter X

Charleston

THE "CRADLE OF THE REBELLION"

As South Carolina's most important city and the scene of the first shots of the Civil War, Charleston had a very special place in the minds of Northern leaders. From the outset it was known as the "Cradle of the Rebellion." In order to erase the taint which they believed it symbolized, its early capture was a prime desire of Union leaders. This was especially true of Gideon Welles and his Assistant Secretary.

The early operations of Flag Officer Du Pont's expedition to occupy Port Royal, beginning in November 1861, have been covered in an earlier chapter. By the summer of 1862 Du Pont was in control of the coast from the North Carolina border to Cape Canaveral, Florida, and his blockade had sealed off every port of importance within those limits except Charleston. Efforts to block its approach channels with sunken hulks failed, and Charleston was one of two Atlantic ports through which blockade runners were making profitable runs. It was a difficult port to blockade for there were three channels to the entrance, separated by shoals, through which the runners could approach and leave port.

The Army sent no important reinforcements to Port Royal and the troops assigned there could do little more than peck away at the fringes of the Confederate defenses, with only minor success. Somewhat strained relations existed between the Army and Navy commanders, although Du Pont granted every request for gunboat support that was made to him.

Charleston was also a symbol to the Confederates and they were determined to defend it to the limit. Its fortifications were strengthened and by mid-1862 no other city in the Confederacy was as well defended against attack from the sea. Wooden ships could not hope to cope with the network of fortifications centered around Forts Sumter and Moultrie at the entrance. Both sides of the entrance were protected by batteries, and any ships that tried to run the gauntlet had to pass at least six forts before reaching the city. It was no New Orleans, with a single strongpoint defending it, and until some solution to the problem of overcoming the network of forts could be found, there was a military stalemate.

By the end of July 1862 Du Pont's South Atlantic Blockading Squadron numbered forty-eight ships, of which eleven were watching Charleston. The Confederates were known to be building rams and ironclads at Charleston and Savannah, and this was a cause for concern. Because of their potential threat Du Pont asked that an ironclad be assigned to him. In August *New Ironsides*, the third ironclad in the program which produced *Monitor* and *Galena*, was ordered to report to him, but it was to be several months before she joined his squadron. Meanwhile, in the Ogeechee River near Savannah there was a Confederate armed vessel, *Nashville*, which was loaded with cotton and ready to dash through the blockade. She was anchored above Fort McAllister, which held off the Union blockaders, but a constant watch was kept should she try to run out.

THE MONITOR PROGRAM

FOLLOWING the battle between *Monitor* and *Merrimack*, pressure was put on Ericsson and other shipbuilders to produce new monitors as rapidly as possible. Assistant Secretary Fox, who had watched the battle in Hampton Roads, was their most enthusiastic advocate. In testifying before a Congressional committee on the new monitor program Fox rashly boasted that the Navy could take *Monitor* herself right into Charleston.

That triggered a wave of newspaper clamor and "On to Charleston" slogans, fatefully to have a result not unlike the "On to Richmond" cry of a year earlier. To Welles and Fox the coming attack on Charleston must not fail. Welles ordered Du Pont to Washington in October 1862 to make sure that he understood what was expected and that he was willing to undertake the attack. At this meeting, after Du Pont had made some pessimistic reports about the Army's activities around Port Royal, Welles insisted that the capture of Charleston was to be a Navy-only affair and that the Army was not to be brought into it. What he had in mind was that the ironclads, when Du Pont got them, would run past the forts to the city and demand its surrender on pain of bombardment. He wanted to repeat, in effect, Farragut's capture of New Orleans.

It was January 1863 before the first ironclad reached Du Pont's squadron. The first of the new monitors to be completed, *Passaic*, broke down en route and had to be towed to Washington for boiler repair. In December 1862 she left Hampton Roads together with *Monitor* herself, in tow of two steamers. The craft ran into a severe storm off Cape Hatteras and *Monitor* foundered, with the loss of sixteen of her crew. *Passaic* weathered the storm but had to be towed to Beaufort, North Carolina, to repair storm damage. *New*

Ironsides arrived at Port Royal on January 17, the monitor *Montauk* on the 18th, and *Passaic* on the 21st.

Before taking on the formidable fortifications of Charleston, Du Pont decided to test the performance of the new monitors. Soon after her arrival he sent *Montauk*, under Commander John L. Worden of *Monitor* fame, to Ossabaw Sound to capture Fort McAllister and to destroy *Nashville*. On January 27, with four gunboats, Worden engaged the fort for nearly four hours. *Montauk* had one fifteen-inch and one eleven-inch gun but her fire appeared to have little effect on the sand works of the fort and Worden broke off the action. The monitor was hit thirteen times by return fire from the fort but suffered no casualties or damage. She engaged the fort again on February 1 for four hours and this time she was hit forty-eight times with only minor damage. She had one dangerous weakness, however, which was that when the turret was struck, bolt heads and nuts sheared off and flew around inside the turret. To stop the flying missiles and protect the gun crews Worden installed a metal shield inside the turret.

During this preparatory period the Confederates threw a scare into the blockading squadron off Charleston. Early in the hazy morning of January 31 two of their ironclad rams, *Palmetto State* and *Chicora*, made their appearance among the blockading ships. *Palmetto State* closed in on *Mercedita*, which had just returned to her anchorage after investigating a suspicious ship. Before *Mercedita* could fully man her guns, *Palmetto State* was under her quarter and rammed her, at the same time firing a seven-inch shell into her which crippled her boilers. When called upon to surrender, Captain Stellwagen had no choice as his ship was completely disabled. He sent his executive officer to the ironclad, which gave a parole to the officers and men. *Palmetto State* then left to join *Chicora*, which was engaged with other blockaders.

Palmetto State made no effort to take possession of *Mercedita* after her captain surrendered, leaving her adrift instead.

This led to a development that lends a comic-opera atmosphere to the affair. The Confederates later expressed extreme indignation that *Mercedita* had left the scene, claiming that she had surrendered. But Du Pont convened a court of inquiry to study the matter and the conclusion was reached that while the captain and crew were surrendered, the ship itself was not. Therefore *Mercedita's* crew took her north for repair, bound by parole not to engage in hostile action until the crew members were officially exchanged.

Chicora was engaged by *Keystone State*, which, after a spirited exchange, had her steam lines cut. She was being hit repeatedly and her captain ordered her colors hauled down in token of surrender. But when *Chicora* continued firing at her, she hoisted her colors again and resumed the battle. As other ships of the blockading group closed in and joined the action, the ironclads retired toward the harbor. Why they broke off the action and retired so early, with little or no damage to themselves, is a mystery for which the action reports give no clue. Both *Mercedita* and *Keystone State* later made their way to Port Royal.

There was an unusual aftermath to this brief action that reveals how much the blockade was hurting and how anxious the South was to get from under its yoke. Later that same day General Beauregard issued a proclamation declaring that the blockading ships had been driven off and the blockade of Charleston was lifted. If true, this meant that under international law the Union would have to go through the formality of issuing new notices of blockade before it could be re-established. Beauregard also claimed that two vessels had been sunk and five others damaged. This proclamation was followed the next day by a statement of the British consul and others that they had gone five miles beyond the usual anchorage of the blockaders and had seen no blockading ships.

It is clear from the reports and logbooks of the blockading

ships that this was not correct. *Housatonic* fired at *Chicora* as she retired toward Fort Moultrie and her log noted the departure of the two ironclads from that fort for Charleston shortly after 4:00 p.m. Only two Union ships received serious damage and they, with the one ship that towed *Keystone State* to Port Royal, were the only ones to leave their blockading stations. Rather than being driven off, it is more accurate to state that the blockaders drove the ironclads back into the harbor. As soon as he received reports of the ironclad attack, Admiral Du Pont ordered *New Ironsides* to Charleston and she arrived the next day.

Lieutenant W. H. Parker, executive officer of *Palmetto State*, was not impressed with the propaganda. "I thought the proclamation ill-advised," he recorded, and "I am constrained to say that this was a badly managed affair on our part, and we did not make the best use of our opportunity." [1] A member of *Chicora*'s crew, in a private letter, noted that no ship was destroyed and expressed disappointment at the result of the sortie, concluding that: "They say we raised the blockade but we all felt we would have rather raised hell and sunk the ships." [2]

On February 28 Commander Worden seized a chance to destroy *Nashville* in the Ogeechee River. The evening before he had seen her run aground while under way above Fort McAllister. At daylight he took *Montauk* close to the fort and had three gunboats enfilade the fort while he ignored its fire to get within 1,200 yards of the grounded blockade runner. After delivering a few ranging shots *Montauk*'s guns set *Nashville* on fire from stem to stern and she disintegrated when her magazine exploded. The fort's batteries hit the monitor a few times but did no damage. In retiring down the river *Montauk* exploded a mine under her hull. At first it was

---

[1] *Recollections of a Naval Officer* (New York; 1885), pp. 300 and 304.
[2] ORN, Vol. 13, p. 623.

thought that no damage was done, but when she began to take in water she was grounded to investigate. The mud sealed her leak and enabled a patch to be put over a rupture in her bottom.

By this time two more monitors had arrived. Not yet satisfied with their offensive power, Du Pont again sent them against Fort McAllister. On March 3 *Passaic*, *Patapsco*, and *Nahant* bombarded the fort. *Passaic* drew most of the fort's fire, being hit thirty-four times, but the damage was confined to some heavy denting in her deck and some sheared nuts and bolt heads flying around inside her turret. *Patapsco* was hit only once and *Nahant* not at all. The significant result of this bombardment, as with the earlier ones by *Montauk*, was how little damage was inflicted on the fort. Only a direct hit could disable one of the fort's guns; generally all that the bombardment did was to plow up sand and dust.

This, as well as other deficiencies that active service was revealing in the ironclads, was reported to Secretary Welles by Du Pont. *New Ironsides*, in particular, was very sluggish in shallow water. The monitors were suffering frequent machinery breakdowns and their rate of gunfire was very slow.

But to Gideon Welles and Fox this stream of complaints seemed to them to be only alibis for inaction in moving against Charleston. They assumed that Du Pont was losing enthusiasm and they became more and more impatient as time went on. Welles and the President were also concerned, needlessly as we have seen, about the precarious position of Farragut above Port Hudson, where he was believed to be at the mercy of a Confederate ironclad. Early in March Welles increased the number of ironclads assigned to Du Pont to nine but ordered him to send three of them to the Gulf as soon as the attack upon Charleston and Savannah was completed. Late in the same month he sent a letter to Du Pont which expressed his confidence but also revealed his concern at the delay in making the attack.

DU PONT'S ATTACK ON FORT SUMTER

BY EARLY APRIL Admiral Du Pont had *New Ironsides*, seven monitors, and *Keokuk*, an experimental craft which was only partially armored. On April 6 he crossed the bar with all of the ironclads, his flag in *New Ironsides*. Thick weather postponed an attack on Fort Sumter that day, and on the next tidal conditions held him up until noon. On getting under way, *Weehawken*, which was to lead the column, fouled her anchor chain on a special raft attached to her bow. This was an invention of John Ericsson's, intended to destroy obstructions. It was designed to carry an explosive charge under its leading edge to blow up the obstructions. It was as yet untested, and as it was believed that an explosion might damage the monitor, the charge was removed from the raft for this attack.[3]

Du Pont's plan was to steam the ironclads in a column past Fort Sumter and attack its northwest face. Guarding the eastern entrance to the channel was a network of forts and batteries centered on the permanent Fort Moultrie. Fort Sumter was an islet near the center of the entrance and there were two batteries on Morris Island, guarding the western side of the entrance. Inshore of Fort Sumter both sides of the channel were lined with batteries up to the city itself.

The squadron was under way by 1:15 p.m. and headed up the channel in the following order: *Weehawken, Passaic, Montauk, Patapsco, New Ironsides, Catskill, Nantucket, Nahant,* and *Keokuk*. There was a line of obstructions running between Forts Sumter and Moultrie. These caused the leading

---

[3] The weathered but intact remains of one of these rafts, which was lost in a storm off Cape Hatteras while being towed to Charleston, may still be seen in Dolly's Bay, Bermuda. Its existence attests to the thoroughness of Ericsson's work.

ships to veer off as they approached it and forced *New Iron-sides*, which became unmanageable in the shallow water, to anchor to avoid fouling up the column. She anchored over a mine with a 2,000-pound charge, which the eager defenders at Fort Moultrie were unable to explode. At about 3:00 p.m. Moultrie opened fire, followed shortly by the other forts and batteries within range. The fire of the forts was heavy and accurate and every ironclad was hit repeatedly. The reports on each side conflict on the ranges, but the nearest monitor got within 1,000 yards of Fort Sumter. At 5:00 Du Pont recalled the ships with the intention of renewing the action the next day.

That evening the captains reported to Du Pont, and when he learned the extent of damage the ships had suffered, he canceled any further attack. Worst battered was *Keokuk*. She was under the fire of Fort Sumter for only about thirty minutes when she had to retire in danger of sinking. She was riddled with ninety hits, nineteen of which were near the water line. Amazingly, her captain, Commander A. C. Rhind, reported that she had only nine killed and sixteen wounded, including himself. The ship sank off Morris Island the next morning.

Nahant was the most seriously damaged of the monitors. She was hit thirty-six times but had only seven casualties. Her turret was jammed, the steering gear deranged, and she had numerous bolts sheared off in the turret and pilothouse. *Nantucket*, hit fifty-one times, had her fifteen-inch gun jammed and the turret could be turned only with difficulty. *Weehawken*, hit fifty-three times, had her armored deck pierced to bare wood and the turret weakened by snapped bolts. *Passaic*, with thirty-five hits, had her eleven-inch gun disabled and the turret also weakened by snapped bolts. *Pa-tapsco*, hit forty-seven times, had her rifled gun disabled, her armor weakened, and her turret was jammed for some time. *Montauk* and *Catskill* were hit numerous times but suffered no serious damage. *New Ironsides* was hit fifty-five times but no shots penetrated her armor and the damage was minor.

In contrast to the terrific punishment which the ironclads —except for *Keokuk*—withstood, was the slow rate of fire which they delivered. A total of 139 rounds were fired by them, of which about fifty-five struck Fort Sumter. Only fifty-five rounds were fired by the fifteen-inchers, indicating that these guns required about ten minutes on the average to load. The damage to the fort was extensive but its fighting efficiency was not seriously affected and it had only five wounded. Its troops took to the bombproof shelters for protection. A few rounds were fired at Fort Moultrie and the batteries on Sullivan's Island, and Moultrie had one man killed when a flagstaff that had been shot away fell on him.

The most serious result of the pounding that the monitors received was the general weakening of the armor by the shearing of bolts that held it together. Should they return to fight in their weakened condition there was a real danger of the turrets collapsing under further punishment. Du Pont was convinced by this action that ships alone could not reduce the forts and that Charleston could only be taken by troops supported by the ships. He informed General Hunter, commanding the local Union troops, of this belief and also stated that, due to the condition of his vessels, he was withdrawing them. At the same time he received a glowing letter of praise from the general for his effort. In care of Commander Rhind, who could give a personal account of the action, he also sent off a short report to Welles.

In Washington news of the battle was anxiously awaited. As usual, the first reports were gleaned from Richmond newspapers. These were brief but they indicated that the attack had failed. Gideon Welles was annoyed by the first brief report received, via Commander Rhind, which was lacking in detail but indicated Du Pont's intention of withdrawing the ironclads from Charleston. On April 13 Lincoln sent a telegram to Admiral Du Pont, directing him to hold his position inside the bar and to prevent the erection of new batteries on Morris Island.

The outcome of this action resulted in some acrimonious correspondence between Du Pont and Welles. A Baltimore paper published an account in which Du Pont was personally criticized and which implied that the action could have been renewed on April 8 but for his reluctance to do so. Chief Engineer A. C. Stimers, who superintended the construction of the monitors and had gone south with them, submitted a critical report in which he claimed that the monitors could have resumed the action on the 8th. Admiral Du Pont complained of these criticisms, but when Welles received Du Pont's detailed report, as well as those of the monitor captains, he was inclined to agree with the critics. That the captains backed up their admiral did not impress him. He dismissed their reports as coming from the Du Pont "clique."

The feeling in Washington was not tempered by a signal victory that occurred during this period. It was known that the Confederates were converting a modern iron screw steamer to an ironclad in Savannah, and a deserter informed the Union Army that the ship was about to sortie. The Army then tipped off Du Pont, who sent *Weehawken* and *Nahant* to Wassaw Sound to intercept the ship, now named *Atlanta*. At 4:10 a.m., June 17, she was seen coming down the Wilmington River. *Weehawken* got under way at once, followed by *Nahant*. Captain John Rodgers, of *Weehawken*, reported that after *Atlanta* fired the first shot at about 4:55:

> At 5:15, being distant from him about 300 yards, we commenced firing. At 5:30 the enemy hauled down his colors and hoisted the white flag, we having fired five shots; steamed near the ironclad and ordered a boat to be sent alongside.[4]

---

[4] ORN, Vol. 14, p. 265.

Atlanta was aground and fired only four times in this brief action. Four of *Weehawken*'s shots hit, with two of them fracturing the armor and one sheared off the top of the pilot-house. The action was over so quickly that *Nahant* was unable to get into it. It suddenly became a grim instead of a gala occasion for spectators on two steamers that had followed *Atlanta* to see the show. She later became U.S.S. *Atlanta* and gave service on the Union side in the James River.

Welles and Fox either did not or would not understand the limitations of the monitors, nor would they accept reports of the extent of damage done them at Fort Sumter. Keenly disappointed that the monitors had failed to take Charleston, they blamed the commander and determined to relieve him. Du Pont believed that Fox was his real critic in this affair, rather than Welles. By early June Welles informed Du Pont that the government was unwilling to relinquish further efforts to take Charleston and that he was being relieved by Admiral Foote. Having lost confidence in him, Welles was justified in relieving him, although he was blind to the true situation and Du Pont was not at fault. Later events showed that he was shelved for being too realistic in reporting the limitations of the monitors.

Foote, who had distinguished himself on the western rivers, was then in New York. He never fully recovered from the wound he had received at Fort Donelson and he died within a month of his new assignment. The next choice was Rear Admiral John A. Dahlgren, the ordnance expert, who was to have been second in command under Foote. In the fall of 1862 he had asked for command of the attack on Charleston, but Welles then would offer him only the command of an ironclad. Dahlgren was a victim of a requirement that no one could be promoted to rear admiral unless and until he had been voted the thanks of Congress. Normally this could only be obtained by distinguished action in battle, and so it is understandable that Dahlgren was anxious to be freed of his desk job and get a sea command. In February 1863 Dahlgren was given the thanks of Congress for his ordnance work and Lincoln appointed him an acting rear admiral. In that rank he relieved Du Pont on July 4.

DEFIANT CHARLESTON

ON HIS ARRIVAL Dahlgren found that Major General Q. A. Gillmore, then commanding the troops in the vicinity, was planning to move against Morris Island on the southern side of the entrance to the harbor and had asked for naval co-operation. Du Pont declined to commit the ships, pending Dahlgren's arrival, and the latter's first step was to order the ironclads back to Charleston from Port Royal. The attack was launched on July 10 with *Catskill*, *Montauk*, *Nahant*, and *Weehawken* abreast of Battery Wagner, near the center of the island. They engaged that battery throughout the day, with only a short break for the noon meal. Battery Wagner replied with accurate fire and *Catskill*, in the van with Dahlgren embarked, was hit sixty times but without serious damage. Under cover of his own artillery General Gillmore's troops crossed from Folly Island to Morris Island, but at daybreak the next day an effort to storm Battery Wagner was repulsed. The monitors resumed their bombardment but broke it off when no enemy activity was observed.

The attack was renewed on the 18th by *New Ironsides*, five monitors, and four wooden gunboats. Union troops attacked just before sunset and the ships kept up a heavy bombardment until it was too dark to distinguish targets. The troop assault was again repulsed, with heavy losses. Meanwhile a diversionary attack on James Island, up the Stono River, was also repulsed and *Pawnee* was hit numerous times and barely managed to get down the river out of danger. It was obvious that Charleston was being defended with vigor in every direction.

For nearly a month after that second attack the principal activity was an almost daily bombardment of Battery Wagner by the ironclads, with occasional shots at Fort Sumter and Battery Gregg, on Cummings Point at the northern end of Morris Island. General Gillmore moved up and emplaced heavy artillery. On August 17 he opened a heavy fire on Fort Sumter while the ironclads kept Wagner quiet. This bombardment of Fort Sumter, lasting for seven days, knocked out that fort and left it little more than a heap of rubble, with only one serviceable gun left.[5]

Meanwhile, early on August 23 Dahlgren took five monitors to within about 800 yards of Fort Sumter and bombarded it. Sumter fired only six rounds in return but Fort Moultrie's network opened with a heavy fire, forcing them to withdraw shortly after daylight. Two attempts to run past Sumter at night were frustrated by tides and obstructions. During the night of September 5 an attempt by Union troops to land near Battery Gregg was repulsed by an alert defense. By that time the troops had inched their entrenchments to the outer works of Battery Wagner. That battery had been under almost daily bombardment for nearly two months by artillery and the ironclads, principally *New Ironsides*. The pressure on the battery was then so great that both it and Battery Gregg were evacuated the very next night. Admiral Dahlgren then sent a flag of truce demanding the surrender of Fort Sumter, but Beauregard refused, saying that Dahlgren "must take it and hold it if he can." While the monitors were proceeding to attack the fort on September 7, *Weehawken* ran aground near Cummings Point. She was under heavy fire from Moultrie and the other batteries on Sullivan's Island,

---

[5] The partially restored fort is now a national monument.

and the attention of all of the ironclads was directed at covering her until she got clear the next day.

In the two months required to take Morris Island the nine ironclads, including the monitor *Lehigh* which joined on August 30, expended 8,000 rounds of fifteen- and eleven-inch ammunition and received 882 hits, mostly of ten-inch shot. Battered though they were, they proved to be very sturdy and rugged fighting ships, as long as they did not close to point-blank range. *Montauk* was hit 214 times during that period and *Weehawken* received 187 hits. *New Ironsides* was also struck by 214 hits, but the damage received was relatively minor and never put her out of action.

Next occurred an incident that is difficult to understand in view of the good co-operation that existed between Admiral Dahlgren and General Gillmore during the reduction of Morris Island. On September 8 Dahlgren organized a landing party of 500 officers and men to land on and capture Fort Sumter that night. He informed Gillmore of this early in the afternoon, at which time he learned that the latter was planning a similar attack. General Gillmore felt that the operation should be under one commander and suggested that the naval landing party join his troops or at least that the attacks should be co-ordinated. Dahlgren insisted that his attack must be under a naval officer although he did direct his landing force commander to assist in the assault of the troops. When the first wave of sailors and marines landed on the rubble of Fort Sumter that night, they were met with a withering fire from the fort, and the boats that had not yet landed withdrew. The men ashore huddled under the debris and were captured the next morning with four killed, nineteen wounded, and 102 prisoners. General Gillmore's force was held up by low tide in a creek near Morris Island and its attack was canceled after the repulse of the naval party.

What neither commander knew or suspected was that the Confederates were fully aware that the attacks were to be made and were ready for them. They had recovered a signal book from the wreck of *Keokuk* and could read the intercepted messages between the admiral and the general.

Following this setback there was a virtual stalemate that was to last for more than a year. In December 1863 the monitor *Weehawken* sank suddenly at her anchorage inside the bar, from flooding through the hawsepipe due to excessive ammunition forward. The monitors were then being used near the harbor entrance to cover picket boats which were out nightly on the lookout for blockade runners. While that traffic was reduced to a trickle, an occasional runner did get in or out of the harbor. There were raids to destroy salt works or some Confederate outpost, but Charleston itself remained as remote as ever. The Army's "Swamp Angel" battery, set up during the siege of Morris Island, bombarded the lower part of the city, but no serious effort was made to take it by land. The chief events of interest during this period were the ingenious and persistent efforts of the Confederates to sink the blockading ships.

One of the first instances of this was during the night of August 21 when *New Ironsides*, anchored off Battery Wagner, sighted a small steamboat close aboard. It was hailed and the anchor slipped. The craft, called a "torpedo ram," moved along the side of the ship and was taken under fire as soon as the ironclad's guns could bear. The craft slipped away and returned to Charleston. Its skipper reported that he was unsuccessful in exploding his spar torpedo and expressed the opinion that the craft was unsuited for the task.

The Confederates next constructed some small craft for exploding spar torpedoes on the ship's sides underwater. These were cigar-shaped vessels fifty-four feet long and five and one half feet in diameter, powered by a steam engine. They were heavily ballasted to ride low in the water and had an open cockpit about twelve feet long in the center, in which rode the eight-man crew. At the end of a ten-foot rod attached to the bow was a spar torpedo with a seventy-pound charge of powder and an ingenious exploder. The first one was named "David" and that name was retained for others that were built.

Soon after 9:00 p.m., October 5, a small object was sighted near *New Ironsides*. When it failed to answer a hail, orders were given to sentries to fire into it. Soon after there was a heavy explosion which crushed in the ship's side and inflicted other damage. This caused some leaking, but she was a rugged ship and was soon back in service. The explosion threw up a column of water which put out the fire in the David's boiler. Its crew went overboard and its commander and one crew member were captured. The others returned to the David and succeeded in returning it to Charleston. Several more Davids were built, but this was their only success. Ships in the squadron were protected at night by log booms and ropes to keep the craft away from their sides. One David claimed to have hit *Memphis* in the North Edisto River in the night of March 6, 1864, but its spar torpedo failed to explode. It was thought that *Housatonic*, which was sunk during the night of February 17, 1864, was hit by a David, but it was a different kind of craft that sank her.

At Mobile the Confederates built a small true submarine, powered by eight men turning a crank attached to the propeller. It was a crude craft and it lost one entire crew trying to submerge at Mobile. It was moved to Charleston where two more crews were lost before it was successfully submerged and surfaced. Named *R. L. Huntley*, for its builder, it was about thirty-five feet long and five and one half feet in diameter. It carried a spar torpedo, with a ninety-five-pound powder charge, on a rod attached to its bow. It was towed to the mouth of the harbor by a David and it struck *Housatonic* at about 8:45 p.m., sinking the ship almost at once. *Huntley* did not return from this attack and no trace of her was found.

Besides the two ironclads that made the halfhearted attack on the blockaders in January 1863, the Confederates built two other ironclads at Charleston, but neither of them made a further appearance. Their existence, however, forced the retention of a large force of Union ironclads there to protect the blockade. Meanwhile, there was criticism of Dahlgren for his failure to gain any success at Charleston, but he had a powerful champion. Although Lincoln was not given to profanity, when he was approached to approve the relief of Dahlgren of his command he refused with heat and said that ". . . he would be damned if he would do anything to discredit or disgrace John A. Dahlgren." [6]

The first break in the stalemate off Charleston came in December 1864 with the approach of General William T. Sherman to Savannah in his famous march to the sea. As a preliminary to this Major General J. G. Foster, then commanding the troops around Port Royal and Charleston, moved up the Broad River, extending inland from Port Royal, to create a diversion. Dahlgren organized a naval landing force to assist in this, and by early December Foster's troops were in position to dominate the Charleston-Savannah Railroad with artillery. On December 12 a courier from Sherman reached Dahlgren to report that he was approaching Savannah. Two days later Sherman himself was on board Dahlgren's flagship, his troops having taken Fort McAllister from the rear the day before. On December 21, as Sherman was surrounding the city for a siege, Savannah was evacuated by the Confederates.

With Savannah as his base Sherman next planned to move his army across South Carolina and into North Carolina in support of Grant's operations in Virginia. He would bypass Charleston but move in a way to threaten that city and the state capital Columbia. He wanted Dahlgren and Foster to maintain pressure on Charleston and, at the right time, to

---

[6] *Papers of the Military Historical Society of Massachusetts*, Vol. XII, p. 205.

make a landing in Bull's Bay, northeast of Charleston. He did not consent to an attack on Fort Moultrie by Dahlgren, for he was convinced that once he was in its rear Charleston would fall without a fight.

Sherman was ready to move by the middle of January 1865, after Dahlgren had helped him transport his right flank to Port Royal Ferry, near Beaufort. Sherman also wanted a gunboat to ascend the Savannah River to cover the crossing of his left flank, about twenty miles above the city. Assigned to this task was the shallow draft double-ender gunboat *Pontiac*, commanded by Lieutenant Commander Stephen B. Luce. That was a fortunate choice, for Luce was one of the most progressive officers in the Navy. From his experience on this occasion Luce developed the idea that naval warfare could be governed by principles of strategy similar to those of land warfare. He was instrumental in founding the U.S. Naval War College at Newport, Rhode Island, in 1884, the first of its kind. The strong impression that Sherman made on him is well expressed by some remarks Rear Admiral Luce made during a conference in 1899.

In the course of the discussion Luce described his meeting with Sherman at Savannah. When he reported to the general, he was shown an outline of Sherman's proposed operations on a map. These would bypass Charleston, which he predicted would fall like a ripe plum as its communications with the inland were threatened. Luce noted: "I said to myself, 'here is a soldier who understands his profession and we have been fooling around with a problem that we didn't know what to do with.' " [7] The solution to the problem thus became obvious and Luce reported that everyone's reaction to it was "why, of course." He cautioned that his experience "shows you the necessity of a man knowing his business."

While supporting Sherman, Dahlgren suffered his final se-

---

[7] Report of the conference, Luce Papers, Naval War College Library.

rious loss off Charleston. In the evening of January 15, 1865, while covering the picket boats in Charleston harbor entrance, the monitor *Patapsco* struck a mine and sank in less than a minute. She went down so fast that two thirds of her crew of 105 were lost.

Sherman's progress was slowed by rains and mud, but on February 12 General Gillmore, who had returned to relieve the ailing General Foster, and Dahlgren made their diversionary move against Bull's Bay. Dahlgren himself had to return to Charleston before the diversion was completed in order to decipher a message from Sherman for which only he had the key. On February 18 the Confederates evacuated Charleston, and gunboats and monitors entered the harbor. Dahlgren occupied the city with marines and held it until troops arrived. Sherman's prediction proved right—he had "conquered Charleston by turning his back upon it." Believing that it might be better suited for the supply of Sherman's troops, Dahlgren occupied Georgetown, South Carolina, with his marines on February 26.

With the occupation of Charleston the job of the South Atlantic Blockading Squadron was completed, although the long and dangerous task of clearing obstructions and mines from the harbor remained. On March 1, while Dahlgren was returning to Charleston from Georgetown, his flagship *Harvest Moon* struck a mine and sank rapidly. On April 14, by order of President Lincoln, at a special ceremony in Fort Sumter the flag which Major Anderson hauled down in 1861 was raised over the fort by the same then brevet Major General Anderson.

The siege of Charleston, in which the city was vigorously and resolutely defended, in the end proved to be a great waste of Union resources. When the Army failed to exploit Du Pont's success at Port Royal promptly, the strategic importance of Charleston to the Union cause declined materially. Although McClellan listed it for seizure in his first plan of operations, General Halleck later stated that the seizure of Charleston and its defenses was never contemplated. As a result, up to a dozen ironclads were tied down there for most of the war in the futile hope that they alone could take the city. The Confederates did have three ironclads there that had to be covered, and a fourth, which was captured with the occupation of the city, was completed just before the evacuation. But following the capture of Morris Island in 1863, there was no further significant military activity. Forays were made from time to time up the nearby rivers and on one of these the gunboat *Dai Ching,* so named because it was built originally for the Chinese, ran aground and had to be abandoned after a seven-hour fight with Confederate batteries.

During this period a large amount of ammunition was expended in bombarding Fort Sumter and the network of forts and batteries on Sullivan's Island, centered at Fort Moultrie. Dahlgren's ships took part in these bombardments regularly. After it had been battered in the bombardment of August 1863, Fort Sumter received two more major and eight minor bombardments with desultory fire at other times. It was under fire on 280 days and the quasi-official historian of the defense of Charleston claimed that 46,000 projectiles were fired at it. Yet from this tremendous volume of fire the total casualties were only fifty-six killed and 267 wounded, although the fort itself was reduced to rubble. The city itself was subjected to a prolonged bombardment to no useful purpose.

The only plausible explanation for this tenacious and needless destruction was the strong Union sentiment that, as the cradle of the rebellion, Charleston must pay. Gideon Welles and his Assistant Secretary were unyielding in that belief. In December 1864, in a letter to General Sherman, Halleck expressed the hope that by "some accident" the place might be destroyed and some salt sown upon its site which ". . . may prevent the growth of future crops of nullification and secession." [8] Sherman replied that he intended to bypass Charleston, but that if he did go for it, he would take the hint, although he did not think the salt would be necessary.

This is the one instance in the Civil War in which Union naval forces were squandered for no real gain. Du Pont became convinced that the city could not be taken by naval forces alone and Dahlgren soon came to the same conclusion. This view was supported by every senior officer who knew the place, but Welles and Fox would not accept it.

---

[8] Sherman, *Memoirs* (London; 1875), Vol. II, p. 22.

Chapter XI

Foreign Affairs

ANGLO-AMERICAN RELATIONS

MANY DELICATE PROBLEMS of international law and neutrality developed during the Civil War. The conduct of naval operations on both sides was influenced by their respective relations with the neutral European powers. The other nations followed the example of England, and the key to foreign relations during the war is found in Anglo-American relations. It has been noted in an earlier chapter that the policy of Lord Palmerston, the Prime Minister, and Earl Russell, the Foreign Minister, was to avoid becoming involved in the American war and to maintain a strict neutrality. The British minister in Washington, Lord Lyons, was a very able diplomat who did much to maintain relations on a relatively even keel.

William H. Seward, the Secretary of State, was a political Anglophobe and his instructions to his minister in London were sometimes bellicose in tone. Fortunately for the United States its minister to England, Charles F. Adams, was a very able diplomat and he frequently toned down Seward's language in relaying Seward's messages to Earl Russell. The English leaders understood Seward and seemed to have an uncanny knack of knowing when he was bluffing and when he was not.

Shortly after he became President of the Confederacy, Jefferson Davis sent three commissioners to Europe to seek formal recognition of the Confederacy as a sovereign state. William L. Yancy, Pierre A. Rost, and A. Dudley Mann arrived in London about the same time as the news of the attack on Fort Sumter. They had only one private interview with Earl Russell and were completely unsuccessful in their mission.

Anyone reviewing the large volume of correspondence that was exchanged between the United States and England during the Civil War can hardly fail to realize that much of it was written as a matter of form to support a policy. Very thin arguments were often presented with great seriousness and many of the documents offered as "evidence" to support a point are questionable at best. It is possible that, in taking these documents at face value, some historians have found that Anglo-American relations were generally strained, with a number of war scares. In the North, particularly, there was an element that talked openly of war with England and a section of the Northern press followed the same line. Much of the English press was friendly to the South and it too could speak freely and belligerently of avenging some "insult" to the English flag. But there is little solid evidence that the responsible leaders were influenced by this clamor.

Much has been made of the idea, expressed in Seward's often-cited memorandum to Lincoln of April 1, 1861, that the United States should become involved in a war with European countries in order to draw the seceded states back into the Union. That was not nearly so farfetched an idea at the time as it seems today. Wars then were not considered as very serious affairs and they sometimes broke out over what now seem trivial causes. No one could foresee that the Civil War would develop into the first total war in modern times. Seward probably misjudged the strength of Union sentiment in the South, but as his suggestion was vetoed by Lincoln, this can never be proved. Lincoln frequently softened Seward's more warlike papers, and some of his colleagues, including Gideon Welles, were apprehensive that Seward might indeed get the Union involved in a European war. That much of his language was political bluster is suggested by the fact that whenever he was faced with a real crisis he became quite pacific and cautious.

The consistent policy followed by Seward was to insist on nonrecognition of the Confederacy as a sovereign state. In his instructions to Adams, who arrived in England in May, the minister was to make it clear that to treat with the Confederate commissioners or to recognize the Confederacy would be considered a hostile act by the United States. Adams was the sole representative of the United States—all of them, it was to be emphasized. Whenever it was thought that the British might be wavering on this, the warning was renewed. The only time the British leaders seriously considered formal recognition was in late summer of 1862, but news of Lee's setback at Antietam squelched that, and recognition was a dead issue after Gettysburg and Vicksburg.

One of the first and major problems faced by Adams was to frustrate the activities of Commander James D. Bulloch, the able and resourceful Confederate naval agent in England. There were other naval agents, some working with him and some independently, but Bulloch was the key one. He reached England early in June 1861, and by the end of the month he had contracted with a Liverpool shipbuilder to build a ship based on a design for a Royal Navy gunboat. It was given the builder's name of *Oreto*. Bulloch was careful enough to consult legal counsel and to find a way in which the English Foreign Enlistment Act, the basic law for British neutrality, could be evaded. The loophole found was that if a ship was built for the Confederacy, it could not be equipped as a warship within English jurisdiction. Her armament and military equipment had to be obtained separately and sent out of the country in another ship. As eagle-eyed and sharp-eared Union consuls were alert for evidence of Southern procurement of military equipment in England, Bulloch had to be extremely careful and carried on his activity *sub rosa*. While negotiating for the first vessel, he visited the Laird Ironworks at Birkenhead, near Liverpool, and soon had a contract for a second "despatch vessel." This was known simply by her Laird hull number as 290; the Northern press speculated wildly about the number's significance—one suggestion was that 290 Englishmen had contributed to her construction. The two ships became the best-known Confederate cruisers, *Florida* and *Alabama*.

The alert Union consul in Liverpool, Thomas H. Dudley, soon discovered that these vessels had all the earmarks of being intended for conversion to warships. He kept Mr. Adams, in London, fully informed of their progress. Bulloch, having obligated his initial funds, decided that he could then accomplish little more in England. He bought an iron steamer in Scotland, loaded her with munitions for the Confederate Army and Navy, and took her through the blockade to Savannah in November. This was the largest single shipment of munitions that got through the blockade. Bulloch returned to Liverpool in March 1862.

THE *TRENT* AFFAIR

THE MOST SERIOUS strains in Anglo-American relations resulted from naval activites on both sides. In the first of these *San Jacinto*, commanded by Captain Charles Wilkes, was en route home from the African Squadron and stopped at St. Thomas, Virgin Islands, for coal in October 1861. Learning that *Sumter* was recently reported in the Caribbean, Wilkes decided to search for her before proceeding north. At Cienfuegos, Cuba, he learned that James M. Mason, the new Confederate commissioner to England, and John Slidell, commissioner to France, were in Havana en route to England. Both were former United States Senators and were well known in the North before the war as leading secessionists. Wilkes went to Havana where he learned that they were planning to sail for St. Thomas in the English mail steamer *Trent*. Leaving Havana, he stationed *San Jacinto* in the narrowest part of the Old Bahama Channel, through which *Trent* would pass. There, on November 9, he intercepted her and removed Mason and Slidell and their secretaries. In his report of the incident Wilkes stated that he had not seized the ship and sent her to Key West as a prize because of his shortage of crew and the inconvenience to the large number of passengers on board.

Wilkes took his prisoners to Hampton Roads. When the news of his action became known there was wild celebration in the North. The British lion's tail had been properly twisted. Mason and Slidell were very unpopular in the North, and there was so much clamor for severe treatment of them that, with Lincoln's approval, Wilkes was sent to Boston to deliver them to Fort Warren, then being used as a military prison. In Boston Wilkes was feted as a hero and his name was hailed throughout the North. Congress gave him a vote of thanks and Gideon Welles chimed in with a much-cited letter of commendation.

The reason for this letter is of interest. When Welles learned that Wilkes had failed to bring in *Trent* herself, he was irate. Had Wilkes done so, the case would have been handled by admiralty courts as a violation of neutrality. Now, with only the two commissioners brought in, their seizure became a political rather than a judicial matter, and Welles was sure that English reaction would be strong. The United States had gone to war with England over similar incidents in 1812. In this case the shoe was on the other foot, but he felt that Wilkes had invited trouble. At the same time he had shown commendable initiative, a quality which Welles admired and eagerly sought among his officers. After approving the seizure and congratulating Wilkes and his crew, he pointedly noted that ". . . the forbearance exercised in this instance must not be permitted to constitute a precedent hereafter for infraction of neutral obligations." [1] He hoped that through this letter other captains would get the point.

English reaction was indeed strong and vocal. The clamor in the press about the insult to the English flag equaled the jubilation over the incident in the North. Shortly after reports of the seizure of the two commissioners reached England, the government sent off a firm but temperate note demanding the release of Mason and Slidell and an apology.

An excellent example of the flexibility of the political mind is shown by this demand. Before the incident occurred, Lord Palmerston had consulted admiralty lawyers and had found that such a seizure would be in accord with British precedent. Having in mind another Union warship, then operating in the English Channel, he even discussed just such an incident with Adams. But when reports of Wilkes's seizure of the two men were received, the admiralty lawyers conveniently reversed themselves. Before sending the note, it was submitted to the Queen and as a result of the Prince Consort's criticisms it was toned down considerably. It contained a suggested solution for the United States in that it expressed the belief that Wilkes had acted on his own initiative and without express orders.

In a private letter Earl Russell instructed Lord Lyons to give Seward the substance of the note before delivering it and to fix a time limit of seven days for a reply. The note was delivered on December 21 and it received the careful consideration of the President and his cabinet. Lincoln, who had earlier expressed the feeling that Mason and Slidell would prove to

---

[1] ORN, Vol. 1, p. 148.

be "white elephants," decided to accede to the British demand and Seward's formal reply was dated December 26. In a very long and wordy discussion, which was intended to mollify critics at home, he reviewed Wilkes's action and stated that he had acted on his own initiative without the authority of the United States. Seward noted that if he appeared to be arguing the British side of the case, in reality he was only presenting the views of the United States of half a century before and that he was pleased that the British had now adopted them. The note did not contain a direct apology, but it was accepted at once by the British government as satisfactory.

Most historians consider that this incident brought the two countries to the brink of a war which Seward brilliantly averted, but a careful review of the exchange of notes in the case does not fully support this. There was much loud and angry talk and discussion of war on both sides of the Atlantic, but the responsible officials were cautious and deeply concerned by the affair. Much has been made of the fact that England ordered her Navy alerted and sent troops to Canada, but it was traditional to alert the Navy for possible action whenever the British government was faced with a critical situation. There was much loose talk and writing in the North about teaching England a lesson and proposing that a "few regiments" be sent to Canada to take over that colony. Lord Lyons was alarmed that the situation might get out of hand and that Canada might be attacked. In the face of such warlike talk it is not surprising that England took precautions.

When reports reached England that Congress had given Wilkes a vote of thanks and that Welles had expressed "emphatic approval" of his action, this was interpreted in England as indicating that opinion in the United States was firm. But by that time the British demand had been sent. There was tension on both sides and the English leaders were obviously relieved when the American reply showed a willingness to close the incident amicably. There is no doubt that the British were serious about the affair, for Lord Lyons was instructed that if no reply was received at the end of seven days, or if the reply was unsatisfactory, he was to close the legation and return to England. That would have been a serious development but it did not necessarily mean that war would follow. On the American side Seward, whose Anglophobia was well known and who had advocated a war with England only a few months before, became quite docile and conciliatory when faced with this crisis.

A comic-opera sequel occurred when some British troop-ships, en route to Canada, found the St. Lawrence River frozen over and the embarked troops were sent to Canada by rail through Portland, Maine. Earlier Seward had embarrassed Lord Lyons by suggesting that this might have to be done. When the need arose, the request was made by the British consul in Portland, and Seward promptly granted it.

THE CONFEDERATE AGENT

As THE TWO CRUISERS contracted for in Liverpool by Commander Bulloch neared completion, Mr. Adams kept sending evidence regarding their true character, collected by Consul Dudley, to Earl Russell. His stock reply was that the information was turned over to the proper Crown authorities for investigation. It was common knowledge that the ships were intended for the Confederacy but the officials could get no confirmation of this. Bulloch had done his covering up well. It was believed widely that the British were sympathetic to the Confederacy and were turning a blind eye to what were obviously money-making projects for British shipbuilders. When badgered by Adams, Earl Russell insisted that the ships could not be seized on mere rumor, opinion, or assertion. His agents just did not have any evidence that would stand up in court, he maintained. That this had merit was borne out by a case a year later when the Crown seized a suspected vessel and the court released it after a lengthy hearing. Anyone reviewing the evidence collected by Dudley and his agents would agree that it was mainly the kind mentioned by Earl Russell.

Bulloch found *Oreto* ready for sea when he returned to Liverpool. Satisfying himself that there was no contraband of war on board, he hired an English captain and signed on a crew for a voyage to Palermo, the Mediterranean, and the West Indies. The captain was instructed to call first at Nassau in the Bahamas, and one of Bulloch's clerks went along in charge of government property. At Nassau she was to be turned over to Lieutenant J. N. Maffitt of the Confederate Navy. For reasons that will become clear when the operations of the cruisers are discussed, *Oreto* dropped out of sight for several months.

When *Oreto* sailed without any interference from local authorities, Consul Dudley redoubled his efforts to get damning evidence on hull No. 290 at Laird's. She was launched in May under the name *Enrica*, and by the 1st of July she was nearly ready for sea. Bulloch found a trustworthy captain and engineer and they quietly signed on an English crew. Originally it was planned that Bulloch himself would command her but Secretary Mallory decided that he was too valuable in England. Instead Commander Raphael Semmes, whose *Sumter* had been bottled up in Gibraltar by Union cruisers for months, was intercepted at Nassau and sent back to England to take the command.

As *Enrica* neared completion Bulloch chartered a sailing bark which was then loaded in London. This had to be done with extreme care for, in addition to a supply of coal, it carried the guns and other military equipment for *Enrica*. His plan was to sail the two ships independently and have them meet at a rendezvous outside of British jurisdiction.

By late July the evidence against *Enrica* was piling up and in this case the British government showed more interest.

Enough solid information had been accumulated to impress Earl Russell, who referred it to a legal officer for study. Fortunately for Bulloch, that official was ill and the papers lay on a table in his home for four days. When action was finally taken and the ship was ordered seized, it was too late. *Enrica* had flown the coop.

On July 26 Bulloch was warned that it was not safe to leave the ship in Liverpool for another forty-eight hours. He immediately arranged for an all-day trial run for the ship in the Irish Sea. To quiet any suspicion he invited several guests to observe the trials. In the afternoon he told his guests that he wished to keep the ship out all night for further trials and returned to Liverpool with them in a tug. Early the next morning he boarded the tug with some additional crewmen and joined the ship. It was midnight before all arrangements were completed.

Enrica sailed around the north of Ireland, since Bulloch knew that a Union cruiser was at Southampton and was probably on the lookout for her in the English Channel. She headed for the Bay of Praya, on Terciera in the Azores, where she rendezvoused with the storeship. There she was joined by Semmes and renamed *Alabama*. Before long it was known that he was again on the high seas.

This indisputable evidence that the ship had been built in England to be a Confederate cruiser angered Earl Russell, and Bulloch's job became more and more difficult. He had already worked out plans for two ironclads intended to break the Union blockade. His legal adviser assured him that these ships, although ironclads and obviously intended as warships, would not affect his earlier arrangements to evade the Foreign Enlistment Act. He made a contract with Laird's for one to be delivered in April 1863 and one in May. Laird's discreetly asked no embarrassing questions. The ironclads were to have two turrets each and were somewhat larger and better protected than the Union monitors. As they were to have ram bows they became known as the "Laird Rams." Bulloch also contracted for the construction of an ironclad on the Clyde, in Scotland.

At first he was optimistic about the prospects for obtaining the ironclads, but by November he doubted that he would ever be able to get them to sea, and he was worried about how to get their officers and crews together. Consul Dudley and his agents were most inquisitive about the ships, and by January 1863 the British government also showed an active interest, with frequent official inspections. Secretary Mallory offered Bulloch a solution to this problem, or so he thought.

Thanks to the vigorous efforts of Adams, Mason had been unable to make any progress as the Confederate commissioner in England, but in France Slidell had been received openly by French officials and even Napoleon III was cordial to him. Believing that the French would be sympathetic toward Confederate activities, Mallory suggested that the officers and men for the ironclads be sent to France. Bulloch should then see Slidell to ask him to try to get sanction for the ships to be fitted out in France. Bulloch was also to investigate the prospects for having ships built there. With this lead and a quiet go-ahead from the Emperor, he worked out one of his most adroit deals, one that seemed foolproof.

He arranged for a French firm of commercial agents, who represented the Viceroy of Egypt, to purchase the Laird ironclads outright. This firm, conveniently, claimed that it had a secret request from the Viceroy to purchase two ironclads for him. Bulloch thereupon made a secret agreement with the French firm to repurchase the ships in French territory, for which transaction the firm was to be paid a commission. He knew that such a deal would have to pass the scrutiny of English courts and therefore the transaction had to appear to Laird's as a completely legitimate sale. In consequence, Bulloch formally notified the shipbuilders that he was convinced that no ship suspected of being built for the Confederacy would ever be permitted to sail from England, and so, wishing to be relieved from further responsibility for the ironclads, he asked Laird's to sell the ships for a sum that would give him a reasonable profit.

Bulloch's own account of this transaction says that the Russian government made an offer for the ironclads about this time, but it seems unlikely that it could have been a serious offer, for Anglo-Russian relations were currently strained because of a Polish revolt. Shortly thereafter, the Russian government even went so far as to send its Baltic Fleet to the United States, to keep it from being bottled up in the Baltic in case of war with England.

His affairs with Laird's completed, Bulloch went to Paris, had his French firm make an offer for the ships, and in due course a new contract was drawn, with Laird's agreeing to complete the ships for the new owner. Mr. Adams, the consuls, and the British government followed all of this with keen interest. Their curiosity about the sale resulted in increased annoyance to the shipbuilder, who asked the French firm to confirm that it was to be the actual owner of the ships. When this was done an admiralty representative went to Paris and questioned the firm at length. He offered to buy the ships for the admiralty, an indication of how embarrassing they had become to England.

This was in August 1863, and Adams learned, through British sources, that the ships were apparently intended for the Viceroy of Egypt. He sent a request for confirmation of this report to Egypt and the reply was that the Viceroy had not ordered any ironclads. It was also about this time that Adams wrote his "this is war" warning to Lord Russell. The tension rose as the ships neared completion, and in October they were seized by the British government. Since the British government was still faced with the difficulty of proving that they were really destined for the Confederacy, the ships were then purchased by the Royal Navy. In contrast to the furor caused by the Laird rams, the Clyde-built ironclad that Bulloch had ordered was quietly sold to Denmark.

In 1862 Slidell, in Paris, was privately assured that French shipbuilders would not be interfered with if they built ships for the Confederacy. By March 1863 financial arrangements were satisfactorily completed and Bulloch got in touch with a shipbuilder in Bordeaux for the construction of four *Alabama*-type cruisers and two ironclads. Formal contracts were signed in July. Construction progressed rapidly and was apparently undetected until November when a clerk who had left the shipbuilder's employ showed Mr. John Bigelow, U.S. consul general in Paris, papers which clearly revealed that the ships were being built for the Confederacy. Mr. William L. Dayton, U.S. minister to France, protested against their completion. By that time Napoleon's confidence in the eventual success of the Confederacy was badly shaken. In February 1864 the French government notified the builders that the ships could not sail and that the cruisers could not be armed in France but must be sold to some foreign merchant as merchant ships. Later orders directed the sale of all of the ships at once. One of the ironclads was sold to Prussia and one to Denmark. Owing to many delays, the latter was not delivered to Copenhagen until the following November. By then Denmark did not want the ship as her short war with Prussia, over Schleswig-Holstein, had ended. Bulloch, through typically complex maneuvers, then managed to get possession of it. She sailed from Copenhagen early in January 1865 and made a rendezvous with her Confederate crew at Quiberon Bay in France. Late in the month she sailed as C.S.S. *Stonewall*. She called at Ferrol, Spain, where, a few days later, she was discovered by the Union cruisers *Niagara* and *Sacramento*. But Commodore T. T. Craven, of *Niagara*, declined to engage the ironclad with his wooden ships, for which decision he was later court-martialed.

Stonewall made its way across the Atlantic and reached

Havana in May. By that time there was no Confederate government in existence and Captain Page offered to deliver the ship to Spanish authorities if they would advance $15,000 to pay off the crew. This was done and the ship was later turned over to the United States upon reimbursement for the expenses.

Besides *Florida* and *Alabama*, three other Confederate ships were obtained in England. In the fall of 1863 the Royal Navy sold an ex-gunboat. She was bought by Bulloch through an agent and was reported to be fitting out for the China trade. When British authorities became suspicious and ordered her detention, she slipped out of Sheerness, near the mouth of the Thames, just ahead of the seizure order, and went to Calais to become C.S.S. *Rappahannock*. She was held in that port by the French in a dispute over bills contracted, however, and saw no service. Another ship was built on the Clyde, armed off France in 1863, and became C.S.S. *Georgia*. Late in 1864 Bulloch bought a ship built for the Far East trade that had just returned from its first voyage. By methods similar to those used for *Alabama*, she was armed off Madeira and became C.S.S. *Shenandoah*. The operations of these and other Confederate cruisers will be covered in the next chapter.

BRITISH GRIEVANCES

AFTER THE *Trent* affair, and excepting some technical cases involving international law applied to suspected blockade runners, there was only one other serious British grievance against the United States. That concerned recruiting for the Union Army and Navy in the British Isles and especially in Ireland. In November 1862 Earl Russell advised Adams that he had reliable information that United States agents were engaged in recruiting and were offering substantial bounties to prospects. This, he added, was a violation of British law and those engaged in it were liable to prosecution. Adams replied that he knew of no such agents and doubted if there were any. Seward directed him to inform the British government that the United States had no agents of any kind in Great Britain or any other country who were authorized to recruit for the armed services. He added, pointedly, that the United States encouraged immigration and that after an immigrant arrived within its jurisdiction he was free to volunteer for military service.

Earl Russell admitted that he was in error in this case but he was soon back on the subject and the correspondence about it extended to the end of 1864. Replying to Adams's complaint that the British were furnishing munitions to the Confederacy as well as allowing the recruitment of British subjects for *Alabama*, Earl Russell reminded him that the Union had bought more munitions than the South and that Britain had grounds for complaint against both sides on the score of recruiting. In January 1863 he complained about attempts of a Union naval vessel to recruit the crew of a captured blockade runner off Charleston.

The flow of men of military age across the Atlantic reached its peak in 1863 and 1864. The method used for obtaining most of the recruits was an outgrowth of the notorious system of "substitute brokers," coupled with the generous bounties of $300 and up offered by the Union Army and by local officials for volunteers. Men with a knack for picking a fast and easy dollar soon found a fruitful field in England and Ireland. By offering free passage and a well-paying job, they readily interested young men in emigrating, especially in regions such as Lancashire, where unemployment was high. Mr. Adams was able to produce some letters, which were apparently legitimate, asking for laborers for the western railroads or for mechanics with special skills. Since immigrants were not subject to the Union draft they were considered desirable employees during the Civil War and the government formally encouraged such immigration. Many of these immigrants did find civilian jobs, but as many or more were given early exposure to recruiting officers with bounties in mind. Earl Russell complained repeatedly of the number of British citizens serving in the Union Navy.

Reliable estimates of how many recruits were obtained from this source probably cannot be made, but the number of arrivals in the United States from the British Isles in steerage class is revealing. In 1861 and 1862 the number was about 35,000 in each year. In 1863 it jumped to 83,000 and in 1864 it was 94,000. In 1865 the number dropped sharply to 48,000. From Europe in 1862 came 84,000 but in 1863 the figure was nearly double—164,000. The immigration from Europe, unlike that from the British Isles, continued to rise sharply each year and in 1865 it was 214,000. The yearly number of immigrants during the Civil War was less than it had been before the war, and it seems probable that the majority of those who came during the war years were of military age as a result of the inducements offered.

In May 1864 Lord Lyons reported to the Foreign Office that he was getting constant complaints from British subjects in the Union Army about the manner in which they had been recruited. New York was the center of the most flagrant abuses and he quoted a report that brokers there had plundered $400,000 from the bounty fees of recruits by demanding exorbitant commissions. Union authorities investigated each case but usually it became a matter of the man's word against that of his recruiting officer.

Early in November 1863 the Union steam sloop *Kearsarge*, which had been watching the Confederate cruiser *Florida* at Brest, anchored at Queenstown, Ireland. Captain John S. Winslow left the ship for a few days to see the consul at Cork. In his absence one of the ship's petty officers visited his old home nearby and suggested to some of the neighbors that they might be able to enlist on board. Times were hard in Ireland that year and men flocked to the ship to enlist. The executive officer held some of them and had them examined by the doctor. But when Captain Winslow returned he ordered the men out of the ship. Later, when he called upon the local British admiral, his attention was called to newspaper reports that *Kearsarge* was in Queenstown to recruit men. He was given a copy of the Foreign Enlistment Act but he stated that he did not want any recruits. After the ship sailed it was searched and several Irishmen were found and sent ashore in the pilot boat. Confederate agents learned of what had occurred and several "affidavits" attesting that recruiting had taken place were brought to the attention of Earl Russell, who sent a stiff note of protest to Adams. Most of the affidavits were signed with an "X-his mark."

When *Kearsarge* was well clear of Queenstown, sixteen Irish stowaways were found on board. Returning to Brest, Captain Winslow sent them ashore, but when it occurred to him that they might enlist in *Florida*, he recalled them. Early in December *Kearsarge* returned to Queenstown and the men were sent ashore in the pilot boat. Winslow sent a note to the American consul explaining what had occurred, but by then he was involved in a full-scale incident.

This recounting of the *Kearsarge* incident is to some extent based on conjecture, for the records in the case, especially the affidavits of the Irishmen concerned, are confusing, contradictory, and often based on a lack of understanding. Captain Winslow's own conduct suggests that he may have realized that it was not above reproach. He did not return to the harbor of Queenstown and he reported his action of returning the stowaways to the local admiral only by letter. Yet when the Foreign Office got his reports of the incident it was apparently satisfied with them. Some of the men were tried under the Foreign Enlistment Act, a precedent which Mr. Adams cited when he tried to get that office to act against agents recruiting for the Confederate cruisers. When reports of the incident reached Washington, Welles ordered a court of inquiry but he was unwilling to recall the ship from its station. By the time *Kearsarge* was available for the inquiry, Winslow was a national hero—he had sunk the Confederate cruiser *Alabama*—and the incident was all but forgotten.

Most historians now agree that England was reasonably successful in her effort to maintain strict neutrality in the Civil War. The sympathy of most of her influential and ruling class was with the South, and this sympathy probably got greater coverage in the press than its true strength merited. The antislavery sentiment was generally among the lower classes. In September 1863 the Confederate government told Mason to withdraw his mission, as the British government was too unsympathetic and too much under the influence of the Federal government for the Confederacy to expect help or recognition. On the other hand, the British refused to accept the Union contention that it was dealing only with an insurrection. British citizens who wished to trade with the South at their own risk could do so as long as they did not violate the Foreign Enlistment Act. The fact that the United States was awarded damages in settlement of the so-called *Alabama* Claims suggests that the British government might have shown more apprehension about the Confederacy obtaining cruisers in England, but Bulloch's machinations made it difficult, if not almost impossible, to establish to the satisfaction of an English court that the ships were actually intended for the Confederacy. On balance, England did achieve her purpose with considerable credit.

Chapter XII

The Confederate Cruisers

THE END OF *SUMTER*

THE BEGINNING of the Confederate effort to attack Northern commerce at sea was noted in an earlier chapter, when
Raphael Semmes evaded the blockade of the Mississippi in
June 1861 in the converted cruiser *Sumter*. By the time he
reached Curaçao in July, he had captured a number of Northern ships and the news of his activity created consternation
in shipping circles in the North. Gideon Welles's first reaction
was to disregard the commerce raider, but the clamor for action against her was too great for him to ignore. Without
weakening the blockade he did send several cruisers to the
West Indies in search of *Sumter*.

Semmes moved into new waters frequently to elude the
ships that he knew were searching for him. Soon after leaving
Curaçao he captured a schooner which was sent to New Orleans with a prize crew. This craft was recaptured by David D. Porter, still in command of *Powhatan*, blockading the
mouths of the Mississippi. With it Porter also captured
Semmes's reports to his Navy Department. Feeling that
he knew Semmes well enough to outwit him, Porter went to
Pensacola to get permission from his squadron commander to
search for the raider. Porter was shrewd enough to estimate

Semmes's movements and he closed in on him steadily as Semmes worked his way along the Brazilian coast and back toward West Indian waters. At one time in October Porter probably sighted *Sumter*, for he reported trying to overhaul a light seen at night which suddenly disappeared. While returning to his regular blockading station, Porter learned that a ship that had been nearby in the morning before this sighting had been boarded by *Sumter*. Semmes did not report possible contact with *Powhatan*, but he did report boarding a British ship on the pretext that he himself was in search of *Sumter*. The ruse did not work, for *Sumter* was recognized by the neutral ship and reported as such.

From Curacao Semmes had made his way as far as Maranham, Brazil, coaling at Surinam and Trinidad en route. In each place the U.S. consul had done his best to prevent him from getting coal and supplies but Semmes's legal arguments got him by. Leaving Maranham, he had cruised across the track of ships running between New York, Brazil, and the Pacific. He had found little Northern shipping and it was during this period that he may have been sighted by Porter. He arrived in Fort-de-France, Martinique, in November 1861, but moved to St. Pierre, the city that was destroyed by the eruption of Mount Pelée in 1902, in order to get coal. There he was found by the Union cruiser *Iroquois*. The governor of Martinique promptly sent a French warship to the port to preserve neutrality. Semmes knew that *Iroquois* was communicating with the shore while she lay outside the three-mile limit, and he suspected that she had arranged with a Union schooner in port to signal *Sumter*'s movements. The night of November 23 being favorable, Semmes got under way and headed south out of the port. Confirming his suspicion, blue lights were displayed by the schooner and *Iroquois* headed off southward to intercept *Sumter*. After running southerly for a few minutes, Semmes reversed course and ran northward along the coast of Martinique and escaped his pursuer.

Then, feeling that the ship needed drydocking, he crossed the Atlantic to Cadiz, Spain, where he arrived early in January 1862. Here again Union officials put many obstacles in his way but he did manage to get his ship docked for minor repairs. These he did not consider adequate and he went to Gibraltar later in the month. There the U.S. consul was more successful in obstructing him. No local dealer would sell Semmes coal nor could he get it from the Royal Navy. His wrath at the consul was exceeded only by the vigor of his defense of his rights under international law.

Somehow he came across a copy of the first annual report of Gideon Welles in which *Sumter* was referred to as a "piratical rover." He sent a long letter to the *Times*, in London, taking the Federal Secretary of the Navy to task for using the term and defending his ship's status as a legitimate man-of-war. The consistent stand of Union diplomatic and consular agents, and to a lesser extent naval officers, that the Confederate raider was a pirate annoyed local officials everywhere and they obviously did not agree. It was due in part to this annoyance that Semmes and other cruiser commanders could usually supply their needs in neutral ports.

The arrival of *Sumter* at Gibraltar ended her cruise as a commerce raider. She was watched closely by Union cruisers in Algeciras, the Spanish port across the bay. Unable to obtain supplies or to get her damaged boilers repaired, Semmes recommended that she be sold. Weeks later he left her with a caretaker and, with most of his officers, started back to the Confederacy by steamship. *Sumter* had captured only eighteen ships and craft, of which she burned seven, but her cruise sent marine insurance rates upward and accelerated the transfer of ships from the United States flag to neutrals. Rather than stopping Union commerce, as the Confederates hoped would be the case, the raider had merely caused a shift to other flags. British shipping profited most from this shift.

FLORIDA AND *ALABAMA*

How Commander Bulloch had a ship named *Oreto* built in Liverpool along the lines of a British gunboat and sent it unarmed out of England to Nassau was related in the preceding chapter. There it was to be turned over to Lieutenant J. N. Maffitt, CSN. He had been a successful blockade runner when he took over *Oreto* in May 1862. She had been held in port for several weeks as a result of litigation. Minister Adams had sent a full report on her from London, including the fact that her armament was sent out in the merchant ship *Bermuda*. The Federal consul at Nassau went to work and caused *Oreto* to be seized for violation of British neutrality. She was freed on advice of Crown counsel, but seized again a day later. Court proceedings dragged out until August, when the ship was finally released.

Maffitt kept in the background during the litigation, but when the ship was released he took her to uninhabited Green Cay, where she was joined by a schooner which had carried her armament from *Bermuda*. There a week was spent transferring the guns and other equipment needed to convert her to a cruiser. These efforts were complicated by an outbreak of yellow fever which reached epidemic proportions. Having no doctor, Maffitt himself had to treat the victims. On August 17 *Oreto* was placed in commission as C.S.S. *Florida*. She was not yet an active man-of-war, as some critical parts for her guns had been left behind in Nassau. In addition, the ship was short-handed when she left Green Cay; her British crew had not been as enthusiastic about enlisting in the Confederate Navy as Maffitt had hoped. She reached Cardenas, Cuba, from where he sent to Havana for help. He himself became a victim of yellow fever and was delirious for a week. Early in September, after a stop in Havana, short-handed and with yellow fever still raging on board, Maffitt decided to try to run into Mobile—a bold decision.

For this attempt he resorted to a ruse; he would try to run through the blockaders off Mobile in the guise of a British warship, which *Florida* resembled. Commander George Preble in *Oneida*, the senior officer in the three blockading ships off Mobile, saw *Florida* approach, but his suspicions were not aroused until she failed to slow down and exchange the usual courtesies. When *Florida* suddenly headed for his blockading line at full speed, Preble opened fire and set off in pursuit of her. The other blockaders joined in the chase. *Florida* was hit several times but managed to reach safety under the guns of Fort Morgan, at the entrance to Mobile Bay.

When Gideon Welles learned that *Florida* had eluded the blockade his ire turned on Preble, whom he blamed for allowing her to get through. He secured Lincoln's approval to summarily dismiss Preble from the Navy and had the general order announcing the dismissal read on all ships of the Navy. Preble, a grandnephew of the hero of the war with Tripoli, Commodore Edward Preble, worked hard to clear his name and to gain reinstatement in the service. Several months later Welles, without making any recommendation himself, forwarded to the President a large number of letters from senior officers and political figures urging Preble's reinstatement. Lincoln then restored Preble to his former rank.

It was January 1863 before the damage to *Florida* was repaired and she was ready for sea. By then there were a dozen blockading ships off the port with strict orders to capture her. Maffitt waited nearly two weeks before a northeast storm created the favorable weather conditions that he wanted to run through the blockade. Early in the morning of January 16 he managed to get past about half of the blockaders when a flash of sparks from his funnel gave him away. Fast blockaders chased *Florida* all of the next day and were gaining on her by dark, but Maffitt eluded them during the night.

He intended to operate in the Northern shipping lanes to Europe, but while steaming north from Nassau he ran into a bad storm in the Gulf Stream. He then decided to head for Barbados. Only a few days after he left Nassau he was chased by a Union cruiser but again managed to elude it at night. He ranged down the Brazilian coast, coaling from a captured bark which he then used as a tender, but by the time he reached Pernambuco he found that Semmes, in *Alabama*, was ahead of him. By then it was May.

At this time one of his officers, Lieutenant C. W. Read, proposed taking the brig *Clarence*, which had just been captured, into Hampton Roads to try to capture a Union gunboat. Maffitt had already decided to clear the South Atlantic and head back for the Northern shipping lanes and he approved Read's scheme. Armed with a single small gun, Read worked his way north and appeared off the Virginia capes early in June. Within a week he captured eight small vessels. He burned six and sent their crews to New York in the seventh, a schooner. The remaining craft, *Tacony*, was a better sailer than his own, so he transferred his armament to it and burned *Clarence*. Then he learned from captured newspapers that Chesapeake Bay was too closely guarded for him to enter it safely, so he moved northward.

News of his presence off the coast created consternation. Secretary Welles ordered all available ships out in search. During the night of June 15 *Tacony* was hailed twice by a Federal ship but escaped detection by the simple ruse of reporting that she had seen the raider chasing a ship the afternoon before. *Tacony* captured several vessels off Nantucket and then worked her way into the New England fishing fleet. After burning several fishing vessels, whose destruction could give little aid to the Confederate cause, Read headed for Portland, Maine. But first he burned *Tacony*, transferring his armament and crew to a captured fishing schooner. From some lobstermen he picked up he learned that the revenue cutter *Caleb*

Cushing was in Casco Bay and that a passenger steamer was at the dock ready to sail for New York the next morning.

Read concocted the bold scheme of capturing *Caleb Cushing* and then using her to capture the passenger liner. At night he boarded *Cushing*, captured her, and made for sea. But the alarm was spread, and the next day she was cornered by Union gunboats. Hopelessly outclassed, Read burned *Cushing*, took to the boats, and was captured with his crew. His short cruise had caused a panic on the Union seaboard and nearly forty ships were sent in search of him. His early successes apparently went to his head for his final venture was obviously foolhardy, if spectacular.

Meanwhile Maffitt had trouble getting coal and supplies in Brazilian ports, thanks to alert Union consuls. After cruising for a time in the vicinity of the equator, he shifted to the Northern coast for a planned rendezvous with Read. Late in June, as Read was taking *Caleb Cushing*, Maffitt was making captures in the approaches to New York. Northern newspapers, found on board his prizes, told him of Read's exploits. On July 8, off Nantucket, *Florida* was sighted by the Union gunboat *Ericsson*. *Florida* fired several shots at her but, being heavily outgunned, *Ericsson* evaded action and contact was soon lost in a fog. Maffitt then prudently headed for Bermuda. When he arrived there on July 15 he was advised that a national gun salute would be returned gun for gun. In an endorsement to the governor's offer, Maffitt stated that this was the only foreign salute received by the Confederate government. In view of England's refusal to grant formal recognition to the Confederacy, the governor of Bermuda seems to have overdone his hospitality on this occasion.

Maffitt left Bermuda late in July and a month later he entered Brest, France, where he hoped to get major repairs for his ship. There he requested his own relief due to illness and Lieutenant C. M. Morris took command. *Florida* remained at

Brest until February 1864, after which she cruised through Madeira, Teneriffe, Martinique, and back to Bermuda in May. Morris cruised in the Northern shipping lanes until late June, when he returned again to Bermuda. He next operated off the Virginia capes, and early in July he captured the passenger and mail steamer *Electric Spark* off the Delaware capes. He put the passengers on a captured schooner and that night scuttled the steamer, the only Union steam merchant ship lost to the Confederate raiders. *Florida* had meanwhile been seen by a tugboat that had escaped, and knowing that the alarm would soon be given, Morris headed south. On October 4 he entered Bahia, Brazil, in which port the Union cruiser *Wachusett*, under Commander Napoleon Collins, was lying.

Wachusett was in the West Indies Squadron, which had been organized in September 1862 under Rear Admiral Charles Wilkes, with the special mission of destroying the Confederate cruisers. It was not long before Welles noticed that Wilkes was inclined to search for the raiders in waters where he might also find blockade runners, whose capture would provide prize money. Welles felt it necessary to send Wilkes a strong reminder of his mission.

Although Collins was in a neutral harbor and a Brazilian gunboat had stationed itself between *Wachusett* and *Florida*, the temptation was too great for the Union commander. He later reminded Wilkes that the latter had once told him not to be too particular about neutral waters in case an opportunity presented itself. During the night of October 6 Collins quietly got under way with the intention of ramming and sinking *Florida* and then slipping out of the harbor. But instead of the desired head-on ram, *Wachusett* struck a glancing blow. Half of *Florida*'s crew was ashore, and after the exchange of a few small arms shots, Collins captured the cruiser. He towed her out of the harbor and took her to Hampton Roads.

Brazil strongly protested this brazen action and the United States could only acknowledge that Brazil's neutrality had been violated. A promise was made that *Florida* would be returned to Brazil, but before that could be done she was rammed and sunk by an Army transport in Hampton Roads. Whether this was an accident or a deliberate scuttling was never established, although two courts of inquiry investigated it. Collins was court-martialed for violating Brazilian neutrality, found guilty, and sentenced to be dismissed from the service. Gideon Welles proved that he was not too displeased with the incident, for he promptly disapproved the court-martial proceedings and restored Collins to duty.

When Raphael Semmes reached Nassau after leaving *Sumter* at Gibraltar, he found orders to return to England and take command of *Alabama*, then about to be slipped out of Liverpool by Bulloch. When he reached England *Alabama*, alias *Enrica*, had already sailed, but Bulloch chartered a steamer and went with Semmes to Terciera where *Alabama* was nearly ready to put to sea as an armed cruiser. As soon as her armament was on board Semmes took her outside territorial waters on August 24, 1862, and formally commissioned her. By offering high pay and a share of prize money he signed on a substantial crew, made up of sailors who had been with the crew of the ship that brought out *Alabama*'s armament and the crew of the steamer chartered by Bulloch. Semmes's officers had either been with him in *Sumter* or had been quietly collected by Bulloch in England.

Semmes set off at once on a commerce raiding cruise. He got into the Northern whaling fleet off the Azores, where he captured and burned several ships, and cruised for a time on the Newfoundland Banks, where he captured more ships. After a severe storm his coal was low and he headed for Fort-de-France, Martinique, where he had a rendezvous with a supply ship. He arrived on November 18 to find that the supply ship had been there for some time and that her mission was well known. The next day Semmes gave her a new rendezvous, and just in time, for that afternoon the Union cruiser *San Jacinto* arrived off the port. That night Semmes slipped out of the harbor without being seen, although the captain of *San Jacinto* had stationed picket boats on each side of the harbor entrance. Signal rockets were supplied to the picket boats and to two Union merchantmen that were in port. The picket boat near the south entrance did fire its signal rockets, but *San Jacinto* had a fruitless search in rain squalls.

Alabama was coaled near a barren island off the coast of Venezuela and then headed for the Windward Channel off Cape Maysi, Cuba, where Semmes hoped to bag a California steamer carrying gold from Panama to New York. After several days he did capture *Ariel*, outbound from New York with about 700 passengers, including 150 Union marines. After taking off some securities and currency, he released the ship in bond and paroled the military passengers.

From Northern newspapers on *Ariel* Semmes learned that an expedition of 20,000 troops, under Major General N. P. Banks, was about to sail for the Gulf of Mexico. He deduced its destination as Galveston and decided to try to get in among the transports, which he knew would have to anchor outside the bar. He arrived off Galveston at nightfall January 11, 1863, to find only five blockaders. One headed for *Alabama* to investigate and Semmes led it well offshore. In a short but brisk action at point-blank range U.S.S. *Hatteras*, a converted merchantman, was sunk. It was a venturesome thing to do on Semmes's part, for a lucky Union shot might have disabled his ship. The action was also not consistent with his mission, which was to attack merchant ships, not to engage Union warships.

Alabama was now overcrowded with many prisoners on board, so Semmes sailed for Jamaica where he landed the prisoners, coaled, and repaired the damage received in the action. Late in January he worked his way slowly from Jamaica to Bahia, which he reached in May, after capturing and burning twenty ships. There he got into a quarrel with Brazilian authorities for using the island of Fernando do Noronha as a base, since he had left his anchorage there to capture and burn two passing ships. One of his prizes was armed and made into a tender, renamed *Tuscaloosa*. Leaving Bahia, Semmes next cruised toward the Cape of Good Hope. *Tuscaloosa* was sent off independently to rendezvous with *Alabama* at Capetown. Semmes arrived off Capetown at the end of July and spent the next two months cruising off that port but made only one capture.

That one, however, was made within sight of Capetown and the townspeople were thrilled spectators of the capture. The Union consul complained that it was made inside territorial waters, but Semmes was able to satisfy local and sympathetic authorities that it was not. Semmes later sent his prize to an uninhabited bay well up the coast and sold her to a resident of Capetown for much-needed cash.

While Semmes was engaged in this *sub rosa* venture, *Tuscaloosa* arrived at Capetown. The energetic Union consul, Mr. Walter Graham, immediately claimed that she was an uncondemned prize and should be held for her owner. In this he was supported by local Royal Navy officers but the colonial attorney general refused to accept this interpretation and released her. She cruised without success between Africa and Brazil for several months and returned to Capetown in January 1864. In the meantime London had ruled on her status and she was then seized, ending her career.

While operating off the Cape, Semmes had another fortunate escape. The fast and well-armed Union cruiser *Vanderbilt* had been sent on an independent search for *Alabama* but had been held in the West Indies by Wilkes, on his own authority, for several months. The route *Vanderbilt* was supposed to follow was very close to Semme's course. At St. Helena, Commander C. H. Baldwin, *Vanderbilt*'s skipper, received a report that *Alabama* and another Confederate cruiser,

Georgia, were in the vicinity of the Cape of Good Hope. *Vanderbilt* arrived there at the end of August and for a week played hide and seek with *Alabama*, being in and out of the same ports only a day or two apart. Baldwin then decided that Semmes had gone into the Indian Ocean and he set off toward Mauritius.

Semmes, however, remained in the vicinity of the Cape until late September, when he decided to shift to the China Sea in search of Union clippers. As he approached the Strait of Sunda he learned from an English ship that the Union cruiser *Wyoming* was patroling the strait. Although outgunned, Semmes decided to try to surprise her at night and sink her. But he did not find *Wyoming* and had to be satisfied with taking three prizes early in November. Meanwhile, reports of *Alabama*'s presence in those waters spread fast, and arriving in Singapore just before Christmas, Semmes found twenty-two Union Merchant ships in port, most of them laid up. By then he had already decided to return to Europe where some badly needed repairs could be made to the ship.

After leaving Singapore, Semmes captured and burned a ship under British register which had only recently been transferred from American register. This change in register was an old trick to evade capture, but in this case it was legitimate and the local British admiral ordered his ships to capture *Alabama* if the action was repeated. By then Semmes was already in the Indian Ocean returning to the Atlantic. He was at Capetown in March 1864, and near the end of April he made his last two captures. *Alabama* had captured sixty-four ships in her career as a raider, burning all but ten of them, and she was the best known and most feared of the Confederate cruisers. She arrived at Cherbourg, France, on June 11.

The Union cruiser *Kearsarge* was then at Flushing, in the Netherlands, and a message from Minister Dayton, in Paris, sent her steaming full speed for Cherbourg. She arrived on the 14th, whereupon Captain Winslow received word from

Semmes that if *Kearsarge* stayed outside the three-mile limit until *Alabama* coaled, she would come out and fight. Winslow was more than willing, and his ship remained outside territorial waters waiting for *Alabama* to sortie. Word of the impending battle spread and sightseers from as far away as Paris converged on the port. It was a gala atmosphere on Sunday morning, June 19, when, just as church services were about to begin, *Alabama* was seen steaming out of the harbor. With *Alabama* following, Winslow moved out to sea to be well clear of French waters. About seven miles offshore Winslow turned and headed for *Alabama*, hoping to run her down. *Alabama* changed course to avoid collision, and the ships found themselves parallel to each other, on opposite courses about half a mile apart. *Alabama* opened fire first, but fire soon followed from *Kearsarge*. In order to keep broadsides bearing, the ships steamed in a circle with the range gradually dropping to about 400 yards. After seven circuits, in a current which carried them to westward, the battle was over and *Alabama* went down. Although the ships were fairly evenly matched, *Kearsarge*'s gunnery was much superior, with her fire more deliberate and accurate. Also, about a year before this battle, Winslow had ranged anchor chains along her sides to give added protection to her machinery. These chains were covered with a wooden sheathing. As a result *Kearsarge* suffered only slight damage. Her luck held as well, for a shell from *Alabama* which lodged in *Kearsarge*'s rudder post, and might have disabled her had it exploded, turned out to be defective.

When *Alabama* was obviously sinking, Winslow called to the nearby spectator yacht *Deerhound* to help rescue her crew in the water. The yacht picked up Semmes and forty-one others, including thirteen officers, and at his request took them to Southampton. Gideon Welles fumed at this "unneutral" action of the British yacht but privately Winslow was pleased that Semmes had escaped capture. They had been former shipmates and friends, and Winslow was concerned that, if taken, Semmes would be tried for piracy. *Kearsarge* recovered seventy men, and two French pilot boats rescued fifteen. Winslow put the wounded into the hospital at Cherbourg and paroled the rest of the men. For this he was censured by Welles, who felt that they should have been held for trial.

There were many charges and recriminations about this battle but it was as fairly fought as it could be. Semmes simply overplayed his luck and vanity, and lost.

OTHER RAIDERS AND RESULTS

Alabama AND *Florida* were the most famous of the Confederate commerce raiders but others are worthy of attention. Working independently of Bulloch, Commander Matthew F. Maury had a ship built on the Clyde but he got no bargain in that one. She slipped away from England in April 1863 and off the French coast met a tug carrying her armament. There she was commissioned as C.S.S. *Georgia* by Lieutenant W. L. Maury. Less fortunate in getting a crew, she started her cruise short-handed.

She headed for the South Atlantic and made her first capture south of the Canaries. In early May she was in Bahia at the same time *Alabama* was there. *Florida* was also in the same waters at this time. *Georgia* continued her cruise along the Brazilian coast, into the South Atlantic, and to the Cape of Good Hope, where she arrived a few hours after *Alabama* had left for the China Sea. Learning that *Vanderbilt* was in the vicinity, Maury let discretion govern and slipped away under cover of a homeward-bound British tea fleet. *Georgia* proved to be a rather poor commerce raider; she took only eight prizes and her bottom was fouled much sooner than normal. She ran into Cherbourg to go into drydock, but several months passed before she got permission to dock and a close examination showed her unfit for further service as a cruiser. She then set off for the coast of Morocco, where she was to transfer her battery to C.S.S. *Rappahannock*, a rendezvous that never took place. During the long wait off Morocco one of her parties ashore was attacked by a band of Moors and the ship shelled the shore for an hour, giving her the dubious distinction of starting and ending the Confederacy's only foreign war. After a long wait she went to Bordeaux and arrived in Liverpool early in May 1864, where her crew was paid off. Bulloch had her armament removed and put her up for auction. An Englishman bought her and converted her to a merchantman and then chartered her to the Portuguese government. U.S.S. *Niagara* seized her at sea and sent her to the United States as a prize. There she was condemned by the prize court, an action that was later confirmed by the Supreme Court.

Rappahannock was the ex-Royal Navy gunboat that Bulloch contrived to buy and which got out of England a hop and a skip ahead of the sheriff, so to speak. She had machinery trouble in the Channel and made her way into Calais late in November 1864. By then the sympathetic treatment of Confederate ships by European nations had cooled measurably. Her captain ran afoul of French authorities in a dispute over charges, which resulted in her being held in port. She never got to sea as a raider, and after hostilities ceased she was sold in England and her purchase price credited to the United States government.

The least justifiable cruise of a Confederate commerce raider was that of *Shenandoah*, an East Indiaman purchased by Bulloch after one voyage. With most of the Union merchant fleet already off the oceans, Confederate naval planners turned to the almost untouched whaling fleet in the Pacific. The whaling industry was in the doldrums and it is difficult, if not impossible, to see how attacks on that fleet could possibly have helped the Confederate cause. The chief victims were to be the owners, which in many cases were the captains of the ships. Yet someone conceived the idea of destroying as much of this fleet as possible. *Florida* was en route to the Pacific for this purpose when her career was ended by *Wachusett* at Bahia.

The newly bought East Indiaman and her supply ship met off Madeira in October 1864, where, after the usual transfer of armament, she became C.S.S. *Shenandoah*, commanded by Lieutenant J. I. Waddell. She had trouble shipping a full crew but did recruit some men from ships she had captured in the South Atlantic, after which she made her way to Melbourne, Australia. There Waddell wrangled with local authorities over breaches of neutrality in trying to recruit men, but he got away in February 1865 after augmenting his crew through subterfuge. He followed the known track of the whaling fleet as far north as the Bering Sea. *Shenandoah* made a number of captures, most of them after Lee had surrendered and the fate of the Confederacy was sealed. On June 23 Waddell captured a ship which had San Francisco newspapers on board, reporting Lee's surrender. They also reported Jefferson Davis's proclamation that the war would continue, which Waddell felt would justify his continuing to operate as a raider. It was not until August that he spoke to a British ship which told him of the capture of Davis and the collapse of the Confederacy. Waddell then had *Shenandoah*'s guns dismounted and made for Liverpool. The ship arrived there in November and was turned over to British authorities, who later surrendered her to the United States.

Two other raiders warrant brief mention. In July 1864 the fast blockade runner *Atlanta* was converted to a commerce raider at Wilmington, North Carolina, as C.S.S. *Tallahassee*. Early in August she ran the blockade and cruised off New York and New England, taking a number of prizes, mostly small craft, later making her way to Halifax. By this time the fortunes of the Confederacy were obviously on the wane and British authorities at Halifax were more strict in enforcing neutrality. *Tallahassee* was given twenty-four hours in port, later extended to forty, and she was allowed only enough coal to get back to Wilmington. Her appearance resulted in another Northern scare and every available ship was sent to sea in search of her. She left Halifax only a few hours before the arrival of a Union cruiser and managed to rerun the blockade at Wilmington late in August. In October, under the name of *Olustee*, she made another short raiding cruise. Sighted by a Union cruiser off Cape Charles, she was chased for two days. She eluded that pursuer but was again chased by Union ships before she got back to Wilmington. She was then reconverted to an unarmed blockade runner and became, fittingly, *Chameleon*.

Meanwhile another fast blockade runner was converted to a commerce raider at Wilmington. This was *Chickamauguagua*, commanded by Captain John Wilkinson, one of the most successful blockade runners. She ran out late in October and had bagged only four prizes when Wilkinson learned that Union ships were in search of her. He made for Bermuda, where he had to use all of his evasive skill to circumvent the tightened neutrality restrictions. There he lost many of his crew through desertion, could get only a limited supply of coal, and returned to Wilmington after a mere three weeks' cruise. She too was reconverted to a blockade runner.

The forays of these ships out of Wilmington were objected to by local Confederate Army commanders because they believed that the forays would focus attention on Wilmington and bring on a strengthening of the blockade there. That is just what happened.

With a handful of commerce raiders, the Confederates succeeded beyond what must have been their most optimistic expectations. The cruisers destroyed only about five per cent of the Union merchant fleet, but created such a panic that nearly half of that fleet was transferred to neutral flags. Most of the remaining Union ships were laid up in port. It is significant that, except for a revenue cutter, only two steamships were captured and one of these was recovered.

The strength of the American merchant marine, which at its zenith had rivaled England's, had begun to decline in the 1850s. The Confederate cruisers gave that decline such impetus that the merchant marine has never fully recovered its once proud place. Its great glory rested with the unsurpassed clipper ships, the most beautiful ships that ever sailed the seas. But iron and steam were beginning to replace wood and canvas in shipbuilding, and while American shipbuilders pioneered some notable steamships, Europeans took the lead after the Civil War.

The Confederate cruisers conducted the most successful military operations of that ill-fated cause, but they accomplished little of real military value. Union trade was inconvenienced, but it actually increased during the war. The main effect of the commerce raiders was to harass owners and operators of shipping without in any serious way hurting the Union military effort. As for destroying fishing and whaling vessels, the only possible motive must have been vengeance. That is the blackest mark against the Confederate cruisers and their sponsors.

The Union cruisers made a poor showing in running down the raiders. Gideon Welles refused to divert naval strength from the blockade, but fifty-eight ships in all were used to search for the cruisers, with twenty-nine of them assigned expressly to that task. At least one class of ships, of which *Kearsarge* was one, were designed for this purpose. Some of the vessels assigned were sailing ships and supply vessels, but obviously a substantial part of the Navy was used in searching for the raiders, with not one being intercepted in the open sea. It is true that they were looking for clever and resourceful commanders who, branded as pirates and promised treatment as such, had a special incentive to avoid capture.

From the beginning of the war Seward, through Adams, built up a case for holding England responsible for allowing the ships to be built and to escape from England. At the end of the war the United States demanded reparations for the damage done by them, but England showed little interest in recognizing such claims until the growing might of Prussia became a threat to England's position and caused a change of attitude. In 1869 a treaty was signed submitting these claims to arbitration, but it was not ratified by the Senate until 1871, during the Grant administration. Although the claims involved all of the cruisers, they came to be known collectively as "The *Alabama* Claims," after the most famous of the commerce raiders. The United States presented indirect as well as direct claims that totaled about $130,000,000. The arbitration commission awarded $15,500,000, which was more than enough to cover the actual physical losses caused by the cruisers obtained from England.

Chapter XIII

The Union Blockade

THE BLOCKADE RUNNERS

THE EXPLOITS of the Southern blockade runners have been so romanticized that the claims of their successes must be taken with reservation. To defy the might of the United States Navy naturally evoked hearty Confederate cheers, and for the blockade runners to do so repeatedly was a good reason for pointing with pride to their feats. Here, however, we are concerned with the sober impact of the Union blockade and its part in the final outcome of the war.

Geography itself reduced materially the magnitude of the job of enforcing the blockade, great though it was. The entire Southern coast from Virginia to the Rio Grande is fringed with a chain of low islands which produce an internal and intricate system of protected waterways. These waters were too shallow for seagoing ships and were restricted to small shallow draft craft. A large number of these were captured in the early months of the blockade, but because of the nature of the coastline the blockade concentrated mainly on the seaports. By the end of 1861 the only important ports available to the South, although they too were under blockade, were Wilmington, North Carolina, Charleston, South Carolina, Mobile, Alabama, New Orleans, and Galveston, Texas. Munitions and other goods run through the Texas ports were of benefit chiefly to the troops and forces in Texas because to reach other parts of the South they had to be hauled over long distances by mule team. Brownsville, Texas, was a very special case which will be discussed in some detail later. Most of Florida can be disregarded as, during the Civil War, the only developed part of that state was the northern belt. Key West remained in Union hands and was the base for the East Gulf Blockading Squadron.

Existing but incomplete Confederate customs records show that there was considerable shipping activity in 1861 after the proclamation of the blockade. For the first few months this seems to have been an unorganized rush to get as much goods as possible in and out before the blockade was tightened. Much of this traffic consisted of coastal runs and was not strictly blockade running, by which is meant trade with neutral ports. The voluntary Southern embargo on the export of cotton during this period served not only to reduce the volume of trade but also assisted in the establishment of the blockade.

In August 1861 Mr. Charles K. Prioleau, of Fraser, Trenholm and Company, the Confederate fiscal agent in Liverpool, decided to test the blockade by sending a suitable steamship to Charleston. It was loaded partly with cargo for the government and partly with private cargo for the parent company, Fraser and Company, of Charleston. For this experimental run an experienced local pilot was sent to Liverpool and the ship made the voyage without interference. It went to Savannah, however, instead of Charleston. There it was loaded with an outward cargo of cotton and ran safely back through the blockade. The object of the voyage had been to show that the blockade was not effective and thus encourage others to trade, but the run proved to be so profitable that Fraser and Company bought and operated a fleet of blockade runners of its own.

Encouraged by that demonstration, Commander Bulloch, in

Liverpool, bought the iron screw steamer *Fingal*, which was loaded with munitions and supplies for the Confederate Army and Navy. Bulloch himself sailed in the ship and ran into Savannah on November 12, just a few days after Du Pont seized Port Royal. It was planned to load her with cotton to be credited to the Navy account, and to run the blockade outward. But delays in collecting the cotton, caused by the already near chaotic condition of the railways, prevented her from being ready to sail until late December. By that time the port was closely blockaded, and in January Bulloch reported that Savannah was completely closed, with its approaches being covered by Union batteries. *Fingal* was then converted to the ironclad *Atlanta*, which was captured in June 1863, after a few shots by the monitor *Weehawken*.

With the fall of New Orleans the number of important Southern ports was reduced to three: Wilmington, Charleston, and Mobile. Geography made Wilmington the best suited for blockade runners. The town itself was inland on the Cape Fear River. Off the mouth of the river was Smith Island, and reaching to seaward of the river were the extensive Frying Pan Shoals. These features provided two channels from the river to the sea. The Western Bar Channel ran southwesterly and was covered near the entrance by Fort Caswell. New Inlet was the northeasterly channel and it was protected after 1862 by Fort Fisher. The distance by sea between the two channels was about fifty miles. That required two separate blockading groups or divisions, one to cover each channel. The loaded blockade runner could drop down to Smithville, now Southport, near the river mouth, observe both blockading divisions, and choose the channel which appeared to offer the better chance for a safe passage. Charleston also had more than one channel and the runners there had the protection of the network of forts guarding the entrance. Mobile had a single main channel but it too was well guarded by forts at the entrance.

In the first year of the war the tactics of blockade runner and blockader were amateurish, but in 1862 there developed the pattern of blockade running that was to flourish in 1863 and through most of 1864. The huge profits that trade with the South could provide became apparent early and this attracted English speculators. Profiteering Yankee dollars also found their way into the trade.

Suitable steamers were purchased, mainly in England. At first the ships were loaded in England and run directly across the Atlantic to the selected Southern port, but this method was soon replaced by a system of transshipment. Bermuda, about 675 miles from Wilmington and about 775 miles from Charleston, became one transfer center, while Nassau became the largest depot. It was about 515 miles from Charleston and about 570 miles from Wilmington. Havana was the principal depot for the Gulf ports. Halifax was another port sometimes used by the blockade runners. Large ships brought goods from England to these depot ports. There the cargo was loaded onto a blockade runner, which then ran into one of the Southern ports where the cargo was sold. The runner was then loaded with cotton, the main item of export, but also carried naval stores and some tobacco. This would be run out to a depot port, from which it was shipped to England, thus completing the cycle.

Except for the intention to run the blockade and the act of running through it, blockade running was not illegal so long as the ships were properly registered and otherwise met the shipping laws. The blockade runners, being merchant ships, were unarmed. Runners from Nassau usually cleared for Halifax and those from Bermuda for Nassau. No one was fooled by this device and British authorities overlooked some irregularities while British subjects were reaping the profits that the trade yielded.

Profit was the motive that built up the system of blockade running. The inbound cargoes consisted mainly of luxury goods—French wines, brandies, silks, and similar items which found a ready market in the South. The cargo was auctioned in the port and was bought up by speculators. Cotton, costing six to eight cents a pound, was then loaded for the outward run. It brought increasingly high prices in Nassau or Bermuda, from twenty-five cents to as much as a dollar a pound at one stage. Most of the blockade runners granted a portion of their cargo space to the Confederate government, but several public agencies found it necessary to own or have an interest in some of the ships. Greed often limited the amount of cargo space allotted to the government, but this was not put under strict regulation until early in 1864.

It soon became apparent that specially designed ships were desirable for this trade and the profits ran so high that ships were built for the sole purpose of blockade running. Although varying in detail, these ships had similar characteristics. Shallow draft was a first requirement, not over nine feet when loaded, to insure a safe passage over the sand bars in the harbor entrances. High speed was also a necessary feature. A speed of ten knots would enable a ship to outrun most of the blockading ships, but as time went on fourteen knots were needed, and some runners were built that could make up to eighteen knots. Another characteristic was a low silhouette; they had only short masts with a minimum of rigging to provide stations for lookouts. Most of them were painted light gray to reduce their visibility, a practice that was adopted by the navies of the world by the time of World War I. At first the Union Navy had very few ships that could match the runners' speed, but since some fast runners were captured from time to time, those suitable for the purpose were armed and converted to blockaders. By the end of the war some forty of these converted vessels were in service. Through these and other fast ships that were built during the war the blockaders were able to keep pace with the blockade runners.

Non-smoking coal was another requisite for the blockade

runners. The best coal for this purpose was Northern anthracite, but the Union banned the export of that coal early in the war. The next best was Welsh semi-anthracite, but even it was in short supply at times. The runners dreaded using Southern soft coal, which made heavy smoke.

More important than the ships were qualified captains and pilots. They had to be daring and resourceful men, but as the pay was very high for blockade running, the trade attracted some of the most venturesome seamen to be found. Ships owned by the Confederate government were usually commanded by naval officers. They proved to be among the best of the blockade runners, with an almost perfect record of success. The naval officers got no extra pay for this hazardous work but they did get paid in gold. English naval officers, on extended leave at half pay, were also attracted to this lucrative business. To evade their own neutrality laws they used assumed names, but some of them were discovered and reported to the British government.

From the outset most captains and pilots felt that attempting to run the blockade in moonlight was too risky. That cut the period for active running to about two thirds of each month. The procedure for running into Wilmington was typical and was used at the other ports, with modifications to meet local conditions. Getting inshore of the Gulf Stream well before dark, the captain got an accurate position for his ship and set a course direct for his selected channel, usually New Inlet, and timed his run to reach it in darkness on a flood tide. In the early days, when few blockading ships were on station, he would approach as close as possible without risking detection and then depend upon surprise to dash through the blockaders in the darkness. This might draw a few shots, but it was over so quickly that there was little actual risk. Later, as the number and alertness of the blockaders increased, more subtlety was required. A night landfall would be made well outside the line of blockading ships and then, taking advantage of the shallow draft, the ship would run just outside the line of breakers toward the protection and haven of the fort. The danger in this was that in case of early detection the alternative to surrender was to be driven ashore and destroyed. The century-old bones of blockade runners may still be seen, at very low tide, in some places along the Carolina beaches.

Captain John Wilkinson, one of the more successful blockade runners early in the war, noted in his *Narrative of a Blockade Runner* that if the blockading fleet had stationed its ships along the landward edge of the Gulf Stream, they would have made more captures than they did from their stations inshore at the inlets. This was finally recognized, but it was not until June 1864 that an outer patrol line of fast cruisers was established off Wilmington, stationed to intercept outbound runners at daylight. The number of captures increased sharply after that.

Since this was a clandestine business it is not possible to determine accurately how many of the specially designed ships were built for blockade running. Union records show that over 1,400 ships and craft were captured or destroyed while engaged in blockade running, 295 of them steamers. Some of these were regular steamships whose design fitted them for this work. Confederate customs records show that in 1861 there were twenty-one steamers engaged in running the blockade to Carolina ports, in 1862 there were forty-five, and in 1863 there were seventy-three. A notebook captured in a blockade runner in October 1863 listed seventy-five ships engaged in running the blockade, which for Civil War statistics shows a remarkable consistency. The year 1864 was the peak year when ninety-eight steamers were engaged in the trade. The number dropped to twenty-four in 1865. Taking into account the number captured or destroyed, the probability is that more than 200 ships were built especially for this purpose.

That is an impressive figure and it indicates how lucrative

the trade was. But the nature of these ships was such that even over a period of three years their combined carrying capacity was not high. *Bat*, captured on its first trip inbound in October 1864, was a typical blockade runner, as the design finally evolved. She was 230 feet long, had a beam of twenty-six feet, a draft of six and one half feet, and a speed of thirteen knots. Her maximum capacity was 850 bales of cotton, with much of it as deck load. Fantastic profits made such a small ship worthwhile, but the total volume of cargo carried by this type of vessel during the course of the war was only a fraction of prewar shipments.

ABUSES AND REGULATIONS

THE TREMENDOUS quick profits made in blockade running attracted a horde of speculators and adventurers. It was chiefly the English who took the initiative in building up the fleet of special blockade runners, and a number of English companies were formed to finance and operate the ships. By 1863 a successful run or two would return enough to pay for the ship and any further successes returned pure profit. It was the usual practice to pay a very high insurance premium for the first trip of a runner, to guard against total loss in case of capture, but once the cost of the ship was recovered, it was on its own.

The cost of operation ran high, reflecting in part at least the risk involved. A captain or pilot got as much as $5,000 in gold for a single round trip and a seaman received $150 per month with a bonus for a successful trip. Freight rates were correspondingly high, ranging from $300 to $1,000 per ton. By the middle of 1863, when organized blockade running was at or near its peak, the monthly expenses of a typical runner were about $80,000. If it made two successful round trips it stood to gain about $170,000 from cotton, other freight, and passengers.

With such large and fast profits as a motive, the inbound cargo consisted of goods which commanded the highest prices in Southern ports. The needs of the Confederacy became secondary except in the ships operated by Fraser and Company or those operated by or for the Confederate government. Since payment for the goods was demanded in gold or cotton, the blockade-running trade made a substantial contribution to the inflation which plagued the Confederate economy.

Nassau was the principal center for the trade. It was almost equidistant from Charleston and Wilmington, and with skilled Bahaman pilots on board, the runners could use inner channels and passages free from interference by Union cruisers. Nassau's docks and every other available space were piled high with cotton bales and other goods. There, as in Bermuda and Havana, the Confederate government had an agent who handled government-owned goods. There too, as in the other centers, the United States consul reported regularly on the activity, but every obstacle was thrown up to prevent his obtaining information. As the recipient of such sudden prosperity, it is no wonder that Nassau's sympathies were strongly with the South. Union cruisers hovered about the islands waiting to seize suspects, but when they came into or communicated with Nassau they were received with hostility. The British government made many usually justified complaints of Union vessels violating the neutrality of the Bahamas.

The normally quiet town of Wilmington was transformed by the trade. In addition to the speculators in search of a fast dollar, gamblers and other hangers-on descended on the city, ready to cut themselves in on the profits. Fights and murders were frequent and it was unsafe to go about at night. The agents and employees of the blockade-running companies lived luxuriously and drained the countryside of foodstuffs with their abundant supply of money. Many permanent residents rented their houses at high prices and moved out of town. Charleston, a much larger city, was less affected by this trade, and about the only commercial activity to be seen there in the middle of the war was at the warehouses where the weekly auctions of blockade goods were held.

The very high prices which the scarce goods brought denied them to all but the wealthy and those in favored positions. Visitors to Charleston or Fort Fisher during this time wrote of what was jokingly referred to as a "blockade dinner," with ample food and fine wines. In contrast to such glimpses of luxury the diaries of many Southern women reveal the hardships caused by the blockade; they mention doing over old dresses, weaving homespun cloth, or improvising substitutes for tea and coffee. These moving descriptions vividly reveal the lack of what had been normal daily necessities but which had not been produced in the South. Adequate supplies of such materials were simply not coming into the country and could not be found. One captain realized a fantastic profit on his own account from a chance shipment of a few boxes of common yellow soap.

The Confederate government made no systematic effort to export its own cotton until early in 1863 when it became necessary to bolster its credit and to straighten out its fiscal affairs. It was then that several government agencies, including the Army and Navy, bought their own blockade runners and obtained an interest in others. These ships were liable to the same neutrality restrictions as warships and their true ownership was concealed, usually by keeping them under nominal British register. The chaotic situation brought about through the encouragement of private blockade running also became a matter of concern. In the fall of 1863 the government required all blockade runners to allocate from one third to one half of their outbound cargo space to the government and a fair share of the return cargo space was also reserved for government account.

Under pressure of the need for further controls, the Confederate government imposed strict regulation upon the trade in February 1864. The importation of a long list of luxury goods, including alcoholic beverages, was forbidden. One half of the cargo on each outward and inward run was to be on government account and at rates fixed by the government. The export of cotton was put under strict regulation. It was a drastic law but it, or something similar to it, should have been in force long before. Confederate fiscal affairs did improve as a result of this law but, as with so many reforms that that government undertook, it came too late.

The new law created considerable indignation in Nassau and the other centers of blockade-running traffic. Some of the English companies threatened to withdraw from the trade rather than comply with it. Most of these threats were idle, as the quick profits still to be made kept most of them in the trade. Blockade running continued until the Confederate ports themselves were occupied by Union forces.

HOW TIGHT WAS THE BLOCKADE?

SOME HISTORIANS have taken the limited successes of the blockade runners as indicating that the Union blockade was not effective. The late Professor Frank L. Owsley, in his *King Cotton Diplomacy*, insisted that it was only a paper blockade that could be run easily and at little risk at any stage of the war.

Statistics on the cargoes of blockade runners brought into the Confederacy and descriptions of huge piles of cotton bales at Nassau are impressive but they also can be misleading. In its long struggle for European recognition and intervention in the war, the Confederate government and its agents constantly hammered on the theme that the Union blockade was only a paper one and that it was illegal because it did not effectively seal off the Southern ports. Their citing of statistics was a propaganda device to support that theme, but no volume of statistics could indefinitely conceal what happened within the Confederacy during the war.

The generation that lived through the prohibition era in the United States will understand the difficulty of assessing the true effectiveness of the blockade. Indeed there is much in common between the two blockades, if the effort to stop the importation of liquors during the Great Experiment can be classed as such. The rum runners of the 1920s displayed great ingenuity in evading the law and the traffic attracted an undesirable element of speculators and gangsters. The forerunner of the familiar naval landing craft of World War II was designed and built for rum runners in the Gulf of Mexico. No one knows how much illicit liquor was smuggled into the United States during prohibition, but genuine foreign liquors could be bought anywhere in the United States—for a price. That experiment demonstrated the impracticability of sealing off the United States to any product for which a sizable demand existed and for which adventurers were willing to take the risks necessary to supply that demand.

The demand for essential as well as luxury goods was far greater in the South during the Civil War than for liquor during prohibition. It was this demand and the huge profits to be made from satisfying it that attracted the speculators and produced the specialized blockade runner. Except for the naval officers who commanded the government-operated runners, there was little patriotic motive in this activity. Many of the boldest and most skillful captains succeeded in running the blockade repeatedly. Professor Owsley has listed twenty-two blockade runners that ran the blockade more than eight times. What he failed to note, however, was that twenty of the runners on his list tried it once too often. Seventeen of them were captured and three were destroyed by being run aground and burned. Of the two that survived, one was commanded by an English naval officer.

In June 1863 Mr. S. C. Hawley, United States consul at Nassau, reported that between March 10 and June 1 of that year there had been twenty-eight sailings from that port, of which thirteen were lost, eight being captured. He computed the average expectancy of a blockade runner to be about four and one half voyages. That seems to be a fair estimate for the period, but many of them were captured or destroyed on their first attempt. In September 1863 *Connecticut* captured the runner *Juno* outbound from Wilmington. It was standard practice in the runners when capture was imminent to throw all papers and mail overboard. In this case a personal letter from the purser was found on board. In it he said: "I consider it quite a farce to call it a blockade when a vessel can go in without being fired at." [1] In forwarding this letter Commander J. J. Almy, with obvious satisfaction, noted that its writer, on the day after his own capture, watched *Connecticut* chase ashore and destroy another runner. This "probably caused some change in his mind" about the blockade being a farce.

When Admiral Dahlgren moved his ironclads inside the bar off Charleston and maintained nightly picket patrols in the entrance to the harbor in 1863, blockade running practically ceased. Wilmington, with its favorable double entrance channels, then became the center of the traffic. In July 1864, when Rear Admiral S. P. Lee, commander of the North Atlantic Blockading Squadron, set up an outer patrol line of fast cruisers to intercept outbound runners at daylight and inbound runners before dark, there were thirty-two blockading ships off Wilmington. An inner line of shallow draft ships was

---

[1] ORN, Vol. 9, p. 214.

stationed as close to the forts as they could get safely. Their mission was to warn other ships, by means of rockets, of runners coming out. Farther to seaward was another line of ships stationed to intercept and chase the runners. Should a runner evade this line, it still had to pass through the distant line as well as evade other cruisers at sea or off the destination.

During the first year and a half of the blockade the risk of capture for a fast runner was not very great, but by 1863 there was a very real and definite risk in running the blockade. By then the Union Navy had ships with sufficient speed to catch most runners and the efficiency of the blockade improved with experience. Only constant alertness and expert ship-handling on the part of the runners prevented the capture of more of them. The accounts of the half-dozen blockade-running captains who wrote memoirs testify to the risk and to the skill and alertness needed at all times to avoid capture. As one chronicler has expressed it, the captains ". . . had to be men who could stand fire without returning it, [have the] cunning of a fox, the patience of Job, and the bravery of a Spartan warrior." [2]

Gideon Welles wisely concentrated the blockade off the important Southern ports. Schooners and other small craft ran the blockade throughout the war by using the inner waterways and making their runs offshore where there was no blockading ship. Most of the blockade runners captured were of this type but many of them made successful runs. In the aggregate, however, that traffic was of little importance. A schooner might carry out as few as six or eight bales of cotton, as many of those captured did. Such a run, if successful, might give an owner a good profit, but the total volume was too small to be of significance to the war effort.

One phase of the blockade received far more attention than its true importance warranted. Matamoras, Mexico, was across

---

[2] James Sprout, *Chronicles of the Cape Fear River* (Raleigh, North Carolina; 1916), p. 387.

the Rio Grande from Brownsville, Texas. Half of the mouth of the Rio Grande was Mexican territorial water and could not be blockaded. Like Nassau and Bermuda, Matamoras became a large depot for exchanging European goods for cotton. Unloaded at Matamoras, the goods were ferried across the river, but they faced a long haul by mule team before they could be of use to the Confederacy. Lieutenant Colonel Freemantle, of the Coldstream Guards, came through the blockade by this route, and he spent several months traveling through the South in 1863. His diary of this adventure has a vivid description of the trek from Brownsville to San Antonio. The great problem, aside from the uncertainty of supply of mule wagons, was scarcity of water. In April when he was in Texas, water was hard to find and it is obvious that in the dry season the wagon traffic between Brownsville and northern Texas towns was very uncertain if it existed at all. Brownsville was evacuated by the Confederates in June 1863, and occupied by Union troops early in November. They were withdrawn in August 1864, when Grant ordered the abandonment of operations in Texas, and the blockade off the Rio Grande was then resumed.

The chief beneficiaries of the trade through Matamoras were the cotton speculators in Texas. Munitions and other military supplies obtained through that port were useful to Confederate troops in Texas, but in the Civil War Texas was strategically unimportant. With the defeat of the South east of the Mississippi, Confederate activities in Texas could be expected to wither on the vine, and that is just what happened.

What gave Matamoras its prominence was the running dispute with England over the application of international law to ships bound for that port. The United States exploited the doctrine of "continuous voyage," that is, if a ship's cargo was ultimately destined for the Confederacy, its clearance for an intermediate neutral port did not protect the ship or cargo. One of the most celebrated cases, complicated by Welles's refusal to surrender the ship's mail, was that of *Peterhof*, seized off St. Thomas in January 1863. She was bound from London to Matamoras with a mixed cargo of articles in demand in the South. She was condemned by the prize court but the decision was modified four years later by the Supreme Court, and the United States had to compensate the owners. That was but one of the many disputes over the rights of neutrals in this trade, in which the cargoes, at least, were usually condemned.

England, as could be expected, strongly defended the rights of its shipping as a neutral, although she respected the decisions of the American courts. The United States, as a belligerent, defended its own right to search and seize ships operating under suspicious circumstances. In doing this she adopted and extended some of Britain's practices during the Napoleonic Wars—practices which the United States had then opposed. When England again became a belligerent in World War I she, in turn, seized upon and expanded American precedents established in the Civil War. The United States, again in the neutral role, hotly protested the British extensions.

The best index of the effect of the blockade on the South is what happened to the Southern economy. By insisting on being paid in gold for their imports, the blockade running companies helped to drain the Confederacy's slim gold reserves and reduced it to trade by barter, with cotton as the principal medium. But even the substantial amount of cotton run out through the blockade was but a fraction of the prewar exports. In 1860 the South exported well over 3,000,000 bales of cotton to Europe. Professor Owsley computed that in the years 1862, 1863, and 1864 over 1,000,000 bales of cotton (nearly double other estimates) made their way to Europe through the blockade. In other words, in each of those years cotton shipments were only about ten per cent of a prewar year. Cotton plantings were greatly reduced in the war years, and in April 1863 Jefferson Davis issued a plea for the people to grow food instead of cotton and tobacco. For this and other reasons there was much less cotton to export, but with the Southern economy geared to this staple, the Union blockade did deal it a crippling blow.

Not only cotton but the entire economy of the South was directly affected by the blockade. Ordinary necessities of life such as shoes, clothing, and housewares were unobtainable except at prohibitive prices. The high prices, of course, were due in part to the fiscal policy of the Confederate government in resorting to printing press money and allowing a runaway inflation, but every contemporary account of life in the South is filled with examples of shortages and improvisations. When we read of women substituting thorns for unobtainable steel needles, to cite one homely example, we can only admire the courage and stamina of the Southern people during this period.

In the early years of the war a substantial quantity of arms and ammunition was run through the blockade, and the Confederate Army was adequately armed, at least until the final few months of the war. The lion's share of the credit for this must go to Brigadier General Josiah Gorgas, Chief of Army Ordnance, who performed a miracle in this field by building and operating arsenals in the South. His diary reveals the difficulty of obtaining machinery and equipment and his concern whenever a blockade runner was lost.

In other respects the Confederate Army did not fare so well. As early as the Battle of Antietam in September 1862, many of Lee's soldiers were without shoes and not enough shoes could be obtained to meet their needs. Other items of equipment, such as uniforms and blankets, were also in short supply, and the shortages increased as time went on. In the final months Lee's troops were in rags and critical food shortages developed. Government-operated blockade runners were sent on emergency runs to bring in food for his army. One of Grant's first orders, after Lee's surrender at Appomattox, was for rations to be issued to Lee's half-starved soldiers.

Sole credit for the economic chaos that began to develop early in the war and increased as the war continued cannot, of course, be given to the Union blockade. Yet it should be recognized that it was the chief instrument for bringing about that condition, directly or indirectly. It was only after the South had been weakened internally through economic collapse that the Union armies began to gain the ascendancy over the armies led by Lee and the other Southern generals. Without the relentless pressure of Union sea power, distant and unseen though it was, that result could not have been achieved. The blockade was the active instrument of that sea power, and it was one of the major factors that brought about the ultimate collapse and defeat of the South.

The Confederate Navy made a gallant but futile effort to defeat the blockade. Its cruisers were very successful in driving Union shipping from the seas, but they did not succeed in drawing blockading ships away from Southern ports to search for them. A tremendous effort was put into building ironclads with which it was hoped to drive off the blockaders. The ironclads were genuinely feared by the Union ships and "ram fever" was a prevalent malady in the wooden ships assigned to the blockade. But for many reasons, most of them technical, the ironclads failed to live up to expectations and had no material effect on the blockade.

Chapter XIV

Mobile Bay

PRELIMINARIES

W HEN FARRAGUT was ordered to take New Orleans in January 1862, the order specifically mentioned the capture of Mobile as a follow-up measure. Circumstances kept him in the Mississippi and no early action against Mobile could be taken. It was second only to New Orleans as the South's largest cotton-exporting port before the war. Its early seizure would have dealt another crippling blow to the Confederacy and saved the Union many headaches that followed from the failure to do so.

After the capture of New Orleans Farragut was committed by Lincoln's own order to open the Mississippi, an operation that was frustrated by the Army's failure to cooperate by providing the troops necessary for taking Vicksburg and other key positions. For Farragut himself, Mobile remained high in priority, and he was prepared to move against that city when, in August 1862, he was told by Welles to defer action against Mobile and to insure the security of New Orleans. His hopes for early action were raised again in December of that year when Major General N. P. Banks, with 20,000 troops, arrived to relieve Butler, whose controversial administration of New Orleans had forced this change. Banks's zest for offensive action proved to be noticeably low and he was no more co-operative than Butler. Farragut was thus forced into the relative inaction of supervising the blockade of the western Gulf.

Blockading there was an even harder problem than off the Carolina ports. From Pensacola to the Rio Grande is about 600 miles, not counting the delta of the Mississippi. Behind this coast is an intricate network of inland waterways in which shallow draft craft, mostly schooners, could move safely to find an exit or inlet which was not covered by blockaders. Because of the shallow waters, steamers could use only three main ports, of which Galveston and Matamoras were too far distant from the center of military operations to be of material importance.

Mobile was by far the most important Gulf port used by the blockade runners. There, as off the Carolina ports, the runners were bold and ingenious, and their chances of success were about the same as those running from Bermuda and Nassau. Most of the blockade runners captured in the Gulf were small sailing craft, but a substantial number of steamers, using Havana as a depot port, were also taken. The monotony of the blockade was sometimes broken by a lighter moment. In October 1862 *Caroline* was captured after a six-hour chase off Mobile. When brought aboard *Hartford*, her captain protested vehemently to Farragut that he was not headed for Mobile but for Matamoras, as his clearance papers showed. To this fantastic claim the old admiral replied: "I do not take you for running the blockade but for your damned poor navigation. Any man bound for Matamoras from Havana and coming within twelve miles of Mobile Light has no business to have a steamer." [1]

---

[1] Reproduced by permission from Charles L. Lewis's *David Glasgow Farragut*. Copyright © 1943 by U.S. Naval Institute, Annapolis, Maryland. Vol. II, p. 145. A milder version is in Loyal Farragut: *The Life of David Glasgow Farragut* (New York; 1891).

After the fall of New Orleans the Confederates expected that Mobile would be next on the Union schedule and feverish efforts were made to strengthen its defenses. These, thanks to Farragut's inability to obtain Army assistance or approval for an early attack on the city, ultimately became quite formidable. The city itself was at the head of Mobile Bay, about twenty miles from the entrance to the bay. On a long tongue of land extending out from the mainland is Mobile Point, forming the eastern side of the entrance. On it stood the masonry Fort Morgan,[2] with forty-five guns, including those in a water battery outside the walls of the fort. On the eastern point of Dauphin Island, about three miles to the westward of Fort Morgan, was Fort Gaines with twenty-six guns. Guarding the entrance to Mississippi Sound, through Grant's Pass, was the unfinished Fort Powell, on a sandy island between an arm of Dauphin Island and the mainland.

After the loss of New Orleans Rear Admiral Franklin Buchanan was ordered to command the naval defenses of Mobile. To strengthen and improve the defenses of the bay he had obstructions, in the form of piling, placed from Fort Gaines eastward toward Fort Morgan. Off the row of piling, in deeper water, a mine field was also planted. This left only a narrow channel, 500 yards in total width, from the mine field to Fort Morgan.

At Selma, on the Alabama River, the Confederates built one of their largest naval stations, and in 1863 five warships were under construction there. Most important of these was the ironclad ram *Tennessee*, one of the most formidable craft built by the Confederate Navy. She was launched in February 1863, and taken to Mobile where her machinery, guns, and armor were installed. She was 209 feet in length, had a beam of forty-eight feet and a draft of fourteen feet. Her armored casemate, seventy-nine by twenty-nine feet, had six inches

---

[2] Now preserved in an Alabama State Park.

of iron armor and five inches elsewhere over two feet of solid wood. She had two 7⅛-inch pivot guns and four six-inch rifled guns.

Shortly after his capture of Vicksburg, Grant proposed that he attack Mobile with the help of the Navy. He thought that it would be an ideal base for operating deep in the South. Halleck vetoed the proposal, but Grant felt so strongly about the idea that he made two more requests, which were also refused. After Chattanooga he renewed his proposal and once again it was refused. In August 1863 Banks also proposed that he attack Mobile, but he was ordered to move into Texas instead.

With no hope for an operation against Mobile in the foreseeable future, Farragut took advantage of what was to be a lull in his campaign. After more than a year's active service most of his ships were badly in need of extensive repair. Seven of them were sent north for this purpose after the capture of Port Hudson, and Farragut himself arrived in New York in *Hartford* in the middle of August 1863.

In September, while he was conferring with Welles in Washington, a report came in from Commodore H. H. Bell, whom Farragut had left in command in the western Gulf, that he was co-operating with General Banks in an expedition to Sabine Pass, on the Texas-Louisiana border. Farragut read the report and predicted that the expedition would be a failure and would end in disaster, as too much was expected of the Navy. He proved to be an accurate prophet. Everything that could do so went wrong, and two of the four shallow draft gunboats taking part were captured, without one Union soldier being landed.

Delays in repairing *Hartford* and in filling out her crew kept her in New York until January 1864. A sense of urgency developed after December 20 when word was received in Washington, through a deserter from Mobile, that Buchanan intended to break through the blockade with *Tennessee* on

January 20. Farragut, in *Hartford*, left New York in a snowstorm on the afternoon of January 5 and arrived at Pensacola on the 17th.

There he found that the situation was not yet serious. He was given full reports on the progress of *Tennessee*, which was unable to get over a sand bar below Mobile, as her draft was two feet deeper than the water over the bar at high tide. Further reports told him of two other ironclads under construction, similar to but smaller than *Tennessee*. Neither was completed, and a third ironclad, which was started by the state of Alabama at the beginning of the war and then turned over to the Confederate Navy, had a hull so rotten as to be unserviceable. Besides *Tennessee* Buchanan had only three wooden gunboats, converted from river steamers.

Up to this time Farragut had been scornful of ironclads and their power, but now, faced with an imminent meeting with one, he too had a touch of "ram fever." He asked Welles for monitors and also asked Porter for two of the Eads-built river monitors from the Mississippi. He reported that he would not attempt to operate against Mobile until he was reinforced. No troops would be available for some time, as General Banks was then planning an expedition up the Red River to Shreveport. On one of his visits to New Orleans Farragut learned of Sherman's plan to attack toward Atlanta. With the belief that a feint attack on Mobile's defenses might keep troops from being sent against Sherman, he ordered a bombardment of Fort Powell. This had the desired effect, for Major General D. H. Maury, commanding at Mobile, immediately asked for reinforcements. The bombardment was kept up for two weeks but ended abruptly with the reported appearance of *Tennessee* in the lower bay. This proved to be a false alarm, but it showed the jittery feeling that existed about the ironclad. Farragut reported that he himself had identified the ship, but *Tennessee* was still above the bar and could not be seen from outside the bay.

When Grant assumed command of the Union armies in the spring of 1864 he developed a broad plan of operations. On the assumption that Banks's expedition up the Red River would be short and successful, he directed Banks to move against Mobile. Sherman was told of this order early in April and he was pleased, because if Banks could open the Alabama River, that would go far to solve his future supply problem. At the end of March Grant ordered Banks to abandon operations in Texas and to concentrate all his efforts on Mobile. But the expedition up the Red River in April and May 1864 turned into a severe defeat for Banks and he never did move against Mobile.

During the night of May 17 Buchanan succeeded in getting *Tennessee* over the bar and into the lower bay. His plan was to run through the blockade the same night and capture Fort Pickens and Pensacola. The ship ran hard aground in the lower bay after crossing the bar and was discovered by the blockaders the next morning. Anxious days passed, but Buchanan made no further move. He seemed to have been overawed by the number of ships that Farragut had assembled and to have believed that an attack on the Mobile defenses was imminent. He dropped all pretense of offensive action to prepare for the expected blow. Although he was criticized in some quarters for his inaction, his gallant if futile later action erased whatever resentment there may have been against him.

Farragut's reports of the appearance of *Tennessee* in the lower bay produced prompt action in Washington. Gideon Welles ordered the monitor *Manhattan*, then fitting out in New York, to proceed at once to the Gulf. Similar orders for the monitor *Tecumseh*, then in the James River, followed. Welles also ordered Porter to send river monitors to Farragut. Porter protested that his monitors were not seaworthy and not suited to Farragut's purpose, but he finally did send *Winnebago* and *Chickasaw* on the way. Early in June Sherman asked Major General E. R. S. Canby, in command in western Mississippi, to make a feint at or, even better, to attack Mobile in conjunction with Farragut.

These measures were as yet unknown to Farragut as he prepared to meet the immediate threat posed by the Confederate ironclad. He believed that Buchanan was waiting for a dark night and smooth sea to sortie, and on June 14 he issued orders to meet that contingency. He then had seventeen ships off Mobile, including four big sloops of war. But Buchanan was also waiting for Farragut's attack, which he expected at any moment. Thus a naval stalemate developed off Mobile that was to last for the next month and a half. General Canby, who superseded Banks in May, came over from New Orleans to confer with Farragut about future operations against Mobile and promised to furnish troops for that purpose.

Knowing by then that monitors were on the way to reinforce him, Farragut waited for their arrival before launching his attack. The first monitor arrived at Pensacola on July 8 and that was the signal for him to prepare his ships in earnest for the attack. He planned to use the same tactics he had used in earlier runs past fortifications. Each large wooden ship would have a smaller gunboat moored on the off side while running past Fort Morgan, as was done at Port Hudson. The ships removed nonessential gear and rigging. Anchor chains were ranged along the exposed side to protect the machinery and sand bags were used to give added protection wherever it was thought desirable. The armored monitors were to run past the fort in a separate column.

Major General R. S. Granger, assigned to command local Army operations, arrived off Mobile on August 1, and 2,400 troops arrived the next day. These were all that could be spared at the time, for General Canby had been ordered to send reinforcements to the Army of the Potomac. It was agreed that the troops should be landed on Dauphin Island and from there prepare to invest Fort Gaines. Seven gunboats were assigned to cover the troops which landed during the afternoon of August 3.

Farragut then had three monitors in company. The two river craft each had two turrets with two eleven-inch guns in each turret. *Manhattan* had a single turret with two fifteen-inch guns. *Tecumseh*, similar to *Manhattan*, was then at Pensacola getting last-minute voyage repairs. Farragut postponed his attack on her account, but on August 4 he announced that the attack would be made the next day. That afternoon *Tecumseh* arrived to complete his force of monitors.

THE BATTLE OF MOBILE BAY

AUGUST 5 produced ideal conditions for Farragut. There was an early-morning flood tide that would carry damaged ships past the fort into the bay. There was also a southwesterly wind to carry the smoke of battle into the eyes of Fort Morgan's gunners. Every ship was ready and each captain knew exactly what was expected of him. Farragut wanted to lead the main column himself in *Hartford*, but he yielded to the advice of his captains who felt that *Brooklyn* was better suited to lead. She was the only ship with four bow chaser guns and she had a minesweeping device on her bowsprit.

The main column for running past the fort consisted of seven large ships, each with a gunboat moored to her port side. To the right was the column of four monitors, led by *Tecumseh*. Four gunboats took station southeast of Fort Morgan and six others were stationed off Fort Powell to block Grant's Pass. The squadron got under way at about 5:30 a.m. and headed for the entrance without confusion or incident. At about 6:30 the leading monitors opened fire on the fort, which did not reply at once. Half an hour later Fort Morgan opened fire on *Brooklyn*, beginning the general engagement. Each large ship opened fire as she came within range and the action gradually developed into a general battle.

Smoke soon obscured the scene from on deck and Farragut climbed into the port main rigging to have better visibility. Fearing that he might have a bad fall if wounded, Captain Drayton of *Hartford* sent a quartermaster aloft to pass a line around the admiral and secure him to the rigging. This much-publicized incident was merely a safety precaution while Farragut was in an exposed position where he had a better view of what was going on. The pilot was also in the main top for the same reason, and he had a voice tube to the captain on deck.

Everything went exactly as planned until about 7:30 when *Brooklyn* reported that the monitors were ahead of her and fouling her track. What developed was really caused by *Tennessee*, followed by Buchanan's three gunboats. The iron-clad was steaming down the bay just clear of the mine field and headed for the column of wooden ships. Commander T. A. M. Craven, in *Tecumseh*, noted *Tennessee*'s approach and gallantly put his rudder over to head directly for her. This change of course, instead of keeping the ship on a track between the buoy marking the eastern end of the mine field and Fort Morgan, took it just inside the field. *Tecumseh* struck a mine and sank within two minutes, taking ninety-three of her crew, including Commander Craven, with her. There were only twenty-one survivors.

Brooklyn also got off the intended track, for shortly after *Tecumseh* was sunk, suspicious objects were reported in the water ahead of her. Captain Alden backed his engine to avoid them. Farragut, from his post in the rigging, saw all of this and instantly made the decision to continue the run, with *Hartford* in the lead, which he had wanted to do from the first. In the confusion the fire of his ships slackened while that of Fort Morgan increased in accuracy and intensity. As

Hartford passed *Brooklyn*, the latter reported that there was a line of torpedoes (mines) across the ship's track.

The famous slogan, "Damn the torpedoes, full speed ahead," was not attributed to Farragut until fourteen years after the event. There are several versions of just what he said and did at this time. That an oral order from his position in the rigging could be heard on deck through the din of battle is doubtful. What is certain is that by order, gesture, or in some form the spirit of that command was transmitted and *Hartford* led the column into Mobile Bay. While he had waited for the arrival of the monitors, Farragut had had night reconnaissances made of the mine field. No mines were found, and he decided that if any were there, they were probably inactive from being in the water so long. He therefore decided to take the risk and lead the column directly across the field. It was a courageous and bold decision to make, but it paid off handsomely, as no ship in his formation struck a mine, or at least none was exploded. By his firm and quick decision the momentum of running past the fort was not lost.

Fort Morgan, *Tennessee*, and the three gunboats maintained a heavy fire on the Union ships as they steamed past. They were hit repeatedly but only *Oneida* was seriously damaged. She was the last ship in the column and a shot from Fort Morgan exploded her starboard boiler, but she continued into the bay. *Tennessee* tried to ram *Hartford*, but she evaded the attempt through superior speed and maneuverability. *Hartford* fired a salvo at the ram at point-blank range, only to watch the shots bounce harmlessly off her armor. *Tennessee* also tried to ram *Brooklyn*, now second in the column, and then engaged each of the large ships as it passed.

When out of range of Fort Morgan, Farragut had the gunboat alongside *Hartford* cast off to chase a Confederate gunboat that was holding a position ahead of the column and firing accurately into it. Other gunboats followed suit, and within a short time all of Buchanan's gunboats were accounted for. *Selma* was captured by *Metacomet*, Lieutenant Commander J. E. Jouett commanding. When Lieutenant P. U. Murphey of *Selma* came aboard to surrender, he drew up before his old friend to say: "Captain Jouett, . . . the fortunes of war compel me to tender you my sword." Jouett would have no part of such formality and replied: "Pat, don't make a damned fool of yourself. I have had a bottle on ice for you for the last half hour." [3] Another gunboat was beached in a sinking condition and the third took refuge at Fort Morgan. It escaped to Mobile that night.

Farragut ordered *Hartford* to anchor about four miles northwest of Fort Morgan at about 8:35 and the other ships started to conform. It was his intention for the crews to have breakfast and then prepare to destroy *Tennessee*, which remained near Fort Morgan. He planned to go himself in *Manhattan* to make a night attack with the three monitors. Buchanan saved him the trouble, for at about 8:45 *Tennessee* was seen to be under way and headed for Farragut's squadron. Recalling the furor that rose over the way in which *Merrimack* was lost in 1862, Buchanan felt that he had to attack. Farragut sent a dispatch boat to round up the monitors, which were to the eastward, with orders for them to attack the ram. Signals flew wide and fast for ships to get under way and attack, with the larger ships ordered to ram the ironclad. As Farragut reported: "Then began one of the fiercest naval battles on record."

Buchanan hoped to surprise Farragut's ships, but they were too alert for that as they converged for the attack. *Monongahela* was the first to ram *Tennessee* but did more damage to herself than to the ironclad. *Lackawanna* crushed her stem in ramming. When *Hartford* closed in, Farragut again went into the rigging and was again lashed to it. An aide stood nearby with a drawn revolver to pick off any sniper in *Tennessee*

---

[3] J. M. Morgan and J. P. Marquand: *Prince and Boatswain*, (Greenfield, Mass.; 1915), p. 104.

who might try to shoot the admiral. *Hartford* struck a glancing blow, and as she was preparing for another try at ramming, she was rammed by *Lackawanna*. That was too much
for Farragut. Turning to an Army Signal Corps officer who
was on board to facilitate signaling between the ship and
troops ashore, he asked: "Can you say 'for God's sake' by
signal?" Given an affirmative answer, Farragut ordered:
"Then say to the *Lackawanna* 'For God's sake get out of our
way and anchor.' " [4]

Tennessee was rammed four times but as her casemate
construction was continued well below the waterline, the
principal damage was suffered by the Union ships that rammed
her. Gunshots at point-blank range did no more than dent
her armor.

While this hot and furious fighting at close range was going
on, the monitors joined in the attack. *Manhattan*'s fifteen-inch
guns proved to be the only ones that could penetrate the
ram's armor. One of her shots let daylight into the casemate
but did not fully penetrate to the interior of the ship. The
hero of the occasion, if any could be singled out, was Lieutenant Commander George H. Perkins in *Chickasaw*. He
placed his monitor directly astern of *Tennessee* and doggedly
held that position while his eleven-inch guns fired at the after
side of the casemate at a range of less than fifty yards. The ram
took a battering there, with the casemate structure weakened and gun port shutters jammed. Buchanan was wounded
by a salvo that hit when he was examining the damage in that
part of the ship.

A fatal weakness in the construction of *Tennessee* was that
the tiller chains to her rudder head were exposed in open
channels on the flat afterdeck. Shots from the monitors carried these chains away, as well as the relieving tackle that was
rigged to replace them. With his ship then helpless to steer,

---

[4] *Battles and Leaders*, Vol. IV, p. 397.

her captain, Commander J. D. Johnston, asked Buchanan's permission to surrender, which was done at about 10 o'clock.

Thus, in little more than three hours' time, Farragut was in control of lower Mobile Bay. It was a magnificent victory by any standard, and it was entirely Farragut's, for at this time the troops ashore had taken no part in the battle. The hopelessly outclassed Confederate ships made a gallant effort, but the result was a foregone conclusion.

In running past Fort Morgan and in the engagement with *Tennessee* Farragut's squadron suffered fifty-two killed and 170 wounded, not counting those lost in *Tecumseh*. A supply ship which tried to follow the warships through the channel against orders was disabled by a shot from Fort Morgan, grounded, and later burned by the Confederates. The Confederate losses were surprisingly light—twelve killed and twenty wounded. Fort Morgan had only one killed and three wounded.

The forts still blocked free access to Mobile Bay and Farragut wasted no time in tackling that problem. Five gunboats bombarded Fort Powell while the main squadron was running past Fort Morgan, and in the afternoon *Chickasaw* was sent to bombard it from the rear. Its commander decided that his position was untenable and he received permission from Fort Gaines to evacuate the fort. During the night the guns were spiked and the garrison was evacuated to the mainland without loss. Time charges blew up the fort, and the way was opened for Union supply vessels to enter the bay from Mississippi Sound.

Fort Gaines was next on the schedule. In the afternoon of August 6 *Chickasaw* and the gunboats opened a bombardment of this fort, which did not make a spirited reply. Very early the next morning a flag of truce was carried to *Hartford* to ask for the terms of surrender. Brigadier General R. L. Page, who was also a commander in the Confederate Navy and who commanded Fort Morgan, sensed that something was wrong and signaled orders to hold Fort Gaines. Getting no reply, he went to that fort by boat late in the afternoon to find that its commander was on board *Hartford* signing the surrender. He ordered the fort to be held and relieved its commander of his command on the spot, but it was too late; the fort was surrendered. The conduct of both subordinate commanders was severely criticized in Confederate circles, but with the perspective of time it appears that they may have used better judgment in a hopeless situation than did General Page.

To a joint demand for the surrender of Fort Morgan, General Page replied that he would hold out as long as he had the power to resist. Farragut and Granger then arranged that the troops would be landed about three miles east of Fort Morgan, from which position they would invest the fort on the land side, co-ordinating their attack with the ships'.

While the troops were getting ashore and preparing their positions, Farragut had his ships and monitors keep up a slow bombardment of the fort, beginning on August 9. This consisted of lobbing a few shots into the fort at regular intervals night and day. It was intended to harass and divert the garrison rather than as a serious effort to subdue the fort. Ironically, *Tennessee* was towed into position and joined in the bombardment. Fort Morgan answered this bombardment with spirited fire from time to time, and it was especially attentive to *Tennessee*.

By August 21 General Granger had his artillery, mortars, and troops in position for the assault. Farragut then stationed his ships so that Fort Morgan literally was surrounded by land and sea. At daylight on August 22 a very intense co-ordinated bombardment began and was continued around the clock. The power and effect of this bombardment soon became apparent. The walls of the fort were breached in several places, wooden buildings were set on fire, and all but two of its guns were knocked out. When a fire threatened the powder magazine during the evening, General Page had his entire powder supply wetted down. By daylight August 23 he had taken enough battering and raised the white flag. The fort was formally surrendered unconditionally the same afternoon.

The outstanding feature of these operations in Mobile Bay was the close co-operation between the Army and Navy commanders. Farragut, of course, had wanted to make this attack for two years, but he had been unable to get approval or the necessary troops until now. When General Canby relieved Banks, he became an enthusiastic supporter of Farragut, and the only reason he did not furnish more troops than he did was that his command had been stripped to reinforce Grant in northern Virginia. He also had to contain Confederate troops west of the Mississippi, as well as maintain the security of New Orleans.

AFTERMATH

FIRM POSSESSION of the lower part of Mobile Bay meant that the Union Navy's mission in the Gulf was, for practical purposes, completed. Mobile was sealed off as a port for blockade runners and the blockade there became absolute. Farragut wanted to occupy the city as a matter of prestige, but he believed that 20,000 troops would be required to accomplish this and he knew that they were not available. While his ships were harassing Fort Morgan, in preparation for the final attack, he made a personal reconnaissance up the bay with some light gunboats and monitors. He found that he could not get within two miles of the forts protecting the city itself because of shoals and obstructions. The Confederates sank the unfinished ironclad *Nashville* across the main channel, which sealed off the approach to the city in the western side of the bay.

Farragut's health was failing during the operations in Mobile Bay, and late in August he advised Welles of his condition, hinting that he be allowed to go north for a rest. Before this letter reached Washington new orders were on their way to him. For more than two years Welles and Fox had wanted to seize the defenses of the Cape Fear River in order to deny Wilmington to blockade runners. They were unable to do anything about this for the usual reason that they could not get the necessary troops assigned. By the late summer of 1864, however, the Army became interested in Wilmington and Grant promised to provide troops for an operation against Fort Fisher. Rear Admiral S. P. Lee, commanding the North Atlantic Blockading Squadron, had no experience in this type of operation and Welles and Fox wanted a naval commander who had proven himself. Grant also lacked confidence in Lee.

At Fox's urging, but without consulting Farragut, Welles ordered him to Beaufort to relieve Lee, to arrive there by the end of September. Farragut received this order only nine days before he was required to be in Beaufort. Understandably irked by the receipt of such an order out of a clear sky, he objected to the plan outlined to him. He insisted that it would not work and reported that he felt unequal to the task; it was then given to Rear Admiral David D. Porter.

In the same letter he reported that General Canby expected to be ready to move against Mobile itself in the near future and expressed the hope that he would be allowed to finish the job in Mobile Bay. But Canby was kept busy in Arkansas and Missouri, and the expected troops did not materialize. In fact there was to be no change or activity in Mobile Bay for several months. With nothing but inaction in sight, Farragut left his old command early in December and arrived in New York on December 15, ending his active war service.

In January 1865 Grant finally ordered Canby to move against Mobile. As early as the preceding September Canby had outlined to Farragut his ideas for taking the city. He proposed to move up the eastern side of the bay and to secure a lodgement on the Alabama River. He believed that this would force the abandonment of Mobile. Now, ordered to move and with adequate troops available, he revived this plan. He would be supported by the Navy, now under the command of Rear Admiral H. K. Thatcher. Naval support could not, however, be provided on the western side of the bay, where the forts protecting Mobile were considered to be much stronger than those to the eastward.

The head of Mobile Bay consists of a delta with several rivers and channels formed from the confluence of the Tombigbee and Alabama Rivers. The easternmost of these short rivers are the Blakely and Tensas, on which were two principal forts and some lesser batteries guarding the approaches to Mobile. Operations against these forts began on March 21 when, convoyed by gunboats, General Canby's troops were landed about seventeen miles from the mouth of the Fish River, which flows into the eastern side of the bay. They moved overland and assaulted Spanish Fort, the strongest of the defenses. Some very heavy fighting occurred there before the fort was evacuated on April 8. Fort Blakely was abandoned on April 11 and Mobile was evacuated the next day. It was then occupied by Union forces on the same day, three days after Lee's surrender at Appomattox. General Canby used about 45,000 troops in this operation.

Admiral Thatcher's gunboats and monitors were active throughout the campaign, bombarding shore positions and covering troops movements. They paid a heavy price through losses to mines. The various channels and rivers were swept and reported clear, but either some mines were missed or the Confederates succeeded in laying new ones at night. On March 28, after shelling Spanish Fort, the river monitor *Milwaukee* struck a mine while withdrawing and was sunk. The next day another turreted ironclad, *Osage*, was sunk at the edge of the channel. On April 1 the tinclad *Rodolph* was sunk by a mine while towing a barge with equipment for raising

Milwaukee. Subsequent to the occupation of Mobile a gunboat, two tugs, and two launches were lost to mines.

Just why the attack on Mobile was launched so late in the war is something of a mystery. When Grant ordered it taken, Sherman was already on his way across the Carolinas from Savannah, and the possession of Mobile, other than for prestige, could have had no influence upon the outcome. Its value to the Confederacy was lost when the entrance to Mobile Bay was secured by Farragut nine months earlier. In his *Memoirs* Grant acknowledged this. In commenting on its capture he noted that he had wanted to take it for two years but regretted that the effort was made only when it was too late to matter.

Chapter XV

Operations on the Western Rivers

July 1863–December 1864

TRADE AND PATROLS

IN JULY 1861 a Federal law was enacted prohibiting trade with citizens of the South except as the President might prescribe under regulations prepared by the Treasury Department. When Southern territory was occupied by Union forces in the Mississippi Valley, a brisk and largely illicit trade rapidly developed in that region. From mid-1862 onward, Grant, Sherman, Buell, and others complained of this activity, but they were unable to get any real corrective action. Lincoln and Secretary Chase believed that the people in "liberated" territory should be permitted to trade for the necessities of life and other goods which were otherwise unavailable to them. Their motive in this may have been good, for it was an effort to obtain good will for the Union, but the abuses far outweighed the gains, and no one could keep munitions and other illegal goods from flowing through the lines into Confederate-held territory.

As with the blockade runners, cotton was the magnet. Cotton, bought for a few cents a pound in the South, returned a huge profit in New England. Speculators descended on the region, bent on quick profits. Medicines, clothing, shoes, and other goods were in tremendous demand throughout the South. On one occasion in 1862 Sherman reported to Grant that individual farmers were coming into Memphis with single bales of cotton and pleading to be allowed to dispose of them so that they would be able to buy necessities. Sherman was so moved by these pleas that he relaxed the regulations for them.

It was the speculators who created the abuses and flouted the law. Greed won over scruple. These traders supplied whatever items were in greatest demand, including munitions, which were smuggled into the Confederacy. The military commanders were convinced that not only were the guerrillas, who were very active along the rivers, armed and equipped through the illicit trade, but also the Confederate armies on both sides of the Mississippi. The situation got so far out of hand that in March 1863 Congress enacted a new law regulating trade. Lincoln then issued a new proclamation authorizing citizens in the South, loyal to the Union, to ship out cotton to designated ports in Federal possession: Beaufort, North Carolina, Port Royal, Key West, and New Orleans. The authorized trade was to be conducted under the supervision of the Treasury Department. The War and Navy Departments were directed to co-operate with the Treasury in handling the trade. In compliance with this, Admiral Porter, commanding the Mississippi Squadron, issued orders to his gunboats to assist in the observance of the new regulations, but they were not to interfere with the trade except to prevent violations. After the fall of Vicksburg and Port Hudson and the opening of the Mississippi, the illicit trade increased rapidly all along the river.

Under the new regulations the loyal citizen could obtain a permit from a Treasury agent to ship out his cotton and he would then be permitted to buy limited supplies for his family needs from the proceeds. But speculators had no trouble in obtaining permits from the Treasury agents to pick up cotton on their own account, and open charges of connivance on the part of the agents were made by military and naval observers. Since large quick profits were to be made in this trade, there were, no doubt, grounds for such charges. In October 1863 the Treasury regulations were modified to permit Army officers commanding districts and posts to endorse permits for taking out cotton. After this, suspicion grew that some of these officers were secretly engaged in the cotton trade, and the nature and volume of permits issued by some of them gives some credence to those suspicions. Whatever was the true situation in this respect, more cotton reached the North than England received by the blockade runners.

There was little that the Navy could do about the practice, for the Treasury regulations did not include naval participation in controlling the trade. Porter maintained vigorously that his officers and ships had a clean bill of health. In a few cases, when one of his commanders was caught communicating with the shore under suspicious circumstances, Porter relieved him at once. His gunboats were not averse to seizing cotton, but it was all sent to Cairo, Illinois, and delivered to the district attorney for adjudication in the courts. Porter maintained that all of the cotton seized by the gunboats was either the property of the Confederate government or of known supporters of that government, making it legitimate contraband. In his *Incidents and Anecdotes*, however, he tells a yarn implying that the crews of the gunboats had stencils reading "C S A," the marking for government-owned cotton. In his *Memoirs* Rear Admiral T. O. Selfridge freely admits that his crew made "C S A" stencils. It is obvious that many a bale of privately owned cotton was transferred to government ownership by means of the stencils and was taken on board a gunboat to be sent north. To cover questionable cases Porter ordered that a reserve of cotton be held at Cairo to satisfy the claims of loyal citizens.

The worst feature of the trade was that the South was being

supplied with all sorts of contraband of a military nature, and by 1864 the situation was of scandalous proportions. Porter had standing orders for his gunboats to be alert for traders landing contraband and to seize any steamer found doing so. But his gunboats could not be everywhere and their interference, mild though it was, was not welcome. When guerrillas captured, looted, and burned a trading steamer in Arkansas, he issued an order that no trader was to land to load cotton unless under the protection of a gunboat. This order was openly flouted. Whenever the gunboats seized a craft caught disregarding the order, the seizure was vigorously protested by the Treasury agent or the Army commander who had issued the trading permit. Unless it could be proved that contraband was involved, the steamer had to be released.

The abuses became so widespread that in May 1864 Major General C. C. Washburn, then commanding the Memphis district, ordered that no boat could land between Cairo and the White River except where there was an Army garrison. He also closed the lines at Memphis. People could come into Memphis from the countryside but no one could leave the city, except by river, without a special pass from his headquarters. At the same time he reported his opinion that "Memphis has been of more value to the Southern Confederacy since it fell into Federal hands than Nassau." [1]

Others expressed similar convictions. Sherman complained that Cincinnati was furnishing more contraband to the South than Charleston. Major General D. E. Sickles, on a special observation mission for Lincoln, advised him from Memphis at about this same time that all trade behind the lines should be interdicted. He estimated that before General Washburn issued his order restricting Memphis, goods to the value of $500,000 a week passed through the lines there in exchange for currency and cotton. A little later General Canby at New Or-

---

[1] ORA, Vol. 39, part iii, p. 22.

leans reported to Stanton that he had reliable evidence that New Orleans contributed more to the Confederate effort than any other port except Wilmington.

The effect of all this on the Navy was demoralizing, for the gunboat captains saw what was going on but could do very little to stop the trade. Often one of them would seize a suspicious vessel only to have its release ordered summarily. Porter backed his officers as best he could, and his complaints to the Navy Department increased in vigor and bitterness. He had to use the gunboats to protect legitimate trade, and as guerrillas were active along the rivers, they also had to be dealt with.

One revealing incident aroused the indignation of Lieutenant F. S. Hill, commanding *Tyler*. He reported in November 1864 that he had received reliable reports that some Confederate Army officers were at a plantation in Arkansas, near Island No. 68. In the dead of night he landed a party to seize them. The party surrounded the house and Negro quarters without giving an alarm. The house was thoroughly searched but the quarry was not found. They had thoughtfully chosen to stay in the stable, a fact which was not noticed by the raiding party until too late. Hill was presented to a lady who proved to be the mother of two of the officers he was after. She showed him a permit to ship out some cotton and demanded that his gunboat cover and protect the loading of the cotton. The permit was duly signed by the Treasury agent in Memphis and countersigned by General Washburn. A steamer was at hand to load the cotton and he had no choice but to comply with the standing orders but, as he expressed it, "with very bad grace."

Still another headache to the squadron was protecting the supplying of leased plantations. The Federal government had called for planters to go south to operate the abandoned plantations along the rivers. These were leased to the planters and were under Treasury supervision. Thus, when he issued an order supporting General Washburn's order that goods could be landed only at Army posts, Porter received a strong protest from the Agent for Plantations at Natchez, who pointed out that if the new order was carried out, his leased plantations could not be supplied. Porter had to modify his order to meet that objection.

New regulations to broaden and tighten the trade were issued in 1864 but the basic pattern was unchanged. Most observers placed the blame for the extensive illicit trade on the Treasury regulations and the Treasury agents appointed to administer them. In a letter to Sherman in October 1863 Porter complained of the conduct of the Treasury agents and concluded that "A greater pack of knaves never went unhung." [2] Porter could exaggerate on occasion, but in this instance his opinion was shared by the top Army commanders in the region. On another occasion Porter criticized the laxity in issuing permits. Manifests were worthless in checking shipments when, as he pointed out, a permit to land "several packages" could cover almost anything.

The highest military and naval commanders condemned the laxity in controlling the illicit trade, and there is no evidence that any of them, with the possible exception of Butler at New Orleans, made a personal profit from this trade. As the naval commander, Porter got the admiral's share of prize money received for condemned cotton, but that was a legitimate reward.

THE RED RIVER EXPEDITION

IN THE SUMMER of 1863 Lincoln and Seward became deeply concerned about developments in Mexico where Napoleon III was about to establish an empire with Maximilian on

---

[2] ORN, Vol. 25, p. 521.

the throne. They decided that it was necessary to display the Union flag in Texas and Lincoln so ordered. In August Halleck directed Banks, at New Orleans, to move into Texas. He warned Banks not to divide his forces and advised against taking Galveston or other coastal points. The best approach, he felt, was up the Red River to Alexandria and Shreveport, Louisiana, from where a drive could be made into Texas. Banks found too many obstacles in this approach and preferred to move against the Texas coast. The ill-fated attack at Sabine Pass in September was the result of this decision. In November Banks sent an expedition which occupied Brownsville and other key points south of Galveston.

Early in 1864 the idea of moving up the Red River was revived. Sherman believed that it would help to clean out Confederate forces in Arkansas and Louisiana. As the plan finally evolved in January, Banks, with the help of the Navy, was to move against Shreveport. His command was reinforced by a corps from Sherman's army and the attack was to be coordinated with one by Major General Frederick Steele from Arkansas. By March preparations were completed, and General Banks informed Porter that he intended to be at Alexandria on March 17. Heavy rains then delayed his departure for several days.

By March 7 Porter assembled, for this expedition, fifteen ironclads and four other gunboats at the mouth of the Red River. On the 11th he was joined by the corps from Sherman's army under Brigadier General A. J. Smith. Early the next morning the gunboats started up the river with the transports following. The first major obstacle was Fort de Russy, a few miles below Alexandria. The ironclad *Eastport* and several gunboats were sent ahead to remove obstacles in the river while part of the troops were landed about thirty miles below the fort to drive back an outpost. Late in the afternoon of March 15 *Eastport* and *Neosho*, after breaching the obstacles, reached the fort just as General Smith's troops were surrounding it after a fast march overland. Most of the Confederate troops in the vicinity escaped, but the fort itself was captured after a short fight.

Porter sent his fastest gunboats toward Alexandria in an effort to head off the retreating Confederates, but they arrived as the last of the transports evacuating the city passed through the rapids just above the city. Alexandria was occupied on the 16th. Banks's troops did not arrive until ten days later, and Porter kept the gunboats busy by having some of them round up cotton in the vicinity.

The naval part of the expedition started up the river on April 2, after Porter ran thirteen of his gunboats through the rapids with considerable difficulty. As the gunboats steamed upriver they were followed by a group of transports with a division of troops embarked. Banks's main column moved along roads near the river. Trouble was expected at Grand Ecore, about midway between Alexandria and Shreveport, but when Porter's force reached that point, the works were found to be abandoned and it was occupied without opposition on April 3. At about the same time Banks's main force reached Natitoches, near Grand Ecore.

With six of the smallest gunboats Porter then moved up the river on April 7, escorting twenty transports with troops which were to land at Springfield Landing three days later. By that time, it was expected, the main body of troops would be at Springfield. Porter reached the landing on schedule. He would have continued on to Shreveport with the gunboats, but the river was obstructed at that point by a large steamer which had been sunk across the channel with its keel broken. The Confederates playfully left a large sign on the hulk inviting the gunboats to a ball in Shreveport.

As he was starting to remove the obstacle, Porter received word from General Banks that his army was falling back to Pleasant Hill, about sixty miles in Porter's rear. After jumping off from Natitoches, Banks's army had been met, on

April 8, by a strong Confederate force between Pleasant Hill and Mansfield, and had been defeated. It would have been a rout if General A. J. Smith had not saved the day on April 9 and driven the Confederates back. The action developed into the spectacle, as Porter described it, of two armies running away from each other with both claiming a victory. Thoroughly dismayed, Banks fell back to Grand Ecore and the protection of the gunboats.

When Porter received the report of the retreat, orders were received also for the troops with him to return to Grand Ecore, 110 miles below by water. In the winding and snag-filled channel the river craft could make only about thirty miles per day. Flushed with their victory, the Confederates harassed the squadron all along the way. This did not become serious until a large party attacked the ironclad *Osage*, hard aground with a transport alongside trying to tow her off. *Osage* was joined by the gunboat *Lexington*, and after a two-hour fight, in which the embarked troops took part, the raiding party was driven off with heavy losses. Aside from this incident the upriver group returned to Grand Ecore without loss. As the river was falling, Porter then started the larger gunboats back to Alexandria.

On April 15 *Eastport*, one of his most powerful ironclads, struck a mine and sank. Porter himself then returned to Alexandria to order up two salvage vessels for an effort to save her. They arrived in a few days and did succeed in getting *Eastport* refloated. She made her way slowly toward Alexandria with frequent groundings. During this time Banks's army was falling back to that city, and although faced with the prospect of stronger Confederate attacks, Porter hoped that he might still save the ironclad. When *Eastport* once again ran hard aground and could not be gotten off, he ordered her blown up and destroyed.

Returning to Alexandria, Porter had a truly critical problem. Normally the Red River should have risen at that time of year but had fallen instead. Part of this was due to diversion of some of the headwaters by the Confederates. Twelve of Porter's craft, most of them ironclads, were caught above the rapids. There was only about four feet of water in the rapids and seven feet was needed for the gunboats to pass through. Porter feared that he would be abandoned by the Army and that he would have to destroy this formidable force. That was a real and pressing possibility until a solution was offered by an enterprising Army engineer.

Lieutenant Colonel Joseph Bailey, Acting Engineer of XIX Corps, proposed to build a dam across the river below the rapids, leaving a narrow passage through which the gunboats could run. He had experience in logging operations in Wisconsin and elsewhere and was sure that he could back up enough water above the dam to accomplish the task. Porter later denied it, but there is good reason to believe that at first he pooh-poohed the idea. Still, no one else came forth with a workable solution to his problem, and in his desperation he agreed that it should be tried. General Banks assigned 3,000 troops to do the job. Trees were felled on the left bank and sunk in the water with their crowns upstream. These were interlocked with other logs and covered with debris. Old mills and buildings were torn down to build cribbing for the right-bank wing of the dam and these were filled with bricks, stones, and other debris.

Bailey promised to complete the dam in ten days. Although Banks assured Porter that the Army would not abandon him, as the days passed his tension and anxiety increased noticeably. For once Porter was a frightened man. Miraculously the dam took shape and after only eight days it was almost finished. Two stone barges at the outer end of the right-bank wing then gave way. Foreseeing failure of the dam, Porter quickly ordered some of the lighter draft gunboats to try the run and four of them got through.

Colonel Bailey cheerfully set out to restore the damage and to build a set of wing dams several hundred yards above the main dam. On May 12 the remaining gunboats succeeded in getting through the passage and below the rapids. It was a brilliant example of military engineering for which Colonel Bailey was promoted to brigadier general. Porter was extremely grateful for being extricated from what probably would have been a career-wrecking disaster. The officers of his squadron in the Red River afterward presented General Bailey with a ceremonial sword.

With the gunboats safely below the rapids Banks announced that his troops would withdraw from Alexandria the next morning. Gunboats covered this withdrawal and the crossing of the Atchafalaya River at Simmesport, where General Smith's corps embarked in transports for their return to Sherman's command. Thus ended, in what appeared to be abject retreat, the Red River expedition.

Porter was bitterly critical of General Banks's conduct of this campaign and placed its failure squarely upon his shoulders. Banks was defeated in the only battle he fought with a major enemy force and his tactical dispositions seem to have been at the root of that defeat. But his withdrawal from Grand Ecore and Alexandria was not of his own choosing. Grant took command of the Union armies in March and he never believed in conducting extensive operations west of the Mississippi. While at Alexandria late in that month Banks received orders from Grant to take Shreveport in a hurry and to return Sherman's troops by the date first agreed upon. At the end of March Grant ordered him to abandon all operations in Texas and to return to New Orleans in order to attack Mobile in co-operation with Farragut. In this order Banks was told to return Sherman's troops at once and to present himself in New Orleans by May 10. Grant later modified this peremptory order, but by the time Banks received the change it was too late. Since the gunboats did not get below the rapids at Alexandria until May 12, it required moral courage for him to remain there with his troops until the boats were safe.

Porter's own conduct and judgment in this campaign are not above criticism. In taking most of his ironclads above the rapids at Alexandria he gambled that the water in the river would rise as it normally did at that season of the year. The water did not rise, and in his eagerness to get at his enemy he disregarded the signs of possible trouble. In the winding channel of the Red River it is difficult to understand why eleven ironclads were necessary or what they hoped to accomplish above the rapids, especially since most of them could not go above Grand Ecore. Understandably, Porter was more than grateful to Colonel Bailey. In reporting his rescue to Welles he wrote: "Words are inadequate to express the admiration I have for Lieutenant Colonel Bailey. This is without doubt the best engineering feat ever performed." [3]

FINAL OPERATIONS

WHILE PORTER was occupied with most of his ironclads in the Red River, Confederate forces east of the Mississippi erupted against Union positions on that river. Early in the morning of April 12 General Nathan B. Forrest attacked Fort Pillow. The gunboat *New Era* was nearby and did its best in defense of the fort, but the garrison numbered less than 600 and it was overwhelmed by mid-afternoon. Half of the garrison was Negro troops, of which few survived. Forrest was accused of permitting their slaughter after they had surrendered. He denied this, but the evidence is strong that his troops did get out of hand. The raid, for such it proved to be, was for the purpose of capturing guns and supplies. Two days

---

[3] ORN, Vol. 26, p. 132.

later, when more gunboats appeared on the scene, Forrest withdrew from the fort. At the same time Columbus and Paducah, Kentucky, were threatened by his cavalry, but gunboats were sent to those points and no actual attacks developed. When he learned of the attack on Fort Pillow, Porter sent ironclads there, but before they reached the fort the need for them had passed.

After the Union gunboat *Petrel* was captured under questionable circumstances while reconnoitering in the Yazoo River near Yazoo City on April 22 there was a lull in activity, especially so after Porter's return to the Mississippi. Guerrillas continued to be troublesome and there was some harassment from hit-and-run batteries set up on the river banks. These kept the patrolling gunboats busy. In June the Union gunboat *Queen City* was surprised by Shelby's force in the White River and captured. A few days later she was blown up on the approach of avenging gunboats. Guerrillas were very active in Arkansas at this time and continued to be for some months. Otherwise affairs were well in hand, and early in July Porter left for an extended leave of absence, leaving Captain A. M. Pennock at Mound City in temporary command of the squadron.

Early on August 22 Forrest, with about 2,000 troops, made a raid on Memphis. He narrowly missed capturing the commanding general but was driven out within a few hours with no important results. From then on, except in Arkansas, the main theater of operations moved away from the Mississippi and shifted again to the Tennessee and Cumberland Rivers. Since June, Sherman had been operating against Joseph E. Johnston and in a series of skillful tactical actions had besieged Atlanta. In doing so, he left Confederate General J. B. Hood in his rear, to be taken care of by Major General George H. Thomas at Nashville. Earlier in the year Sherman had four shallow draft gunboats built at Bridgeport, Tennessee, for the purpose of patrolling the Tennessee River above

Mussel Shoals. They were manned by the Army but their officers and leading petty officers were assigned by the Navy. They began active patrolling late in July.

Late in September Sherman asked Porter to keep gunboats active on the Tennessee as far as Eastport, Mississippi, as he expected to reoccupy the place as a cover for future cavalry movements. Porter promised to do what he could, although he doubted that the gunboats could get as far as Eastport in the low stage of water in that river. This exchange took place just before Porter was detached to take command of the North Atlantic Blockading Squadron. His relief, Rear Admiral S. P. Lee, from that squadron, did not arrive in his new command for about a month after Porter's departure.

On October 10 about 1,200 troops in three transports, escorted by the tinclads *Key West* and *Undine*, arrived at Eastport. There was no sign of Confederate activity, but as the troops began to land, a battery in the hills opened an accurate fire on them. Both gunboats returned the fire at once and there was a brisk fight for about half an hour, after which the damaged gunboats and transports retired. It was an ominous portent of things to come on the Tennessee. Hood had begun to close in on Nashville.

Late in October an attempted crossing of the Tennessee River by Hood at Decatur, Alabama, was repulsed with the help of one of the gunboats on the upper river. Anticipating that a crossing would be attempted in the vicinity of Mussel Shoals, General Thomas sent urgent requests that the river below the shoals be patrolled by gunboats. The water was too low for ironclads to operate and the task was given to tinclads. On October 30, at a point only about fifty miles above Paducah, a roving battery of Forrest's cavalry disabled *Undine* and captured two transports. *Undine* was grounded on the opposite bank, set on fire, and her crew took to the woods. She was captured and repaired, however, by Forrest's troops.

By November 4 Forrest had shifted his battery to a narrow

slot on the river below Johnsonville, Tennessee, then a Union supply depot. On that date a lively action took place in which the gunboats *Key West, Tawa,* and *Elphin* were set on fire and lost after giving a good account of themselves. Before that happened the gunboats recaptured *Undine,* but she and several transports at Johnsonville had to be burned to keep them from falling into Confederate hands. Lieutenant Commander Leroy Fitch, still active on these rivers, came up from Paducah with six gunboats and joined the fight from below the slot. He decided that the Confederate position was too strong for the gunboats to force a passage, and after watching the fate of the craft above the slot, he withdrew. The Tennessee River was closed to Union forces for the time, although Forrest himself withdrew to Corinth after this action.

Realizing the gravity of the situation, Admiral Lee sent a call down the Mississippi for a shallow draft ironclad and rushed repairs on two others at Mound City. He proposed to operate one each in the Tennessee and Cumberland Rivers and to keep the third for use where most needed. Before any of them could be sent up, however, events in Tennessee forced a concentration of effort in the Cumberland River. Hood's pressure increased and General Thomas pulled his forces back to Nashville.

This development alarmed Grant, who saw Louisville and the entire Union position in that region threatened, and he sent orders to Thomas to attack Hood. Thomas insisted that he needed his cavalry, which was being built up and outfitted in the rear, before he could attack. As the tense situation seemed to worsen Grant was on the verge of relieving Thomas of his command when he received reports of the latter's success at Nashville. In that development the river gunboats had a significant part.

By early December Fitch had two ironclads and five gunboats at Nashville. On December 3 he learned that Hood's left flank had reached the river and had emplaced a battery at a point about four miles below the city in an air line, but eighteen miles by river. Fitch decided to hit the battery that night with an ironclad, backed up by the gunboats. His craft moved down the river without lights and were undetected until the ironclad *Carondelet* opened fire at point-blank range from a point in the river opposite the battery. The gunboats shelled the position until the generally inaccurate fire of the battery was silenced. After daylight the gunboats returned to continue the action but found the position abandoned. Three steamers, previously captured by the battery, were recovered.

On the 6th Fitch decided to take a convoy of steamers down to Clarksville, covered by the ironclad *Neosho* and gunboats. Moving well ahead of the transports, he found the battery position reoccupied. He ran past the battery in the ironclad and then returned to a position off its center. *Neosho* remained there for two and one half hours firing grape and canister into the battery's position at ranges of only twenty to thirty yards. The battery's guns, high on the river bank, could not be reached by *Neosho*'s fire in that position, so *Neosho* retired up the river and Fitch sent the transports back to Nashville. Then, renewing the action, he stationed *Carondelet* above the battery where she could enfilade the guns while *Neosho* dropped down opposite the battery and reengaged it at close range. The battle was continued until nearly dark, when Fitch broke it off and returned to the lines below the city. The fire of the battery was reduced but not completely silenced. *Neosho* was hit more than 100 times during this action but suffered no serious damage.

In the face of the growing tension over the fate of Nashville, Admiral Lee, in *Cincinnati*, arrived at Clarksville on the 7th en route to the city. The ironclad could go no farther because of shoals above the town and Lee took no direct part in the action which followed. While Thomas was making his final preparations to attack Hood, Fitch's gunboats patrolled the river above and below the city. He was told on the 14th that the attack would be launched the next morning and was asked to drop down the river to hold the attention of the batteries while Union troops attacked them from the rear. The scheme worked to perfection. Fitch maneuvered the gunboats before the batteries without making a serious effort to attack them. He kept their attention until afternoon, when Thomas's cavalry closed in and captured the position with only slight opposition. This was an important break in the battle.

The fighting continued until the next day, when Hood's lines broke and his army left the field in a rout. The gunboats on the upper Tennessee assisted in the reoccupation of Decatur, cutting off Hood's retreat at that point, and then ran down to the upper Mussel Shoals. Admiral Lee rushed up the Tennessee to Florence, Alabama, and the lower shoals. Some of Hood's troops had crossed the river near Florence before he arrived, but most of them crossed through the shoals where the gunboats could not reach them.

Hood's defeat at Nashville ended large-scale military operations in the Mississippi Valley. Some of his command were sent to Mobile, some to join Johnston in the East, and Forrest's cavalry retired into Mississippi. The gunboats contributed much more to this defeat than their limited part in the actual fighting would seem to indicate. The Confederates had a healthy respect for their guns, especially those of the ironclads, and they deployed their troops to avoid them, insofar as possible. The gunboats kept the rivers open for traffic most of the time and the bulk of supplies and equipment for Thomas's army was delivered by water transport. Thomas himself was very complimentary about the naval performance in his support.

Conceived and operated initially as an Army project, the Mississippi Squadron rapidly grew too large for the Army to manage and under the Navy it became a powerful and efficient force. Once the major Confederate forts on the Mississippi were subdued, the squadron kept that river open for Union traffic, threatened only by hit-and-run guerrilla activity. This severed the South almost completely. No substantial reinforcements were sent from west of the river to the hard-pressed Confederate armies in the East. An intercepted message from Jefferson Davis in 1864, ordering every effort to be made to send troops across the river, showed how urgently these troops were wanted.

As the Union gunboats seized or destroyed every steamer, boat, or raft that could be found, the means for crossing the river simply did not exist. The gunboats could not be everywhere, but their appearance all along the river was frequent enough so that the only crossings that did take place were by small boat, and even this was dangerous. Only the merest trickle of the large volume of munitions and supplies that went through the blockade to the Texas ports could be sent where they were most needed. An example of how tight this secondary blockade was is illustrated by an experience of the gunboat *Avenger*, commanded by Lieutenant C. A. Wright. In November 1864, near Bruinsburg, Mississippi, he spotted a skiff crossing the river. He shelled the Louisiana shore from which the boat had come and, as he reported: ". . . the following captures made yesterday opposite Bruinsburg by this vessel, viz: 154 Enfield rifles (new), 162 bayonets, 116 bayonet scabbards, 4 pair bullet molds, 17 bales wool, 1 Confederate captain, 1 Confederate commissary sergeant, 1 Confederate private, 14 new skiffs (destroyed), 2 wagons (destroyed)." [4] The first five items presumably made their way through the blockade into Texas, but the second five appear to be indigenous to the region.

The splitting of the Confederacy and the tightening of the

---

[4] ORN, Vol. 26, p. 734.

anaconda's coil around its forces in the Mississippi Valley were major blows to the South. It was unfortunate that so much time was needed to find such generals as Grant and Sherman, who appreciated the great advantage naval support could provide and what it meant. Had the pleas of Farragut for help been heeded, the Mississippi might have been opened a full year sooner than it was. No one can say now what that would have taken from the ability of the South to fight on, but one thing is certain—the South's position would not have been enhanced.

Chapter XVI

Virginia and Carolina Waters

1863–65

SUPPORTING OPERATIONS

WHEN THE LAND CAMPAIGN in Virginia shifted away from tidewater after the end of McClellan's Peninsula campaign in 1862, a relative quiet settled over the waters of Virginia and North Carolina. The Union Army held Norfolk, Fort Monroe, and Yorktown in Virginia, but most of the tidewater peninsular region of that state was more or less a no man's land. Union gunboats covered occasional troop movements up the rivers on raids or for reconnaissance.

Comparable conditions existed in Pamlico and Albemarle Sounds in North Carolina. In addition to Roanoke Island, the Union Army had garrisons at Beaufort, which was the base for the blockading ships off Wilmington, and at New Bern, Washington, and Plymouth in North Carolina. A small force of half a dozen shallow draft gunboats were kept in the sounds to patrol and to support the garrisons. The period of relative quiet lasted through 1863, and the primary task of the North Atlantic Blockading Squadron during that year was the enforcement of the blockade of Wilmington.

This situation underwent a change in the early part of 1864.

The Confederates came to life in the region and threatened the Union positions in the state. They attacked the defenses of New Bern early in February and at about the same time a Confederate naval party in small boats got within 100 yards of the gunboat *Underwriter*, at anchor above the outposts at Plymouth in the Roanoke River, before being detected. The party boarded and captured the gunboat, but the forts protecting Plymouth opened fire on her, set her on fire, and forced the raiding party to withdraw. The gunboat's magazine blew up, making her a total loss.

The Union Navy well knew that the Confederates had several ironclads under construction in the rivers of North Carolina. Efforts to have the Army move up and destroy them were unavailing, and the construction went on unmolested. The first of these ironclads to be brought into action was *Albemarle*, in the Roanoke River. She was similar to all of the other Confederate ironclads, with a central sloping casemate pierced for six guns, but she was armed with only two. She had four inches of armor over about fourteen inches of wood.

On April 17 Confederate troops attacked Plymouth, in which attack *Albemarle* was to assist. Three Union gunboats were at Plymouth, assisting in its defense. Lieutenant Commander C. W. Flusser, commanding the side-wheeler *Miami*, was confident that the gunboats could destroy *Albemarle* if she appeared. He planned to lash his own gunboat to *Southfield*, ram with both gunboats at once, and fight at very close ranges. Both gunboats were kept busy shelling Confederate positions near Plymouth, but they expected *Albemarle* and were alert for her.

At about 3:30 a.m. on April 19 the gunboat on picket duty above the town ran down to report the approach of the ironclad. The two gunboats were already lashed together, and when *Albemarle* appeared they steamed at her. In the resultant collision *Albemarle* scraped across the bow of *Miami* and rammed *Southfield* on the starboard side, cutting a fatal gash in her hull. She sank almost at once. *Miami*'s shots merely bounced off the armor of *Albemarle* and fragments from one of them killed Commander Flusser. Unable to damage the ironclad, *Miami* then steamed down and out of the river. *Albemarle* followed for a time but then retired to Plymouth, which surrendered the next day.

Albemarle's next appearance was on May 5. After her first appearance Captain Melancton Smith, with three gunboats, was rushed to Albemarle Sound. When the ironclad came out of the river on the 5th she was engaged by eight gunboats in a running fight that lasted about three hours. Captain Smith's plan was for the gunboats to steam past *Albemarle* in order, passing as close as they could get to her and firing at the shortest range. *Sassacus* rammed the ironclad but did no damage. That gunboat's boiler was struck by a shell and she was disabled, the only serious damage done during the action. *Albemarle* had her armor dented and her smoke stack was riddled. Her captain, Commander J. J. Cooke, broke off what he reported as ". . . the unequal contest in which we were compelled to engage," and retired into the Roanoke River before dark. The Union gunboats still held the sound and they captured a tender which had come out with *Albemarle*.

During the night of May 6 the ironclad *Raleigh* came out of the Cape Fear River convoying several blockade runners. She engaged three of the light gunboats on the inner blockade line without doing any serious damage to them. At daylight, with the approach of the entire fleet of Union blockaders, she retired into the river. She ran aground just above Fort Fisher, broke her keel, and became a total loss.

Although *Albemarle* did not again come out of the Roanoke River, there was a long period of uneasiness on the sounds, for her existence was a constant threat to the wooden Union gunboats and to their control of those waters. Lieutenant

William B. Cushing, who made a reconnaissance up the Cape Fear River almost to Wilmington in June, proposed to destroy the ironclad. His plan was substantially the same idea that the Confederates used at Charleston with the "David" spar torpedo boats. His proposal was approved and he obtained three small steamboats in New York, to each of which was fitted a spar torpedo over the bow. Two of the boats were destroyed by accident and the third was not ready for the attempt until October.

During the night of October 27 Cushing, with a volunteer crew, steamed up the Roanoke River and got abreast of *Albemarle* before he was discovered. The ironclad was moored to the shore just below the town dock and she was protected in the river by a log boom several feet out from her hull. When he was hailed from the ironclad, Cushing ran his boat directly toward her at full speed. At the same time his boat came under heavy rifle and musket fire. It struck the log boom, slid over it, and Cushing coolly hit *Albemarle* underwater with his torpedo. The ironclad sank very quickly. Still under heavy fire, Cushing told his men to jump overboard and fend for themselves. He and a seaman swam away and succeeded in getting back to Union gunboats but, except for two men killed, the boat and the rest of the boat's crew were captured.

When Cushing returned and reported *Albemarle* sunk, Commander W. H. McComb, then commanding the gunboats in those waters, decided to attack the batteries defending Plymouth at once. He moved up the river with six gunboats in the forenoon of October 29, but had to return to Albemarle Sound when he found obstructions near the wreck of *Southfield* below the town. The next day he took the gunboats through the Middle River and into the Roanoke above the town. Early on the 31st he moved down past the town to engage the batteries at close range. When their magazine blew up the crews of the batteries fled and McComb took possession of them and the town. He held it until a garrison was sent from Roanoke Island, and Plymouth thereafter remained in Union hands.

After the gunboats moved out of the James River, following the collapse of McClellan's Peninsula Campaign, there was little naval activity in the rivers flowing into Chesapeake Bay for nearly two years. The land campaigns in Virginia and Maryland during that period were inland, for the most part, and beyond the reach of naval support. The Potomac River Flotilla was a small independent command given the task of keeping that river open for shipping, but it was also kept busy trying to break up the smuggling from Maryland to Virginia. It played a small part in the Rappahannock River after Hooker's defeat at Chancellorsville in May 1863, when its gunboats protected his supply base.

During 1863 and early 1864 small but daring Confederate naval parties made forays into Chesapeake Bay and the Potomac. Their most notable success was to capture two Union gunboats anchored in the mouth of the Rappahannock in August 1863. The craft had been forewarned of such an attempt, but two boat parties succeeded in boarding and taking them in the dead of night. As Confederate gunboats they captured a few Union schooners but were soon withdrawn up the Rappahannock, where the Union Army destroyed them before they could do any more damage. The same group seized and destroyed several schooners at other times but, except for the capture of the gunboats, the raids were of more value for their heroics than for their military significance.

When Grant developed his plan of campaign against Lee in the spring of 1864, a return to the James was included. Major General B. F. Butler was then in command of the Department of Virginia and North Carolina at Fort Monroe. To form the left flank in Grant's campaign, Butler was ordered to move up the James and attack across country to cut the Richmond and Petersburg Railroad. Grant intended for Butler to attack Petersburg itself to insure the cutting off of Lee's supplies.

The Confederates had built three ironclads at Richmond and they were a threat to any Union movement on the river. Therefore when Butler moved up the James early in May, his transports were convoyed by three of Admiral Lee's monitors, the captured ironclad *Atlanta*, and seven gunboats. To preserve secrecy and to mislead the Confederates the transports first moved toward the York River, as if they were to ascend that river. They turned back in time to enter the James after dark, in order to get as far as possible up that river before being detected. The troops were landed at Bermuda Hundred, a short distance above the mouth of the Appomattox River, in the afternoon of May 5. The first Confederate naval reaction to this movement was the use of mines. On May 6 the Union gunboat *Commodore Jones* was blown up by a mine in the James.

Butler made a halfhearted drive toward Petersburg but then changed his plan and attempted to move in behind Lee's forces near Richmond. He was driven back near Drewry's Bluff and dug himself in along a line between the Appomattox and James Rivers near Bermuda Hundred. There he was bottled up by Beauregard.

City Point, at the mouth of the Appomattox, became the base for Army operations on the James. Mindful of the Confederate ironclads in the river above the Union position, Grant ordered obstructions placed in the river on Butler's right flank, near the head of Trent's Reach. While Butler prepared the obstructions, Admiral Lee objected to them being emplaced, since they would force his craft to remain below them, but Grant's positive order settled the matter. The obstructions were lodged near the center of a large loop in the river, with the head of the loop only about half a mile wide. In June, after a series of battles north of Richmond, Grant shifted his own base to City Point, which then became his main base.

The narrow neck of land above the obstructions enabled the opposing ironclads to get within range of each other occasionally. There were a few exchanges of shots between them but no serious damage was done by either side. The situation developed into one of watchful waiting for the Union gunboats, which continued to fear that somehow the Confederate ironclads might get below the obstructions. The Confederate ships did come down several times and exchange shots with powerful Union batteries near the head of Trent Reach. Similarly, Union ironclads, including the monitors *Tecumseh*, *Canonicus*, and *Saugus*, exchanged shots with Confederate batteries on June 21, when the Confederate ironclads joined in an indecisive action. Admiral Lee's main task, after the obstructions were in place, was to insure that the river below was kept clear for the use of supply ships for City Point. Gunboats had to patrol the entire river, for Confederate raiding parties had an annoying habit of appearing on the river bank and shooting at the passing transports and supply ships with light artillery.

FORT FISHER

As EARLY AS 1862 the Navy Department realized that the only way that Wilmington could be sealed off and denied to the blockade runners was to occupy the mouth of the Cape Fear River. Its strong defenses and the geography of the entrance, with its narrow and treacherous channels and bars, were such that it could not be forced by naval ships as had been done at Port Royal and New Orleans. The northeast point of the mouth of the river was defended by Fort Fisher. The construction of this fort had not begun until 1862, but it was to become the strongest single fort in the Confederate arsenal. The older masonry Fort Caswell guarded the southwest point of the entrance. They were the keys of what became an intricate network of defensive works.

In May 1863 Admiral Lee reported that the only feasible way in which the position could be taken was by an adequate ground force supported by naval vessels. He proposed, about the same time, that Smith Island be occupied. General Foster, commanding troops in the sounds, was willing and anxious to do this, but he could not provide the necessary troops. Many from his command had been sent to Charleston. Gideon Welles repeatedly sought to have the War Department provide troops for the Cape Fear River operation, but he was put off on every occasion. Although Lincoln agreed with Welles on the importance of the project, he was unwilling to interfere with the Army's plans.

When Grant came east to take command of the Union armies, Welles found a more sympathetic ear. During the summer of 1864, while Grant was in the midst of his campaign in Virginia, Welles argued that taking Wilmington was more important than taking Richmond. His reasoning was that if Lee found his only remaining source of outside supply cut off, he would have to give up Richmond. This argument had its effect, and Grant, responding to the need to seal off Wilmington as a haven for blockade runners, agreed to provide the necessary troops. Early in September he promised that the troops assigned would be ready to move about the 1st of October.

With this assurance in hand Welles wanted to be doubly sure of success as far as the Navy was concerned. It was at this time that he selected Farragut to command the expedition, only to have the crusty old admiral indignantly decline the assignment. Welles then settled on David D. Porter, from the Mississippi Squadron, who exchanged jobs with Admiral Lee. Porter assumed command of the North Atlantic Blockading Squadron on October 1 and plunged at once into the assembly and preparation of what was to be the most formidable fleet to be used in the Civil War.

The troops were not ready in October and the expedition was postponed several times for many reasons. One of these reasons was that newspapers got wind of the expedition and its pros and cons were freely discussed, both North and South. Grant felt that the essential element of secrecy was lost. Welles urged action before the end of favorable autumn weather, but it was December before the expedition was ready. Grant intended that Major General Godfrey Weitzel command the troops, but as Wilmington was in Ben Butler's department, the orders were issued through him. Butler decided to take part in the expedition himself.

Another reason for the delay in launching the expedition was that Butler had a grandiose idea of loading a ship with tons of gunpowder, running it in close to Fort Fisher, and blowing it off the face of the earth. Porter fell in with the idea and much effort was expended in preparing a ship for this experiment. The expedition continued to be discussed openly in the press and very little of the plan of attack could be kept secret. To make matters worse, the naval vessels and the transports arrived in the vicinity of the Cape Fear River several days before the attack was launched, thus warning the defenders that it was imminent.

Welles's belief in the importance of Wilmington to the Confederacy was confirmed by General Lee. He sent a telegram to Colonel William Lamb, the energetic commander of Fort Fisher, telling him that the fort must be held at all cost. Without it (and the blockade runners) he would be unable to sustain his army and would have to evacuate Richmond. On December 20 Governor Zebulon Vance of North Carolina issued a flamboyant proclamation stating that an attack on Wilmington was imminent and calling upon all men able to bear arms to rally to its defense, in order ". . . to drive back from our doors a fate horrible to contemplate." He assured the people that "Your governor will meet you at the front and will share with you the worst." [1] The governor did visit Fort Fisher on December 29, four days after it was first attacked.

Porter's naval force was assembled at Beaufort by the middle of December. Butler, with his transports, moved independently and arrived a few days later. Winter gales and heavy surf imposed delays and it was not until December 23 that conditions were suitable for the attack. The agreed plan of action was to run the bomb ship in under the fort after dark and to explode it late at night. At daylight Porter would then station his ships within one mile or less of Fort Fisher, in a quadrant extending from near Smith Island to as close to the beaches northeast of the fort as they could get. The troops were to land on the open beaches about four miles above the fort and be prepared to attack after Porter's planned heavy bombardment.

The attack was launched according to plan. The bomb ship, an ex-blockade runner named *Louisiana*, loaded with 235 tons of gunpowder, was run in close to the fort in the night of December 23 and exploded soon after midnight. No one knew for sure what concussion or shock wave would result from the explosion of so much powder, and Porter kept his ships miles at sea until after the explosion. The bomb-ship experiment was a complete fizzle. The explosion did no damage, except to destroy the ship, and hardly disturbed those inside the fort who assumed that some ship offshore had had a boiler explosion.

At daylight Porter's ships, which included *New Ironsides* and three monitors, closed in to their assigned positions. The bombardment opened shortly before noon and continued until after sunset when they retired for the night. Porter reported that the fort was completely silenced under an intense

---

[1] ORN, Vol. 11, p. 785.

rate of fire of 115 shells per minute, which was indeed a very heavy rate of fire.

Near the end of the bombardment Butler appeared on the scene with a few of his transports. He had been at Beaufort for coal and water. On Christmas morning all of the troop transports were present and it was then agreed that the bombardment would be renewed while the troops landed under the protection of some gunboats. The bombardment was conducted at a more leisurely pace than on the first day and continued throughout the day. From the bombarding ships troops could be seen moving about near the fort during the day. In the afternoon Porter received a letter from Butler saying that a reconnaissance of the fort showed that ". . . it was left substantially uninjured as a defensive work by the navy fire." [2] He said further that General Weitzel agreed with him that the place could be taken only by a siege, which was not within his instructions. Butler hurriedly re-embarked his troops the next day and returned to Hampton Roads, leaving about 700 men on the beach, to be recovered by the gunboats.

Porter was furious at being deserted by Butler. He fired off letters to Grant pleading with him to send back the troops under a new commander and to Welles saying that he would remain in the vicinity, hoping that the troops would return. He even sent one to Sherman at Savannah, asking him to send troops to help take Fort Fisher. He was convinced that a handful of troops could have walked into Fort Fisher on Christmas Day, as he had completely silenced its guns. During the two days of bombardment his ships fired more than 20,000 shells, weighing more than 600 tons. The return fire from the fort had been light, as were Porter's casualties, most of which resulted from bursting guns in the ships. From all outward appearances he seemed to have good reason for his confidence.

---

[2] ORN, Vol. 11, p. 251.

General Butler's precipitate withdrawal from the scene, without even a token attack, could not be excused and Grant dismissed him from his command upon his return to Fort Monroe. Yet when we learn from those on the receiving end just what damage was done to Fort Fisher, it appears that Butler was probably wiser than he knew. Colonel Lamb reported that the fort suffered little more than superficial damage. Wooden buildings were burned, three guns were disabled, and some earthworks were torn up, but no bombproof shelter or magazine was endangered. The fort's reason for returning the ships' fire so slowly was that no attempt was made by any ship to cross the bar. The fort's casualties were three killed and sixty-one wounded. Major General W. H. C. Whiting, commanding the Cape Fear River defenses, later compared this bombardment with the second one that took place in January, and he expressed confidence that an assault after the December attack would have been repulsed with great losses to the attackers. The fire of the first bombardment was diffused and scattered and it left the parapet and palisade, or stockade fence around the fort, almost undamaged. Under such conditions an attack by land would have required a strong and aggressive leader to have had any chance of success, and Butler hardly qualified in that respect.

When Grant learned of Butler's action he asked Porter to remain off the Cape Fear River, as the troops would be returned as soon as possible. He gave the command to Major General A. J. Terry, who was ordered to co-operate fully with Porter. General Terry arrived at Beaufort on January 8, 1865, and the two commanders came to a complete understanding for the next attack on the fort. Stormy weather held up the operation for a few days, but on the 12th the combined fleet sailed for Fort Fisher.

Porter was not satisfied with the firing in the first bombardment as he had noticed many shots wasted by being fired at the fort's flagpole. For the second bombardment he modified his plan to concentrate upon destruction of individual targets rather than general bombardment, the practice that was used in World War II. This time he used forty-four ships, with the ironclads stationed only about 700 yards from the fort. The ships were ordered to fired deliberately at their assigned targets until they were destroyed. While the troops were being landed, *New Ironsides* and four monitors bombarded the fort, with orders to dismount all of its guns. After the troops were landed the remainder of the forty-four ships assigned took their stations and joined the bombardment. It was continued until dark when the wooden ships hauled off to anchor. The ironclads kept up a harassing fire throughout the night. On the 14th the full bombardment was resumed and it was concentrated again on dismounting the guns of the fort. During the day it was arranged that the land attack on the fort would be made at 2:00 p.m. the next day. At the end of the day the ironclads again continued to fire through the night.

To assist in the assault on the fort Porter organized a landing force of 1,600 sailors and 400 marines drawn from the ships. They were to attack the seaward face of the fort while troops attacked the land face. The sailors were armed with cutlasses and pistols, with only a few rifles in the force. They were ordered to rush the fort, during which they were to be covered by marine riflemen. In the morning of the 15th the landing force was put ashore, after which the intense bombardment of the fort was resumed. It was not until 3:00 p.m., when Porter received word that the troops were ready for the assault, that the gunfire of the ships was checked. By then the parapet was badly shot up and the palisade was shot away in most places.

When the sailors rushed the seaward face of the parapet they were met by a withering rifle and musket fire. The officers tried to rally their men, but they fell back and took whatever cover they could find. The landing force lost about eighty killed and 270 wounded. Their attack failed, but it did make an important contribution to the eventual outcome. The defenders believed that this was the main attack and concentrated their defenses against it. That allowed General Terry's troops to get into two gun traverses at the northwest corner of the parapet and gain a strong foothold inside the fort before it was realized that they were there. There followed some hard fighting in the fort and it was not until about 9:00 p.m. that it was captured. This was announced to the fleet with three cheers, and they were echoed in the fleet, which followed with an immense pyrotechnic display. Clearing out the rest of the spit on which the fort stood yielded a total of nearly 2,100 prisoners, including General Whiting and Colonel Lamb, both of them wounded.

During the night of January 16 the Confederates blew up Fort Caswell and abandoned their extensive works on Smith Island and at Smithville. On the following night Porter sent Lieutenant Cushing into the river for a reconnaissance. He found Fort Caswell abandoned and hoisted the Union flag over it. As he approached Smithville the few Confederate troops in the town ran out and Cushing took the surrender of the town, capturing a considerable quantity of commissary stores. Sailors held the town for about a week until relieved by troops.

As soon as the channel could be located and buoyed, Porter sent his shallow draft gunboats into the river. He also assigned a party to operate the range lights which were used by the blockade runners. On January 19 two runners came in and were quite surprised to find themselves Union prizes. Still another was taken about ten days later.

Porter was deeply impressed by the strength of the defenses of the Cape Fear River. Fort Fisher [3] fell so easily, he felt, because the three days and two nights of continuous bom-

---

[3] Part of the land face is now preserved in a North Carolina State Park. Through the action of storms and erosion the seaward face has completely disappeared.

bardment disabled all but two of its guns and the garrison was demoralized. Nearly 170 guns were captured in the entire network of fortifications. He considered Fort Fisher itself, with seventy-five guns, to be the strongest fort he had ever seen. With the entrance to the river in Union hands and with his large fleet present, he felt that there was enough strength there to hold it against any force that might be sent against it. He proposed to remain there until a move could be made against Wilmington, which would have to wait until more troops were available.

The actual captures of Fort Fisher and of the Mobile Bay forts were the best co-ordinated and conducted joint operations of the war. Porter and Terry warmly praised each other, and the record shows that there was complete understanding and confidence between them.

Fort Fisher was the most formidable position taken in an amphibious operation during the war. The Confederates had been given ample time to build it up, thanks to the failure of the Union Army to realize its importance earlier in the war. The correctness of Lee's prediction that he could not sustain his army before Richmond if Fort Fisher was lost was borne out, for in less than three months after it fell he was forced to surrender to Grant.[4]

FINAL OPERATIONS

FOLLOWING the capture of Fort Fisher the effort of the North Atlantic Blockading Squadron was confined chiefly to

---

[4] To cap the sunset of Butler's controversial military career he was called before the Congressional Committee on the Conduct of the War in January. He testified that Fort Fisher was impregnable and could not be taken except at heavy cost. As he finished this statement newsboys were heard in the streets shouting an extra edition that the fort had fallen. Butler joined in the burst of laughter that followed.

the James and York Rivers. Porter remained at Fort Fisher while his gunboats assisted in the attack on Wilmington, which was occupied by General Schofield on February 22. Fort Anderson, several miles above Smithville, stubbornly held off the gunboats for a month until it was nearly surrounded by Union troops. After that the gunboats continued to patrol in the Carolina sounds, but the war was fast drawing to a close and there was little for them to do. With Sherman driving across the Carolinas, the Confederate forces were directed at a desperate effort to stop him.

The naval standoff that existed in the James River after June 1864 continued into 1865. When he went to Fort Fisher Porter left two monitors and *Atlanta* in the James Division to protect against the three Confederate ironclads which were above the obstructions at Trent's Reach. A real scare developed at Grant's headquarters at City Point in January when it was learned that the Confederate ironclads planned to run down the river to destroy the huge Union Army supply base at that point. There was only one monitor present at the time, and when Grant learned that the naval commander had moved it down the river away from the obstructions, he intervened. He issued orders to all gunboat captains to move up to the obstructions. He was careful to say that these orders were issued by the authority of the Secretary of the Navy. He did not have that authority but felt sure that Welles would approve his action. Urgent requests were sent to Hampton Roads for more ships, and on the 24th *Atlanta* and *New Ironsides* were sent up the river from Norfolk.

In the evening of January 23 Flag Officer J. K. Mitchell, commanding the Confederate James River Squadron, led the ironclads *Virginia, Richmond,* and *Fredericksburg,* with six gunboats and two torpedo boats, down the river from their anchorage below Drewry's Bluff. On the way they had to run past Union batteries above Dutch Gap. The fire of these batteries gave the alarm, but Mitchell's squadron reached the obstructions about 10:40 p.m. *Richmond, Virginia,* and the gunboats anchored, while *Fredericksburg* continued on to find a passage through the obstructions. A freshet a few days before had made a breach through which the ironclad had no trouble making a passage. She was then anchored, and Mitchell, who was on board, returned to *Virginia* to bring her through. He found her fast aground after dragging her anchor. At about 3:30 a.m. he received word that *Richmond* and two gunboats were also aground. The tide was then ebbing and there was no hope of getting the craft off until the flood tide came in during the forenoon. *Fredericksburg* was recalled above the obstructions in order to be clear of the Union batteries.

Union batteries near the grounded craft fired at them during the night, using searchlights, and at daylight took up a heavy fire, scoring repeated hits. One gunboat was blown up. The Union monitor *Onandaga* and several gunboats which were at anchor some distance down the river heard the shooting during the night but did not move until about 8:30 a.m., when they steamed up and joined the fight. *Onandaga* fired only ten fifteen-inch rounds and eleven rounds of eight-inch from her two turrets. Both of the grounded ironclads were hit so often that an accurate count of the fire could not be kept, but *Virginia*'s report gave the opinion that the two most damaging hits she received were from the monitor. Both penetrated the armor but did not pass into the casemate or hull. At about 11:20 the grounded craft succeeded in getting afloat and the squadron retired up the river.

This was one of the very few instances when Union naval forces did not show aggressiveness in meeting their Confederate foes. The naval commander in the river, in whom Porter had expressed complete confidence as one who had never had "ram fever," appears to have had a severe attack of that malady in this case. He was summarily relieved of his command and was later court-martialed for his failure to take advantage of the opportunity to seek decisive action. Fortunately for him, nature and possibly poor seamanship spoiled the Confederate attack or Grant might have had justification for his concern for the security of his base.

Nothing further of note occurred on the James until near the end of hostilities. Porter returned to that river after the occupation of Wilmington, and when it became apparent that Richmond was about to be abandoned, he ordered the river obstructions removed and his craft prepared to move up to the city. Grant broke through the Confederate defenses at Petersburg on April 2, whereupon the fate of the capital was sealed. The city was evacuated later in the same day. Rear Admiral Raphael Semmes, then in command of the James River Squadron, was ordered to destroy all of his ironclads and gunboats during the night, which he did. Porter meanwhile had the river swept for mines, and on April 4 his flagship, *Malvern*, with President Lincoln on board, moved up to Richmond, marking the end of the Navy's work in the Virginia campaign.

In his *Incidents and Anecdotes* Porter has a moving description of Lincoln's reception by the Negroes of Richmond. In the course of this he mentioned the Emancipation Proclamation and left us this prophetic passage:

> Twenty years have passed since that event; it is almost too new in history to make a great impression, but the time will come when it will loom as one of the greatest of man's achievements, and the name of Abraham Lincoln—who of his own will struck the shackles from the limbs of four millions of people—will be honored thousands of years from now as man's name was never honored before.[5]

---

[5] David D. Porter: *Incidents and Anecdotes of the Civil War* (New York; 1885), p. 296.

Chapter XVII

Conclusion

THE PRESIDENTIAL PROCLAMATIONS which set the strategic pattern of naval operations for both sides in the Civil War were essentially political in nature. In neither case did the resulting policies take into account the material forces initially available or their ability to do the job. But once the die was cast there was little choice for either Navy in what it should contribute to the war effort; how it was done was another matter. Although the Union Navy's most spectacular results were achieved in amphibious operations, the blockade of the Confederacy was its overriding task. This automatically made attempts to thwart that blockade the primary task of the Confederate Navy.

The most noteworthy accomplishment of the Union Navy was the establishment and maintenance of the blockade, an assignment for which it was completely unprepared at the outset. The scope of the blockade, covering about 3,000 miles of the Southern coast, was unprecedented, and early critics claimed that it was an impossible task. With only three ships immediately available at the beginning, there were grounds for such pessimism, yet within three months ships were stationed off the principal Southern ports and a recognizable blockade was in effect. More important, long-range plans, developed by the Board of Strategy, prepared the way for strengthening and maintaining a continuous blockade indefinitely.

Gideon Welles, as a member of Lincoln's cabinet, took part in the discussions that led to the proclamation of the blockade. He preferred a proclamation merely announcing the closing of the Southern ports to the more formal proclamation of a blockade, but political consideration of foreign reaction determined the actual form of the proclamation. The difference was only a legal technicality, for to have closed the Southern ports would have required an effort comparable to that expended on the blockade. While the formally proclaimed blockade admitted that a state of war existed under international law, Northern leaders ignored that admission. They maintained that they were dealing with an internal rebellion in which the rebels had no rights under international law.

For practical purposes Welles had to start from zero to establish the blockade, for most ships of the existing Navy were unsuited for the purpose. One of his first steps was to purchase or charter every available ship and craft that could be armed quickly and rushed into service. Additional ships were bought and built, and within a year the Navy had about 300 ships in service. With such ships and craft the blockade was established, although it was unable to stop all communication by sea with the Southern ports. Geography and the great profits to be made from blockade running saw to that. Both the techniques required for blockade running and for ships enforcing the blockade grew into highly developed specialties. Since the initiative was with the runners, the tactics of the blockaders lagged somewhat, but not by much.

Welles's final report on the war states that 418 vessels were purchased during the war, of which 313 were steamers. In addition, 208 warships were built under contract. These included about sixty-five ironclads of all types. Thirteen ocean cruisers were designed primarily for pursuit of the Confederate cruisers. There was a variety of ships and craft designed and built for the peculiar conditions under which they were required to operate. The Mississippi River shallow draft ironclads and monitors are examples, and the ferryboat principle was used to develop very efficient double-ended gunboats for use on Southern coastal rivers. Some of the craft listed in the *Official Records*, such as the old whaling hulks filled with stone and used as obstructions at Charleston and in some of the channels between the outer banks in North Carolina, have no rightful place in that list and are not considered here. Taking such factors into account, it is a reasonable estimate that the Union Navy operated between 500 and 600 ships and craft during the course of the war. The exact number is not important for, as occurred in World War II, its relative strength as compared to its opponent became overwhelming.

At the outbreak of the war the Union Navy had about 1,000 professional officers of all grades fit for duty, and about 7,500 enlisted men. There was no naval reserve, but the Navy was fortunate in having a large pool of merchant marine officers on which it drew. At the peak of its operations in 1864 the total strength of the Navy was about 6,000 officers and 45,000 enlisted men. As was the case with the Army, the turnover was high and procurement was difficult. In the early part of the war men enlisted for one year only and became very disgruntled if they were not discharged promptly. Curiously, conscription took many sailors into the Army without regard for their status. Welles often appealed to Stanton to release a man from the draft who was already serving as a sailor in the Navy. On the Western rivers many qualified river boatmen also were taken into the Army. The Army agreed in principle to release them to serve in the river gunboats, but it was not always easy actually to get a qualified individual released.

In the eyes of most Northerners at the time, the Union

Navy was subordinate to the Army and its activities and accomplishments were barely recognized, except for some spectacular victory such as New Orleans or Mobile Bay. This irritated naval officers and Gideon Welles. Welles resented Army claims that it had taken Hatteras Inlet and Port Royal, for example, or that Grant had captured Forts Henry and Donelson, although he did capture the latter. It was for this reason that Welles wanted Farragut to take New Orleans without Army help. It was also behind his insistence, in the face of professional advice to the contrary, that Charleston should be taken by the Navy alone. He also wanted a solo try for Fort Fisher, but wiser counsel prevailed.

Lincoln was well aware of the contribution of the Navy to the war effort. In August 1863, after Gettysburg and Vicksburg, reviewing those who deserved credit for the then favorable state of affairs, he wrote:

> Nor must Uncle Sam's web-feet be forgotten. At all the waters' margins they have been present, not only on the deep sea, the broad bay, and the rapid river, but also up the narrow, muddy bayou, and wherever the ground was a little damp, they have been and made their tracks.[1]

Certainly by the standards of the times the over-all Union naval performance in the Civil War was first-rate and noteworthy. Gideon Welles deserves much of the credit for this. He was one of Lincoln's most loyal cabinet officers and he had no political ambition other than to fulfill his assigned task to the best of his ability. He was a good organizer and in his assistant Gustavus V. Fox he had an able administrator. Many considered that Fox was the real brain of the Navy Department, and he did have an active part in all discussions of policy. Fox's contribution to the Navy's effort was great, but there is no doubt that Welles was the policy maker for that

---

[1] *Rebellion Record*, Vol. VII, p. 461.

department. There was no chief of naval operations nor professional operating staff and the Secretary worked directly with the commanders afloat.

Welles was generally a good judge of men and the principal commanders in the war were his personal choice. His temper was short and he was quick to vent his wrath at what he conceived to be a blunder or a reverse. He could also be hasty in his judgment and this sometimes led to unfair treatment of officers in command. He was bothered at the beginning by superannuated and unfit officers in key command positions, but he replaced them as rapidly as he could. If his military judgment was not as high as his other qualities, that is explained by his lack of military experience. In most cases he deferred to the advice of more experienced men, but in some, notably that of Charleston, he was adamant. His motive there was political, for that city was a symbol of secession and, to him, of rebellion.

Another quality which is greatly to Welles's credit, at a time when it was too often lacking, was his scrupulous honesty. The Navy Department was remarkably free of scandal during the entire war. Its policies and practices were frequently challenged by hostile members of Congress, but Welles was able to answer his critics in every case. The few contract frauds that did occur were uncovered by his own agents and he pushed the prosecution of the guilty ones.

The officers of the Union Navy met the challenge that was produced by a different kind of warfare than they were trained for. Head and shoulders above them all was David G. Farragut. In meeting the problems he had to solve, Farragut was thorough and realistic. He never over- or underestimated his opposition, and his plans were clear and concise. He had complete confidence in his own judgment, a confidence which his performance justified. This extended beyond the purely naval field of operations. He believed, for example, that if he could get by an Army position, outflanking it by water, so to speak, that position would have to be given up. That explains his tactics at New Orleans, Port Hudson, and Mobile Bay.

He made sure that his subordinates knew and understood what was expected of them, and then, with full confidence in them, he conducted his operations with a minimum of orders and signals. He could be gruff and blunt and did not hesitate to let a subordinate know when his performance was considered to be below standard. His officers respected and admired him and his men showed a real affection for him. It is worth noting that the two least controversial military commanders in the Civil War are the Confederate general Robert E. Lee and the Union admiral David G. Farragut. The Navy was not to produce a match for Farragut's tactical ability until the great naval leaders of World War II proved themselves.

David D. Porter received the most publicity of any naval officer in the war. That was no accident, for Porter was probably the most publicity-conscious of all the officers. Son of a hero of the War of 1812, he was ambitious to become famous in his own right. He was also the most politically minded naval officer, and before the fighting began he was on friendly terms with many Southern political leaders in Washington. He had a warm and charming personality, which helps to explain why Welles picked him for an important command after his unorthodox experience with *Powhatan* in 1861.

The jump from lieutenant to rear admiral in little more than one year makes Porter a remarkable man by any standard. He was, of course, a very senior lieutenant in 1861 and he became a commander soon after the war began. He knew that, in a service bound to a system of seniority, his appointment would be resented by many. The officers in the Mississippi Squadron were relatively junior and remained so while he commanded that squadron. By the time he moved to the North Atlantic Blockading Squadron his position was well established and there was no friction. Porter's most noticeable quality was his eagerness to get at his enemy wherever and whenever he could. That trait affected his military judgment and led him to near disaster in the Red River. Nevertheless he was a capable commander, but his personal ambition and vanity made him the most controversial naval commander of the war.

Gideon Welles's treatment of Rear Admiral Samuel F. Du Pont was both unfair and unwarranted. In taking Port Royal and occupying other key points within the limits of his command, Du Pont proved that he was an able and aggressive officer. He would have accomplished more if he had been able to get the necessary Army support for the operations that he wanted to conduct. His approach to the attempt to take Charleston with ironclads alone was that of a prudent man who wanted to know the capabilities of his craft before he put them to the ultimate test. The experience of the monitors at Fort McAllister was disappointing and his mildly pessimistic reports were misinterpreted in Washington as a sign of timidity. Even Lincoln inclined to this, for he once remarked that Du Pont seemed to have "McClellanitis." When he did launch the attack against Charleston, he determined to continue it as long as there was a reasonable prospect of success. Then, after receiving reports from his captains after the first day's action, he realized that another day of such punishment might result in the loss of the monitors, and he promptly and courageously canceled a renewal of the attack. It was this decision that turned the ire of Welles against him. Welles did not dismiss Du Pont from his command, but Du Pont informed the Secretary that if there was a loss of confidence in him he wished to be relieved.

When the monitor captains rallied to the support of Du Pont, Welles dismissed this support as coming from the Du Pont "clique." There are several references to personal cliques in the Navy in Welles's diary, but the writer has found little evidence that they existed to any damaging degree. Du Pont had a voice in selecting his captains, but it is only natural that a commander would want subordinates in whom he had confidence. Porter's officers in the Mississippi Squadron were very loyal to him and some of them were very close and trusted aides. One of the reasons given by Farragut for declining the command against Fort Fisher was that he did not know the captains and he would not have time to learn their capabilities. He also had favorites, but that any of these small groups can be classed as a clique rather than personal choices in whom the commander had full confidence is not well supported. Percival Drayton, who was with Du Pont for much of the war, was also a favorite of Farragut, and he commanded *Hartford* at Mobile Bay.

Of the other wartime admirals, Andrew H. Foote showed admirable qualities of aggressive leadership until his wound, received at Fort Donelson, removed him from active command. John A. Dahlgren, Lincoln's confidant, who was selected to relieve Du Pont, undertook the capture of Charleston feeling sure that he would succeed. When his experience confirmed Du Pont's opinion, Welles could only accept the fact—although not with very good grace—that Charleston could not be taken by the Navy alone. S. P. Lee, who commanded the North Atlantic Blockading Squadron for more than two years, performed creditably and he was always ready and willing to support the Army on the rivers within his command. One compensation for the monotonous task of blockading was that he received more prize money as his admiral's share than any other officer in the Navy, since Wilmington, the most active port for blockade runners, was within the limits of his command. Charles H. Davis, who demonstrated his command qualities in the early years of the war, was relegated to relative obscurity by being made a bureau chief in Washington. The other admirals in the Civil War either occupied obscure positions or came into a major command after the main events were completed.

Many of the younger officers, too junior to have important sea commands during the course of the war, performed outstanding jobs in individual commands. Henry A. Walke and Leroy Fitch, on the Western rivers, Captains John Rodgers and Percival Drayton and the younger Stephen B. Luce, to name a few, fall within this category.

Compared with the complex and precise amphibious operations of World War II, those of the Civil War were rather crudely planned and co-ordinated affairs. Except for Roanoke Island, amphibious attacks on the seacoasts and at New Orleans were conducted at the instigation of the Navy. The purpose in each case was either to secure a base for its blockading vessels or to seal off a port to relieve the blockade. Naval officers on the scene recognized the potential value of these bases for Army operations in the interior, but the Army, on the whole, showed little interest. Grant and Sherman, and later Canby at Mobile Bay, did recognize the value of naval support, and they not only sought it but showed complete confidence in it.

These amphibious operations were executed in such a way that the only general co-ordination was employed for the troop landings. Yet, basically, the pattern of the Civil War operation was not unlike that of World War II. The landing was preceded by an intense bombardment by warships in an effort to destroy or silence the defenses. Where conditions favored, the troops were landed out of range of the defensive works and they did not attack until after the bombardment had had its effect. As was the case in World War II, these operations were more smoothly executed and coordinated toward the end of the war, as the commanders profited from earlier experience. The Navy's experience in amphibious operations in the Civil War was used in developing the doctrine that became the basis for all of the American amphibious operations in World War II.

Another feature of Union naval operations deserves brief mention. A study of Civil War naval logistics is beyond the scope of this study, but the Union Navy developed and operated a well-organized and efficient supply system for its far-flung operations. Complaints of shortages or failure to receive needed supplies were fairly frequent in the early part of the war, but they tapered off noticeably as the naval effort got into high gear. With its vessels operating on the high seas, spread out for 3,000 miles along the Southern coast, and on the Western rivers, the Union Navy's supply system was a real accomplishment which contributed materially to the Union successes. Part of this result was due to an extensive overhaul of the Navy Department.

Within a year after Welles became Secretary of the Navy he reorganized the department. It then had eight bureaus: Equipment and Recruiting, Navigation, Ordnance, Steam Engineering, Construction and Repair, Yards and Docks, and Medicine and Surgery. Each was charged with procurement in its field, but there was a great deal of decentralization. Besides the Navy Yard at Washington there were other foundries and arsenals that made guns and ammunition. Purchasing agents in key cities made local contracts for provisions and supplies. The Navy Yards at Portsmouth, New Hampshire, New York, Philadelphia, Norfolk, and Washington were kept busy repairing ships, but considering the low general efficiency of the machinery of the period, those repairs were not excessive.

At Beaufort, North Carolina, Port Royal, Key West, Pensacola, Ship Island, Mississippi, and New Orleans there were depots for the local issue of supplies. The river gunboats were supported by depots at Mound City (Cairo) and Memphis. Limited repair facilities also existed at those points. On the Carolina coast, at least, much use was made of what became known in World War II as mobile logistic support—the use of store ships for issuing supplies locally and well-equipped repair facilities, also afloat. An idea of the magnitude of the job may be obtained from the fact that about 500,000 tons of coal were consumed by the ships in 1864. Figures for other requirements are not readily available, but a rough estimate is that the equivalent of about 300 vessels, with a capacity of about 1,000 tons each, were required in 1864 to keep the Union ships and gunboats supplied. The variety of supplies provided is also impressive. Fresh water was a problem in the smaller vessels and water had to be hauled to them from the North. Even ice was supplied. It was intended primarily for hospital facilities, but occasional mention in the records shows that it was also available to individual blockading ships.

When we turn to the Confederate side of the naval part of the Civil War the story is largely one of tragic frustration. Despite the limited material resources of the South, an impressive effort was made, but except for the successful record of the commerce raiders and the use of submerged mines, the results were largely negative.

When he took office Secretary Stephen B. Mallory had more experience in naval affairs than did Gideon Welles, but his estimates of the strategic results to be gained from the Confederate naval effort were wide of the mark. His hope that the commerce raiders would be able to weaken or disperse the Union blockade, or that the Confederate ironclads would succeed in driving off blockading ships, was never realized. Like Welles, he was severely criticized for his conduct of the office, and he was given a full share of the blame for every Confederate failure or Union success. He also had his critic in the Confederate Congress where the chairman of the House Naval Affairs Committee demanded his ouster loudly and often. Jefferson Davis retained confidence in him or he could not have kept the office throughout the life of the Confederacy. After the loss of New Orleans there was a lengthy investigation of the Navy Department, but about the only solid conclusion reached was that New Orleans had been lost.

Starting with nothing except for the few craft seized by individual states, the Confederate Navy was built up by a high degree of resourcefulness and ingenuity. The commerce raiders, obtained chiefly through the efforts of Commander Bulloch in England, destroyed a substantial amount of Union shipping, but the real object of their operations, to disperse the Union blockade or make it fail, was not achieved. The secondary object, to destroy and drive Union shipping from the seas, did succeed to a high degree, but not with the result expected. The Union flag almost disappeared from the seas, but Union trade and commerce was not destroyed. The economic accident of European crop failures and bumper crops in the growing Middle West caused trade to flourish, even as the Union merchant marine was being harassed by the commerce raiders. The Confederacy could take pride in the accomplishments of its colorful Raphael Semmes, but when these are weighed against the cold facts of economic logic they are seen to have contributed little in a material way to the Confederate cause.

There was one activity in which Confederate success was measurable. That was in the production and use of submerged mines. A variety of mines was designed and constructed with much ingenuity and they were used extensively in the Southern rivers and harbor entrances. The Union Navy had a deep respect for those mines, and while it developed devices to cope with them, it suffered materially from them. Seven ironclads and about twenty wooden gunboats and transports were sunk or destroyed by this weapon. Another eight were damaged, and these losses show that the mine was a dangerous and usually fatal weapon.

The most impressive index of the effort made by the Confederate Navy is the fact that it obtained or built more than 130 vessels and craft. This feat is all the more remarkable when it is recalled that the South was almost without shipbuilding facilities and the craftsmen needed for this very specialized work. Most of its craft were existing river boats converted into lightly armed gunboats with the machinery protected by hay or cotton bales. Many were merely armed hulks. Of necessity there was much improvisation, but the result obtained testifies to the zeal and devotion that was displayed by the Navy. At Selma, Alabama, it established a Navy Yard and an ordnance plant where ironclads were built and naval guns and gunpowder were manufactured.

The ironclad program, in particular, illustrates the great effort that was expended against what a century later seems to have been prohibitive odds. The records list twenty-six ironclads built or under construction by the Confederate Navy by the end of the war. All but one, *Stonewall*, which Bulloch had built in France, were built in the Confederacy itself. Some of them were only partially armored and a few were classed as floating batteries, eloquently illustrating the serious shortage of propulsion machinery. They were built or converted in or near the principal ports and in rivers with access to the sea or the Mississippi River. Several of them were still uncompleted at the end of hostilities or were completed too late to take an active part. Such was the fate of *Missouri*, built at Shreveport, Louisiana, and surrendered at Alexandria. Their design followed closely that of the first conversion, *Merrimack* at Norfolk, with a low main deck on which was an ironclad casemate with sloping sides protecting the guns and machinery. They were equipped with ram bows, and this feature gave rise to the "ram fever" in the wooden ships of the Union Navy, where the potential threat of the Confederate ironclads was highly respected.

Half of the ironclads saw some sort of action. In Hampton

Roads *Merrimack* sank two wooden sailing warships before her fight with *Monitor*. *Albemarle* sank a wooden gunboat in the Roanoke River, but thereafter was strangely inactive until her own destruction. Three ironclads were destroyed in the Mississippi to prevent their capture and another was sunk by Farragut's squadron. Two of the Confederate ironclads were captured and saw later service in the Union Navy. Other brief sorties of ironclads out of Charleston, the Cape Fear River, and in the upper James River near the end complete the record of the ironclads' activity. These inflicted some damage on Union ships but did not seriously impair Union naval activity. The score of three ships sunk, with a few others damaged, was certainly not much of a return for the effort that was put into producing the ironclads. Why was this so?

There were two primary reasons for the failure of the Confederate ironclads to have a decisive or even an important part in the naval war. One was mechanical in nature. Materials were difficult to obtain and in some cases the lack of essential machinery or armor slowed or prevented the completion of construction. Ingenious improvisation went into their construction, but the lack of proper and adequate materials produced an inferior and unreliable craft that was rushed into service. They were underpowered and therefore slow and clumsy to handle. *Merrimack*, originally a modern and fast ship, could barely make steerageway after her hull was cut down and the armor installed. The captured Confederate craft, *Atlanta* and *Tennessee*, proved to be reliable in Union service only after extensive overhaul.

The second reason for their poor showing was psychological in nature. Confederate naval officers were cast from the same mold as those in the Union Navy. They had the same professional qualifications and traditions, while their incentive to succeed was probably greater than for officers on the Union side, for in remaining loyal to their states they had cast off an established career for a new and unproved one. But they were realists enough to know that their makeshift craft were no match for the warships of their opponents, and this undoubtedly created a feeling of awe toward the Union Navy and a sense of futility in trying to accomplish an almost hopeless task.

Captain W. H. Parker, in his *Recollections of a Naval Officer*, has a very moving passage that illustrates this feeling. On the eve of the battle in Albermarle Sound in February 1862, in which he commanded the Confederate gunboat *Beaufort*, he was deeply depressed at the prospects. His comparison of the opposing forces was gloomy and ominous—sixteen Union gunboats to eight Confederate, fifty-four guns to nine. In his despondency he went aboard the Confederate flagship to talk to his commander, Commodore Lynch. Their conversation lasted throughout the evening and at intervals would revert to the immediate problem. As Parker left to return to his own gunboat Commodore Lynch's parting words were: "Ah! if we could only hope for success . . ." [2]

Buchanan, in Mobile Bay, showed a somewhat comparable emotional reaction. He boasted that he would break the Union blockade with *Tennessee* and retake Pensacola, but when confronted by Farragut's twenty-odd ships he remained inactive inside the bay. His own explanation for this was that he was convinced that Farragut was about to attack and that he must be prepared to defend Mobile. But the feeling in Mobile was that his failure to steam out and seek battle was due to his being overawed by the Union force.

This feeling was indicated in other ways. The action reports of the Confederate commanders contained glowing accounts of the gallantry and heroic conduct of the officers and men against vastly superior forces. They were sensitive about

---

[2] *Recollections of a Naval Officer*, p. 228.

their honor and bitterly denounced what they considered to be the unchivalric conduct of their opponents.

The Confederate cruisers operated in a different environment, where the initiative and resourcefulness of the captains were key qualities. They knew that Union cruisers were scouring the seas in search of them and that they could expect no mercy if captured.

To point out that this sense of frustration existed does not imply that the Confederate naval officers were lacking in courage or initiative. Their record of performance shows that they were amply endowed with those qualities. But they were realistic men and could hardly fail to realize the magnitude and difficulty of their task in the face of the overwhelming force that was opposed to them.

We may admire the courage, determination, and perseverance with which the Confederate Navy fought its war, but it has to be admitted that the effort resulted in little more than annoyance to the Union. The Union Navy, on the other hand, tipped the balance in favor of its cause. As the anaconda's coil closed around the South and sealed it off from free access to the materials it needed, the Confederacy was drained of essential goods to the point that it could not continue the war. It was this, in the end, that forced Lee's surrender and the collapse of the South.

This neither implies that the Union Navy could have done the job alone nor reflects on the performance of the Union Army, which had the essential task of meeting and defeating the Confederate Army. It is significant, however, that the Union Army's major victories did not occur until the South was suffering from shortages imposed by the Union blockade. By creating these shortages the Union Navy ensured the ultimate victory of its cause.

Index

i

A NOTE ABOUT THE AUTHOR

REAR ADMIRAL BERN ANDERSON (U. S. Navy, retired) was born in Kansas City, Missouri, in 1900, attended the United States Naval Academy, and became a commissioned officer in 1920. He was on active duty until 1950, and won the Legion of Merit with Combat V for service on the staff of the Commander, Seventh Amphibious Force, Southwest Pacific Area, in World War II. From 1952 to 1960, Admiral Anderson was technical adviser and assistant to Samuel Eliot Morison in the preparation of the fourteen-volume *History of United States Naval Operations in World War II*. He is the author of *Surveyor of the Sea: The Life and Voyages of Captain George Vancouver*, published in 1960.

November 1962